Weekend Walks

in St. Louis and Beyond

Weekend Walks

in St. Louis and Beyond

30 Town and Country Walks
within 150 Miles of the City

Robert Rubright

Backcountry Guides
Woodstock, Vermont

Library of Congress Cataloging-in-Publication Data

Rubright, Robert.
    Weekend walks in St. Louis and beyond : 30 town and
    country walks within 150 miles of the city / Robert
    Rubright.—1st ed.
        p.cm.
    Includes index.
    ISBN 0-88150-448-3
    1. Saint Louis (Mo.)—Guidebooks. 2. Saint Louis
Region (Mo.)—Guidebooks. 3. Walking—Missouri--Saint
Louis—Guidebooks. 4. Walking—Missouri—Saint Louis
Region—Guidebooks. I. Title.

F474.S23 R84 2002
917.78'660444--dc21

                                            2002066441

Text design by Chelsea Cloeter
Cover design by Dede Cummings Designs
Front cover photo by Joseph Sohm © Tony Stone Images

Published by Backcountry Guides
A division of The Countryman Press,
P.O. Box 748, Woodstock, Vermont 05091

Distributed by W.W. Norton & Company, Inc.,
500 Fifth Avenue, New York, NY 10110

Printed in the United States of America

10 9 8 7 6 5 4 3 2 1

In memory of Emilie K. Rubright

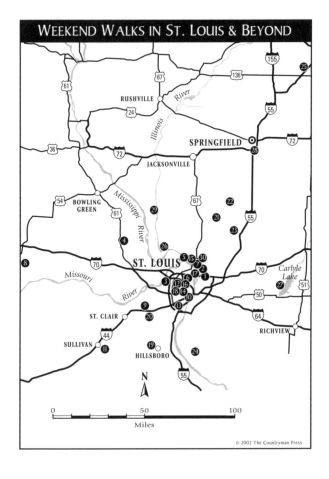

WEEKEND WALKS IN ST. LOUIS & BEYOND

© 2002 The Countryman Press

Contents

Illinois   228

Acknowledgments

A trail guide freighted with local and regional history is really a project in which many bright, insightful, and enthused persons offer generous contributions of their thoughts and their time. Especially when it comes to taking a walk!

Without some of the area's enduring sources of history, such as the main branch of the St. Louis Public Library, the research library of the Missouri Historical Society, and the St. Louis Mercantile Library, this book would not have much of an underpinning.

Special thanks and acknowledgment must go to my friend Esley Hamilton, preservation historian for St. Louis County Parks and Recreation Department and, in my estimation, the St. Louis area's finest individual source of knowledge about old buildings, historic registers, and historic dates and personalities. I want to thank Doris and Charles Danna of Kirkwood, Missouri, for their continuing inspiration and detailed knowledge of architectural and landmark facts and fiction. The book would have been hollow without the commentary of my old friend Ramon D. Gass, the forester/entomologist who became a true hiking buddy. His knowledge of every twig, tree, flower, weed, fern, fungus, and moss continues to bewilder those of us who walk with him. John E. Marshall, a classmate of mine at Westminster College and eventually its vice president and acting president, helped immeasurably with the detailed walk through historic Fulton, Missouri. Richard Gilpin, an attorney in St. Louis and lover of history, helped us develop our initial connections for the walks in Benld and Carlinville, Illinois. Without the eagerness and keen resourcefulness of Noel D. Holobeck, who heads the St. Louis interests section of the main public library in downtown St. Louis, this book would have been much weaker. John Hinkel was very helpful with trail map assistance.

Staff members at other libraries and archives were sympathetic and helpful. Among those institutions: the Frank Bertetti Benld Public Library, Benld, Illinois; Lumpkin Library at Blackburn College, Carlinville, Illinois; St. Charles (Missouri) Historical Society; Madison County Historical Society, Edwardsville, Illinois; St. Louis County Library System; Ferguson (Missouri) Public Library; Callaway County (Missouri) Historical Society; Reeves Library at Westminster College, Fulton, Missouri; Bloomington (Illinois) Public Library; Illinois State Historical Society, Springfield; Overland (Missouri) Historical Society; University City (Missouri) Public Library; University City Historical Society; Richmond Heights (Missouri) Public Library; Ft. Belle Fontaine (Missouri) Historical Society; Archives, St. Louis County Parks and Recreation Department; Hayner Public Library, Alton, Illinois, and Alton (Illinois) Museum of History and Art.

Several of the above groups represent organizations that have been extremely supportive of this book project. I wish to cite the Missouri Department of Conservation, Illinois Department of Natural Resources, U.S. Army Corps of Engineers, and the St. Louis County

Department of Parks and Recreation—especially their unmatched team of site superintendents and park rangers.

Many individuals were very generous of their time and knowledge as this book was being developed. Among them are: Michael Arduser, Jean Ashworth, Paul Bauer, Mary Ann Beahon, Jim Birdsell, Rose Ann Bodman, Ronald A. Brunnert, John Bunnell, Ronald Coleman, Erin Connett, JoAnn Corbett, Ted Curtis, Joe and Pat Devine, Daniel Drees, Robert Emde, Tom Emery, John Fassero, Laurie Flori, Jim Frank, Michael Hethcote, Mark Hodges, Dennis Hogan, James and Margot Holsen, Frank Janson, Pat Jones, Ken Kamper, Ruth Kamphoefner, Ben Knox, Barbara Perry Lawton, Judy Little, Ann Lloyd, Irv Logan, Joseph and Yvonne Logan, Eugene J. Mackey III, J. Marshall Magner, Jim Malone, Morton and Tanya Mallory, James Mathies, William McCartney, Vicki McDaniel, Peggy McDonald, Kevin Meneau, Don Mincke, Mary Newman, John Nelson, Osmond Overby; Richard D. Reed; John Rehtmeyer; Carol Schaefer; Bruce Schuette, Thelma Sibley, Bud Smith, John Solodar, Max Storm, Sister Mary Lu Steuber, Gary Tatham, Steve Tiemann, Carolyn Toft, Pat Westhoff, Virgil Wiegand, Gary Woith, and Helen Wuestenfeld.

Many, many thanks to my son, Ted, who assisted me when computer problems arose, and to my wife, Lynn, for her numerous walks and unending patience.

Introduction

In this book are walks in the St. Louis area that take you through forests, savannahs, glades, wetlands, historic districts, city neighborhoods, parks, conservation areas, and nature preserves. In addition, nine walks that are way beyond metropolitan St. Louis but well worth spending a weekend day to enjoy and explore are found within.

Among the nine "beyond" walks, six are in Illinois (most of them are on or near Interstate 55 north) and three are in Missouri. They include a memorable, history-filled walk in Fulton and hikes on the wilderness trail at Meramec State Park, near Sullivan, and the Blazing Star trail (packed with woodlands and prairie) at Cuivre River State Park, near Troy. The farthest-away walk takes you 150 miles north to Funk's Grove in Shirley, Illinois, less than 10 miles south of Bloomington.

At Funk's Grove there are virgin maple forests, a cemetery filled with Funks—one was the cattle king of Illinois, another founded Funk's Seeds—the nonpareil "Cathedral in the Trees," where you can hike through or stay to get married, and woodlands filled with tall and majestic oaks, hickories, and, in particular, maples. If you hike in February, you might see part of the operation that taps three thousand maples in what is known as "Funk's Timber."

In Springfield, Illinois, we explore the renowned Lincoln Memorial Garden, which has been around just about as long as Lake Springfield itself—since 1935. This lush arboretum and nature area, landscaped by Jens Jensen, considered the dean of Midwest landscape architects in his day, keeps improving with the years. The garden still faithfully adheres to the original Jensen plan that embraced fingerlike walking lanes, council groves, showy wildflowers, native trees, and the beautiful Lake Springfield shoreline. South of Springfield you are invited to explore a trio of walks that happen to all be in Macoupin County: Benld-Gillespie and Carlinville as well as Beaver Dam State Park near Plainview, Illinois.

Macoupin County is rich in old coal mines and the lore associated with them. In the early years of the 20th century, Benld was a wide-open town where coal miners, many of them Italian and Slavic immigrants, walked to work, swam in mine ponds, and drank beer in saloons along the main street. Legend has it that Al Capone and some of his henchmen ran a large still near Benld during Prohibition and that Capone himself strolled the streets of the tiny town. Most old-timers, however, disavow any Capone presence in Benld or Gillespie, ascribing such talk to urban legends or folklore. A walk through Benld, then over to the edge of Gillespie along the old Illinois Terminal Railroad bed, will bring to life for hikers some very poignant regional history. A walk through Carlinville with its million-dollar courthouse, the Blackburn College campus (Blackburn is one of only seven American colleges where students are expected to work their way through school, mostly as employees of the college), and the Standard Addition, the country's largest collection of intact Sears Roebuck catalog homes, is very memorable. Finally, the Macoupin County itinerary is complete with a walk through Beaver Dam State Park, perhaps the smallest and most compact of the Illinois parks but one with a flora-rich lakeside loop, followed by a loop of an active marsh where wood ducks dwell and ospreys swoop down to capture their prey and fly into the nearby forest to devour them.

Another walk beyond St. Louis will carry you to the largest man-made lake in Illinois: Carlyle—one of the country's premier sailboat venues and home to Eldon Hazelit State Park, which maintains a 3-mile lakeside walk with some very panoramic lookout points.

In selecting the 30 walks for this trail guide, I knew that many of them had plenty of historic subtexts. But I was nevertheless surprised at the uniqueness and special features of the walks I found. Among the walks, I have encountered: the first U.S. Army post west of the Mississippi (Fort Belle Fontaine); the confluence of America's two greatest rivers; perhaps the largest collection of hill prairies in the Midwest (Fults Hill); the most extensive American tribute to Sir Winston Churchill (Fulton, Missouri), the longest bike/hike pedestrian bridge in the United States as well as the Mississippi's roughest and most treacherous stretch (Chain of Rocks), the oldest city park west of the Mississippi (Lafayette), and the WPA-built county park with perhaps the most rest room facilities per capita—anywhere (Tilles Park).

One thing to remember about hiking trails and walkways: They're constantly changing. Many of the hikes in this book have varied to some degree since I set out to write about them several years ago. In 1995 I published

Walks and Rambles In and Around St. Louis, a book with 37 outings in Missouri and Illinois. Most of the walks in that book have undergone changes since then.

Wherever you choose to walk, you can enjoy the hike more when you are prepared both physically and intellectually. Here are some guidelines that I try to follow when I take a walk:

1. Walk with somebody! One never knows when a missing trail sign, confusing fork, or overgrown trail vegetation will cause you to lose your way temporarily in unfamiliar woods. If you have a companion, you'll be able to reason together and resume your way more quickly. In addition, walking with two or more, especially in urban woods, is a smart idea.

2. Always carry water, nutritious snacks, a first-aid kit, insect repellant (chiggers, mosquitoes, and ticks have added markedly to the population of Missouri and Illinois), and a strong sun-blocking agent.

3. Your trip will be more enjoyable if you carry an up-to-date wildflower guide tailored to your region. Others may want to take along birding guides (especially during the May and September–October migration periods), tree and shrub guides, and butterfly books. And don't forget your camera in case you want to record some flora or fauna that you've not seen before or want to look up later on.

4. Always pick up a brochure or leaflet at trailheads or visitors centers. Most of the time these publications have useful maps and forewarnings about the terrain.

5. It's always a good idea to wear leg coverings whenever walking in tall grass or a forest with overgrown

trails. Plus always wear a hat, and comfortable water-proof hiking shoes.

Best wishes to you as you begin your walks in St. Louis and beyond!

Missouri

1 · Old Chain of Rocks Bridge

Location: St. Louis, Missouri
Hiking distance: 3 miles
Hiking time: 2 hours
Bicycles: Permitted

The 1.1-mile, two-lane, $2 million continuous-truss Kingshighway Chain of Rocks Highway Bridge (its original name) linking Missouri to Illinois across the Mississippi River at Chouteau Island opened June 25, 1929, for "local and transcontinental motor traffic." From 1936 to 1955, the bridge carried the main route of US 66 into St. Louis. Once here, drivers found their way north to Dunn Road (now the service road on I-270 north) to Lindbergh, or via a "city route" to downtown and then west. Early in World War II, the war department required managers to paint the bridge in earthy camouflage colors to confuse possible enemy bombers.

The new bridge owner, from 1939 on, was the city of Madison, Illinois, which was 4.5 miles east. (An Illinois law permits municipalities to own property within 5 miles of their corporate limits.) Madison, which took title after the previous owners defaulted, earned nearly $7 million in tolls, prompting residents to dub the bridge "the Golden Goose of Madison." In 1968 a new four-lane I-270 span less than 1 mile north forced Chain of Rocks Bridge to close for good.

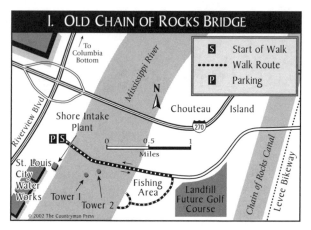

I. OLD CHAIN OF ROCKS BRIDGE

For 30 years the bridge lay abandoned, though Madison officials listened to many proposals for bridge revival: strip mall, flea market with 100 booths, mid-bridge restaurant/lounge, arts-and-crafts festival site, six-story hotel and a truck stop on its Illinois end, a marina, heliport. Madison decided to sell the bridge for scrap in 1975, but a decline in scrap-metal prices canceled the planned demolition. Thus the bridge became Madison's millstone.

Around 1995 the bridge's optimum reuse plan surfaced: Fix its dilapidated infrastructure, open it to bicycles and walkers, and make it a pivotal part of Confluence Greenway—a fast-developing 200-square-mile mostly linear system of trails, levees, parks, historic places, wildlife refuges, scenic byways, visitors centers, and conservation, recreation, and natural areas abutting the Missouri and Mississippi Rivers in six metropolitan-area Missouri and Illinois counties. The bridge, Chouteau Island, and more than 50 miles of bicycle/walking trails are the major greenway components. The greenway itself begins near the Gateway Arch in downtown St. Louis, heads north along the Riverfront Trail to the bridge, crosses it, then splits at the Chain of Rocks Canal east levee. Trail users can opt to travel south on the levee to East St. Louis and cross the historic Eads Bridge to complete one loop of the greenway, or take a left and head along the Confluence Greenway for Alton, and continue on along the Great River Road and bike path through Grafton at the confluence of the Mississippi and Illinois Rivers to Pere Marquette Park, the northern terminus. Greenway linkups to Columbia Bottom, site of the Missouri-Mississippi River confluence, and eventually to a hookup with the Katy Trail in St. Charles County, are on the drawing board.

A water taxi system around the confluence site—to connect with several historic places on the rivers—is also being planned.

Trailnet, Inc., the visionary St. Louis not-for-profit organization, conceived the greenway idea, master-minded a fund drive, leased the bridge, gathered technical expertise, repaired and sealed its concrete deck, installed a sky-blue pedestrian fence, and opened the bridge weekends from April to November. Contemplated for sometime before the targeted 2004 completion date are bridge lighting, cantilevered viewing spots as well as a raised observation deck reachable by elevator or spiral staircase, improved parking, rest rooms, a Route 66-themed roadhouse/restaurant, and a major visitors center on the Missouri approach. Chouteau and nearby Cabaret and Mosenthein Islands are set for redevelopment; major changes will occur in and around Columbia Bottom as well as the Lewis & Clark State Park opposite it in Illinois. "All of this land (about

10,000 acres) is evolving into a massive area that needs to be implemented with the stature of a national park," says Ted Curtis, Trailnet executive director.

In the wake of its restoration, the bridge is being hailed as one of America's longest exclusive pedestrian-bicycling spans and a specific destination for tourists from America and abroad—especially Europeans seduced by images of old Route 66.

Before walking the bridge, here's some context.

The St. Louis Entrance and Neighborhood

From the 1920s to the 1960s, the 85-acre Chain of Rocks, or Riverview Park, occupied a precipitous hillside across from the bridge entrance on Riverview Drive. Among its attractions: a vast lily pond and fountain, 15-foot waterfall, ornate planters, picnic grounds, a garden where white roses spelled out CHAIN OF ROCKS, public swimming pool, and switchback roadways that eased up from Riverview to the top of the park on Lookaway Drive. "Every variety of tree grown in this part of the world may be found in the park," its superintendent boasted. Many northsiders asserted that the park and the bridge constituted a major entranceway into St. Louis.

Near the park, atop the hill, was the Chain of Rocks amusement park (1927–1977). High taxes, vandalism, and competition from Six Flags Over Mid-America brought about its demise. Visitors loved its merry-go-round, roller coaster, rectangular Ferris wheel—"the Swooper,"—and the Dodgem pavilion.

In 1901 the St. Louis Water Works Railway (later the St. Louis & Chain of Rocks Railroad), put on electrical cars to carry water division employees from Baden and,

Viewing the Chain of Rocks Bridge from the Illinois shore

later, Bissell's Point, in North St. Louis. Buses replaced the cars in 1936, but rail service was revived "as a wartime measure" in 1944 and finally discontinued in 1955. The water division has operated on Riverview Drive since 1894. North of the bridge on Riverview in its early days was the North Shore Country Club and the Chain of Rocks Bridge Buffet.

The Chain of Rocks

The Chain of Rocks, also known as Grand Chain or Sawyer's Bend, is a 10-mile stretch of river starting several miles north of the bridge and extending downriver to near the Merchant's Bridge. Before a new canal replaced the chain 50 years ago, the chain was described as "a series of flat rocks shoving out from the Missouri side, sloping and extending about halfway toward the Illinois side." In low-water periods—the river could drop here from 5 to 18 feet in spots—rocks would rise above the river surface to create navigational nightmares; water velocity could double or treble. Within the chain's rapids "there is a demon that could swallow canoes," wrote Edith McCall in *Biography of a River*.

Water Intake Towers

Two inactive landmark-status water intake towers reminiscent of castles on Germany's Rhine River stand in the Mississippi south of the bridge. Water taken in via tower screening gates was tunneled to settling basins and pumping stations on the Missouri shore. The river's main channel originally flowed between the towers, which were 700 feet apart. Since the Missouri and Mississippi merge 4 miles to the north, their respective waters are not considered completely mixed until they reach 30 miles downstream; hence, Tower 1, nearest Missouri, is said to be in Missouri River water, and Tower 2 is in Mississippi water.

Tower 1, dating to 1894, is attributed to St. Louis architect William S. Eames who helped design the 24-building Cupples Warehouse System near Busch Stadium in downtown St. Louis, and possibly his partner Thomas C. Young, who earlier had designed the federal prison at Fort Leavenworth, Kansas and the St. Louis Masonic temple at 3681 Lindell Blvd. The cylindrical, turreted, Romanesque limestone tower rests on river bedrock 100 feet below. Its red-granite substructure is faced with rough limestone. Eight intake gates were operated from the first floor; upstairs contained living and storage units. Julius Miller was tower keeper intermittently for 40 years between 1894 and 1934. He worked from the tower in winter months only to chip ice off the gates.

Tower 2 began operation in 1915 as a backup for Tower 1. Designed by St. Louis architects Roth and

Study, its style is Roman revival, similar in design to some municipal buildings from the period. A fancy stone balcony with wrought-iron railings, an arched doorway; second-floor sleeping quarters, and a tower keeper's penthouse are features of the buff Bedford limestone edifice that's supported by a massive concrete substructure covered with gray Georgia granite. Since 1935 no resident keepers have occupied the towers. In ensuing years, however, water division maintenance crews relished the chance to work out at the towers. "Sometimes the crews would stay for as long as two weeks," an official said in 1968. "They had lively times out there, and there were always lots of card games." Tower 2 once functioned as a lighthouse, river historians say.

Rectangular brick Tower 3 at the city water works on the Missouri shore opened in 1932. Its purpose, according to the water division, was to "remove the problem of ice and sand clogging the two existing river intakes during certain river conditions." Because they could not keep out sand, ice, mud, debris, and germs, the two river towers were essentially made obsolete by the new square tower, though they could be reactivated in a dire emergency.

Chouteau Island

Chouteau Island, at about 3,000 acres, may be the largest remaining open space in metropolitan St. Louis, especially when linked to its neighbors to the south, Cabaret and Mosenthein Islands. Chouteau has been on area maps since at least 1796 under earlier names such as Great Island, Grande Isle, and Big Island. An 1866 island map clearly identifies 4-mile-long Chouteau

Slough, which gave way to the present Chain of Rocks Canal.

A note on an 1873 map describes the island and adjacent farm fields as comprising "some of the most fertile and alluvial land in the world." The island's first-known occupants were Frenchmen in the 1750s. Archivists of the Madison County Historical Society in Edwardsville maintain that in 1802, James Gillham was the apparent first American settler. As the 19th century advanced, the island embraced small farms and one settlement, Old Madison, which was eventually swept away by floods. Farmer August G. Wegener was a busy resident in the late 1800s. Wegener owned a steamboat landing from where travelers could embark for Alton, St. Louis, or East St. Louis. He also operated a lighthouse and was both postmaster and freight agent. And since "he had the best spring wagon and buggy and the finest looking horses in the community," he was Chouteau's undertaker, too.

In 1956 officials momentarily weighed Chouteau's northern tip as part of a proposed Lewis and Clark Park with marina and campgrounds. Farm families lived on the island and worked its fields until 1993, when their homes were battered by the monumental flood. At least 19 or 20 separate farm operations remain, however, along with a landfill set to close in 2002.

Teenager carousing and partying was so pervasive on Chouteau in the 1960s and 1970s that the township sheriff complained, "They've got the idea that anything east of the Mississippi River is Arizona Territory." In 1973 scuba divers recovered nearly one hundred stolen or stripped automobiles from an underwater dumping ground by the island.

In 1998 the city of Madison annexed Chouteau, proffering ideas for serious recreational development. A throughway for the Confluence Greenway, hiking trails, an 18-hole golf course on the landfill site, fishing and picnic areas, a replica of a bridge toll building, and wetlands, prairies, and woodlands were part of Madison's conceptualizing, as were a sports complex, camping facilities, thousand-car parking garage, recreational-vehicle area, and direct ramp to I-270. Chouteau's southern end would accommodate prairie and wetland areas, fishing, camping, picnicking, and trails. Some of the city's ideas have been included in the Confluence Greenway and Chouteau Island master plans.

Chain of Rocks Canal

Created to bypass the notorious chain of rocks, the 8.4-mile canal, which all river traffic must use, opened in 1953 after seven construction years. It was dug out along the route of the Chouteau Island Slough (where steamboats once plied) as well as the Cabaret Island chute to the south. More than 23 million cubic yards of dirt and debris were excavated for the canal; much of the material now supports the levees—part of the Confluence Greenway—flanking the waterway. Lock and Dam 27, at the canal's southern end, contains a 1,200-foot lock that, when completed, was said to be "the largest in the western hemisphere...200 feet longer than those of the Panama Canal." To debut the canal, the city sponsored a 6-mile river parade that drew 150 vessels including pleasure cruisers, towboats, and barge floats.

Access

From I-270 in north St. Louis County, exit at Riverview Drive. Drive south on Riverview for less than 0.5 mile to the Chain of Rocks Bridge parking area, and turn in. The bridge is open daily, sunrise to sunset, from April to November.

Trail

As you approach the bridge, ailanthus trees with lance-shaped leaves (the tree that grew in Brooklyn) occur wild in the scrubby bottomland to the north, shared with cottonwoods, box elders, black willows, and omnipresent shrub honeysuckles. Noxious pokeweeds, some reaching 10 feet, are neighbors, too. In earlier times pioneers made ink from their drooping purplish berry clusters. You should not—the berries, seeds, roots, stems, and leaves can be poisonous to humans. Within the south bottomland much of the same flora can be found, but with more black locust trees bearing sharp thorns on their branches. In May these locusts' perfumy clusters of creamy white flowers add some colorful relief to the mass of green beside the bridge. Once you're on the bridge deck, you'll note that the green spread of water-tolerant trees and often smothering wild grape-vines continues to the Mississippi River edge, where rows of silver maple and young black willow saplings hog the muddy shoreline.

From the right side of the bridge, look out at Tower 1, the rough limestone structure with a conical tower and Romanesque arched windows. "I drove a 1959 Ford sedan out to Tower 1 in 1961, and others drove out in pickups back then," says Carl Schumacher, a city water division engineer and unofficial historian of the now-buried structure known as Homer's dike. (A low-water, broad-crested rock-fill dam, put down stone by stone across the chain of rocks in 1962, was designed to ensure adequate water flow in adverse conditions in the bypassed river stretch. This dam is partially visible in extreme low-water periods; look for it as it extends eastward from the water intake plant on the Missouri shoreline. The dam and pool caused the burial of Homer's dike.) Immediately to the south of Tower 1, in the middle of the river, is Mosenthein Island, which appears as an oval form. Farther south is the St. Louis downtown skyline, accented on the left by the 630-foot stainless-steel Gateway Arch, America's tallest national monument.

Somewhere between Tower 1 and the upcoming Tower 2 is the Illinois state line. As the bridge is developed, an interpretive deck will mark the state boundaries. Look down at Tower 2, the imposing Romanesque hulk that is more than twice the size of Tower 1. Though the tower has been mothballed for decades, work crews still visit occasionally by motorboat. "There's constant interest in the towers," says Schumacher. "One person even explored putting in a bed-and-breakfast at Tower 2, until we said that there is no electricity, no running water, and no toilet facilities—and no way to get there."

The roadway bend toward the middle of the bridge usually slowed down traffic. The main reason for the bend, according to the majority concensus, is that the new bridge needed to be relatively close to the existing intake towers so that boats could navigate the nasty shoals more efficiently. If the bridge were measurably removed from the towers, it would mean that pilots would first have to negotiate the towers, *then* the bridge piers. However, a minority bend theory is that workmen supposedly started building the bridge on bedrock on the Missouri side but couldn't locate bedrock straight across the river in Illinois. Therefore, the bridge had to be bent so that the Illinois end would be securely footed in bedrock.

From the bend, the bridge deck levels off for about a third of a mile until it begins a long descent to Chouteau Island. If you look carefully out to the left from midbridge, you'll see the spot on the horizon where the Missouri enters the Mississippi, although it's difficult to be precise with so much landscape and shoreline in between. On the right-hand side, the Illinois shoreline yields the popular fishing area where fly casters often stand in shallow water near the end of the rock-fill dam. Farther south on the shoreline is the northern tip of Cabaret Island. In 1929 the St. Louis planning commission announced its intention to convert Cabaret and Mosenthein—"twin islands"—into a 2,000-acre park with lagoons, beaches, gardens, forests, and aviation field for "land and water planes" and somehow connect them by land to the Missouri shore. In 1933 promoters pondered creating a new, straighter river channel and allowing the "old channel" between Mosenthein and Cabaret to become a yacht basin. Furthermore, there was talk of hosting a world's fair in the early 1940s at or near the site of the redeveloped islands that were somehow to be attached to Missouri. Needless to say, those plans withered and died.

As you hike down the last stretch of the deck, you'll observe that cottonwoods—some of them 100 feet tall—hundreds of silver maples, and thousands of chirping red-winged blackbirds seem to prevail in the bottomland, especially to the left. Shorebirds—primarily herons and egrets—are attracted to the permanent backwater that lies out to the left. Amid this thick vegetative bottomland/backwater, planners foresee elevated walkways, platforms, and a network of paths.

Leave the bridge deck, and walk straight ahead on the former entrance road, passing an old farm levee on the left as well as an entrance to a remaining farm operation. Take a right onto the first dirt road on your right—just before the landfill operation that's destined to be converted to a golf course—and walk down to the fishing area. Usually there's a crowd of fishermen who've parked their pickups in the dusty lot. Here you're about as close as you can get to the mighty Mississippi, which sometimes roars past at disarming speeds. You can also get a ground-level perspective of the bridge, bend and all. "Hearsay has it that someone found some fossilized shark's teeth on the shore near the low-water dam," says Carl Schumacher. That finding has never been confirmed.

Now you must turn around, and walk back over the bridge. In the next few years you'll be able to walk all over Chouteau Island (which some claim will be the Mississippi River's largest restoration project) and stretch your mileage appreciably. For now, the modified bridge loop must serve as an appetizer.

2 · Columbia Bottom Conservation Area

Location: North St.Louis County, Missouri
Hiking distance: 2 to 5 miles
Hiking time: 1 to 2 hours
Bicycles: Permitted
Note: *During construction in 2002 and early 2003, this area may be closed to public use. Before visiting call the regional office of the Department of Conservation (636-441-4554).*

At Columbia Bottom, 4,300 acres of mostly flood-plain in the shape of a fat mitten, America's two best-known rivers merge. Until the late 1990s when the Missouri Department of Conservation purchased the land from the city of St. Louis, the confluence of the Missouri and Mississippi Rivers had not been very accessible, save for the farmers who leased much of the property, privileged hunters who used the place as a preserve, or various neighbors and others who trekked or trespassed on rough, often muddy terrain to the historic merging.

It hasn't taken long for the conservation department to write a management plan to drastically improve the land and open it as a multiuse facility to hikers, birders, hunters, fishermen, and visitors opting for self-guided auto tours. After the plan's three main phases are

2. COLUMBIA BOTTOM CONSERVATION AREA

N

Missouri River

Projected riverfront trail

Confluence Site (planned observation deck)

0 1 2
Miles

Site of planned boat ramp, parking lot, and trailhead

P

P S
New Visitor Center Site

S Start of Walk
•••••• Walk Route
P Parking
▬ Levee

Wetland

Prairie

Forest

Mississippi River

© 2002 The Countryman Press

fully drawn—sometime in 2004—the area will radically change from its 2002 status: leased, open farm fields; hundreds of acres of riverfront forest; scattered wetlands; a levee by the Missouri river to forestall low-level flooding; more than a dozen miles of farm and service roads and dirt paths; and the confluence itself, a stub of land battered by floods and rendered muddy, scrubby, and preternaturally unattractive. (Across the Missouri River at the confluence, a new 202-acre Missouri state park in St. Charles County is slated to open by 2004, in time for the Lewis and Clark bicentennial. It will have a boardwalk and viewing platform near the confluence site.)

Conservation's creative makeover will provide an entrance road and a visitors center near the present parking lot on the southwest corner, as well as new hiking trails and an access road directly to the confluence, which will include an elevated viewing area, a boardwalk, parking lot, and short trail for handicapped persons. Conservation experts will preserve and expand various wetland sites, plant new grassland, and add trees to existing forested areas along the river's edge—plans that please naturalists and birders. "Once the habitat is improved and roads are put in, the birding community has hopes that Columbia Bottom might become a premier birding location," says John Solodar, a vice president of the St. Louis Audubon Society. "The main attraction could be the shorebird habitat...which is sorely lacking in the St. Louis area."

One thing that the conservation department can't do is alter Columbia Bottom's intriguing history. Some of our great explorers and naturalists have made the turn at the rivers. John James Audubon headed left up the Missouri to study birds and their nesting sites; Lewis and Clark camped for five months across from the confluence in 1803 and 1804 in preparation for their expedition to the Pacific Northwest. Even the body of General George A. Custer, killed at the Battle of Little Big Horn, was shipped east and around the confluence point in 1876. Fur traders, keelboatmen, Native Americans in canoes and pirogues, steamboaters, and military forces all knew the great intersection of the rivers. In the early 19th century, it wasn't unusual to stand at the confluence and see flotillas of up to 150 canoes operated by Sak, Fox, and Pottawatomi Indians. Sometimes tribal leaders deposited their women and children at Columbia Bottom while they took the Mississippi to St. Louis to do business with the American government.

Father Jacques Marquette and Louis Joliet were among the first to write about the confluence. Marquette wrote in 1673 that the site was "an accumulation of large and entire trees, branches, and floating islands." Muddy water from the Missouri "spoils the water of the Mississippi," wrote missionary priest J. F. Buissow St. Cosme in the 1600s. "The Missouri . . . seems to enter the Mississippi like a conqueror, hurling its white waves against the opposite bank without mingling them," observed Pierre Francois Xavier de Charlevoix in the 1720s. One veteran riverboatmen, whose anecdote is among hundreds retold in B. A. Botkin's *A Treasury of Mississippi River Folklore,* declared, "We used to separate the men from the boys at the mouth of the Missouri. The boys went up the Mississippi, and the men went up the Big Muddy."

Steamboats were a common sight in the mid-1800s. Some of them had trouble navigating the snag-ridden, agitated waters of the confluence. Gazetteers chronicled several nearby steamboat accidents, notably the *Amazon* in 1856 as well as the *Julia, Nadine, Argonaut, Bedford,* and *Cora.* Amazon Bend, a sweeping curve in the Missouri north of Columbia Bottom, is named for one of the sunken vessels.

Two tiny Columbia Bottom towns appear on early 19th-century maps: Columbia and Madison. Both settlements had disappeared by the 1860s due to pounding floods and constantly shifting river channels. At least three ferry operations ran from points near the confluence in the 1800s. One, the Madison Ferry, carried passengers to Chouteau Island, situated today at the Illinois end of the old Chain of Rocks Bridge. In the 1870s settlers were willing to give the floodplain another try. Mostly German immigrants, they started small farmsteads and built modest homes. Once again the shifting river swallowed many of the farms; just a handful survived. A few of the leased-farm operations at Columbia Bottom today are worked by descendants of those pioneering farmers.

To make way for the postwar "Air Age," the St. Louis Airport Commission in 1943 designated Columbia Bottom as the place to build the area's second major airport. Freight carriers and "huge transcontinental airships" were to be accommodated at the airport. Two lakes were to be built so St. Louis could become prominent in "international seaplane transportation." Simultaneously, Major Albert Lambert, a civic leader for whom St. Louis's major airport, Lambert Field, is named, was calling on the commission to acquire nearby railroad tracks so that St. Louis could become, in his opinion, the greatest rail and air transport center in the United States.

Airport devotees boasted that the Columbia Bottom acquisition was "one of the largest sites ever selected solely for airport use." The *St. Louis Globe-Democrat* stated, "Ten months out of the year and most years out of the century, this will be almost a park-like area, consecrated as an historic site." Access to the new airport would be via a "Mississippi River Memorial Highway," projected as part of the postwar interregional superhighway system.

However, some area leaders complained that the site was still too far away from downtown St. Louis to easily handle airmail operations—though civic dreamers had earlier proposed that helicopters shuttle both passengers and mail from the roofs of downtown buildings to the new air facility at Columbia Bottom (a transportation method much faster than taxis and trucks, the leaders said). At any rate, opposition to the airport proposal—and reminders that in 1943 nine feet of flood-water covered the proposed site—eventually killed the concept and its grandiose side proposals.

Access

In north St. Louis County, take I-270 to Riverview Drive, the last Missouri exit before crossing the Mississippi into Illinois. Drive 3 miles north on Riverview Drive, which becomes Columbia Bottom Road. At Strodtman Road, park in the existing lot, or look for signs that direct you to new parking facilities or to the confluence area itself.

It's probable that in 2002, major changes will start to occur at Columbia Bottom, especially a new entrance road and a road to the confluence and a suitable viewing platform. Some of the existing routes to the confluence will be eliminated.

Trail

Any new approaches to the confluence will take you by croplands to the levee and the Missouri River, then to the confluence point. As you start your walk, corn, wheat, and soybean fields managed by "permittee" farmers dominate the landscape. "Literally everything inside the levee is cropped," says Michael Arduser, regional natural history biologist with the conservation department, though some unfarmed areas are lowlands that will probably be redeveloped as wetlands. Marsh and harrier hawks cruise the wheatfields searching for prey. Red-tail and sparrow hawks also consider the farm fields as part of their territories as do colorful horned larks, who possess yellow flares between black patches on their heads and breasts. In some of the open

The entrance at Columbia Bottom

fields, coyotes are seen during daylight hours.

As the Columbia Bottom redevelopment progresses, a 250- to 500-acre native prairie will be planted around the center of the property taking over some of the farm-field space. Conservation staffers are contemplating an eventual "wildlife travel lane" over parts of the area, as well as sunflower fields to lure hungry doves as a basis for managed dove hunts. There are plans for controlled deer hunts, as well as hunting for turkey, squirrel, rab-bit, and quail. In 1981 a white-tail buck with nonsym-metrical antlers that measured 48 inches across, the world's record for an nontypical buck, was found dead near Columbia Bottom. The original rack, extremely valuable, is locked in a vault in Jefferson City; a replica is mounted at Powder Valley Nature Center in Kirkwood.

Black willows are seen by the long slough that flows near the levee. In the spring, says Arduser, the slough is a "salad bar" for birds—sometimes hundreds at a time—and other wildlife. As we passed one day, song and white-throated sparrows and juncos fed at the slough. In nearby wetlands, many of which will be expanded as the management plan unfolds, button-bushes and neighboring shrubby dogwoods are thriving. As you draw closer to the levee, you'll be seeing new accommodations for fishermen along the 6 miles of Columbia Bottom shoreline. An existing slough, improved riverbanks, and boat ramps will be available.

Over these flatlands near the levee, Major William B. Robinson, cofounder of Lambert Field, flew his airplanes in the 1920s. "Many times I have landed planes on the bottoms," he once said. "The soil is sandy and absorbs rainwater quickly." (Of course, Robinson failed to mention floodwater and its effects.) In some of the farm fields closer to the levee wild turkeys can be seen—sometimes in huge flocks. Toward the river are hundreds of trees damaged by the flood of 1993, now roosting sites for woodpeckers and hawks and egrets. "I've seen up to 300 great white egrets sitting in some of the willows and sycamores by the river," Michael Arduser notes.

The short walk from the levee to the confluence, or from the planned new parking lot near the confluence, is pretty bland, a trek among "post-flood regenerated" plants. You'll see cottonwoods, silver maples, mulberries, and black willows growing vigorously, along with some aggressive vines. In late spring and early summer, birders will find orioles, indigo buntings, yellow warblers, yellow-bellied cuckoos, and red-eyed vireos flashing in and out of the floodplain woods and thickets. Most probably, a short boardwalk will be erected in this area to make walking easier.

Despite the convenience of a raised viewing platform, the confluence area won't escape heavy flooding.

"In the 1993 flood, the confluence point was under at least 12 feet of water," says Arduser. As you stand near the confluence tip, you can see St. Ferdinand Island to the right—an expansive Mississippi river sandbar visible only during low water. Across the river is the Lewis and Clark State Historical Site off IL 3 near Wood River. The site, on a floodplain timbered area, is in the process of an expansion that includes an impressive new building. It commemorates Camp Du Bois, the winter camp where Lewis and Clark and their corps of more than 40 men trained, drilled, acquired provisions, and packed their three vessels from December 1803 to May 1804 in advance of their famous expedition. But due to shifting channels of both the Mississippi and Wood Rivers, this historic site is only symbolic. Historians believe the actual launching spot is at least 3½ miles north, though the exact spot remains unknown. (Historians also note that Camp Du Bois was in American territory during Lewis and Clark's training time. The narrow section of flatland and floodplain that extends 2 to 3 miles back from the Mississippi River from the mouth of the Kaskaskia River north to Alton is still referred to as the American Bottom.)

Visitors to the confluence can view what some call "eternal flames" that emanate from refinery operations near Wood River and Hartford. The largest open flare is generated by the Prencor refinery as it burns off excess gas from its refining process. Prencor has announced that its plant will close, so the flame may soon be extinguished. Flares are occasionally seen from operations of the Tosco refinery, as well. What hasn't been found is what the authors of *Big Muddy: Down the Mississippi Through America* call America's largest barge, larger than a battleship. According to the authors, the barge, named *The America*, was moored at Wood River, Illinois. So far we've looked in vain for *The America*.

At least 150 years ago, some confluence visitors obviously sampled the water. In their 1858 *St. Louis Sketch Book*, Taylor and Crooks wrote that despite some peculiarities, the Missouri River water that meets the Mississippi at the Missouri mouth "is nevertheless about the best river water in the world. It is said to keep longer, and be sweeter on a sea voyage, than the water of perhaps any other stream; indeed, it may almost be said never to spoil. Once it settles, and the sandy particles are quiet, it soon becomes very palatable, and persons soon become very fond of it—preferring it to any other water."

As some were sipping the memorable Missouri River water, others gathered to watch steamboats race from St. Louis to Alton or up to St. Paul, Minnesota. In 1868 the steamer *Hawkeye State* of the North Line Packet Company traveled 800 miles in 2 days and 20 hours from St. Louis to St. Paul, an unbroken steamboat record.

In 1963 the Mississippi was frozen bank-to-bank just above the confluence, though a channel was cut through the ice. This was one of the few times in at least 150 years that ice had shut down the river so near the confluence, where the converging waters are so fast and turbulent. A frozen Mississippi near downtown St. Louis, on the other hand, was not so unusual. In the 1860s and 1870s squatters pitched tents to sell beer and liquor at midriver to people crossing the ice on foot. Wagon trains and heavy coal wagons set down wooden planks to facilitate their crossing once reported to be 10 to 20 inches thick.

Once you've been to the confluence site and tested the new network of trails, you can—in the not too distant future—retreat to your car and drive over to the new state park on the St. Charles County side of the Missouri River for another view of this historic meeting of waters.

3 · Creve Coeur Lake County Park

Location: Maryland Heights, Missouri
Hiking distance: 5.33 miles
Hiking time: 2 hours

In the early 1900s Creve Coeur Lake (perhaps Missouri's largest natural lake) was a popular playland that drew up to 100,000 St. Louisans on warm weekends and on holidays. In those salad days, visitors arrived on stagecoaches, then horse-and-buggies, then on trains of the Missouri Pacific and Rock Island lines. "Every half-hour, a 12-car train run by Missouri Pacific unloaded its human cargo at the lake and returned to the city, passing on the way another train coming out," reminisced a reporter. Transportation to the lake became much easier when United Railways debuted electric trolleys on its Midland–Creve Coeur Lake line, especially its open-roof "moonlighter" cars. The trolleys, which came from downtown St. Louis and the Delmar loop in University City, operated from 1900 to 1950.

In midsummer, the reporter continued, the lake was a "sight of beauty. A great boardwalk extended down into the water, which was completely covered with the glossy green leaves of water lilies, each about the size of a large platter." Some were saying that a "Demon-Fish or giant water Serpent which crawls through the under-brush about the shores to listen to the conversations of

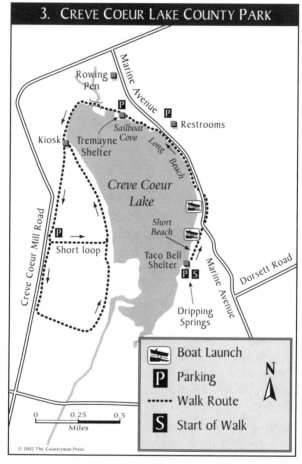

3. CREVE COEUR LAKE COUNTY PARK

Rowing Pen

Marine Avenue

P

P · Restrooms

Sailboat Cove

Long Beach

Kiosk

Tremayne Shelter

Creve Coeur Lake

Short Beach

Taco Bell Shelter

P S

Creve Coeur Mill Road

P →

Short loop

Dorsett Road

Marine Avenue

Dripping Springs

Boat Launch
P Parking
····· Walk Route
S Start of Walk

N

0   0.25   0.5
Miles

© 2002 The Countryman Press

lovers" lived in the lake. That and other myths have been told and retold for years. As the lake developed and prospered—roughly from 1890 to 1920—it at one time or another embraced a hilltop amusement park, hotels, an opera house, an observation tower originally in place at the 1904 St. Louis World's Fair, a racetrack that featured mule races and human footraces, a floating dance pavilion, and plenty of sailboats, canoes, rowboats, and sightseeing launches. Actor Gregory Peck—who lived in St. Louis for a short time as a child—recalled that at one time his grandfather had been "keeper of the boats" on the lake. Fishing camps hugged the shore; anglers took to the water to reel in jack salmon, huge catfish, bass, and crappie. Simultaneously, the west bank held several icehouses that harvested and supplied ice to St. Louisans for years. "Fields of ice, acres and acres in extent, were sliced out and housed," wrote one wide-eyed reporter. Later on, of course, artificial ice making rendered the icehouses obsolete. Around 1913 St. Louisan Thomas W. Benoist used the lake to try out what he said was the world's first flying boat. The two-passenger craft hit speeds of up to 64 miles per hour.

In the late 1920s a 50-acre subdivision known as Creve Coeur Beach was put up near the east and northeast lakeshore. Its unpaved streets had flowery names: Zinnia, Hibiscus, Petunia. Toward the end of its 40 years, the floodplain subdivision reached a state of blight and was torn down in 1974. A section known as Eldorado Beach lay on the west bank; it contained hotels, clubhouses, and shanties. On the east shore condemned shacks were at one point used for simulated assaults by St. Louis County Police SWAT teams.

Plenty of stories survive from the lake's golden years. In 1893 the owner of Creve Coeur Lake House, a saloon, said that his beer-drinking donkey could drink 100 glasses of beer in a single sitting. There were also stories about how the lake was named—that Creve Coeur meant "broken heart" in French and that there

were numerous tales of unrequited love and sacrifice
that led to broken hearts. Others said that the lake had
been named after a well-known Frenchman, the Count
de Creve Coeur. Preservation historian Esley Hamilton
points to an 1872 map of St. Louis County and notes
that there were then an upper lake (now dried up) and
a lower lake, which seen together resembled two sides
of a broken heart. He theorizes that that's how the place
got its name. In Prohibition days a criminal element fre-
quented the lake, prompting old-time police officers to
joke about how mob members would throw their hit
weapons into the lake and how many "Saturday-night
specials" the lake bottom might yield if it were drained.
In 1954 the lake was so silted and dry, it was described
as a mudflat. No weapons were found.

As the popularity of the resort ebbed in the 1930s,
the state of Missouri tried in vain to buy the area and
make it a state park. In 1944 a group of men that included philanthropist A. P. Greensfelder pooled $13,600,
purchased 400 acres from the Public Service Company
(which had owned the amusement park), and presented the land to the county as a gift. "Creve Coeur Lake
Memorial Park" opened in June 1945 on the bluff overlooking the lake, the first park owned by St. Louis County. It wasn't until the 1960s that the county sold bonds
to help buy the land around the lakeshore, condemn
the dilapidated buildings, dredge the lake, and promote
the area as a renewed recreational site.

Birders gravitate to the lake; a stray sandhill crane
was spotted in a swampy stretch near Dripping Springs
a few years ago. Photographer Martin Schweig Sr., a former president of the St. Louis Audubon Society (Audubon's first chapter in America) is an avid birder. "In the

1930s, I'd get on the Creve Coeur trolley—it had open sides and was a wild, bumpy ride for a nickel—and ride to the base of the observation tower above the lake. The trolley would circle the tower and head back to St. Louis. We'd slide and tumble down the hill to the lake. I remember in the mid-1930s seeing a rookery with hundreds of herons on the west side of the lake and lotus lilies growing all over the water." Back in those days, Schweig added, "our birding club would put up signs that warned against poison ivy—just to keep non-birders out of our territory."

Another veteran St. Louis birder, Rose Ann Bodman, who edited the monthly birding column for the Webster Groves Nature Study Society bulletin for 20 years, recalls that she and Phoebe Snetsinger, who would become the world's champion birder—tallying more than eight thousand species before her untimely death several years ago—visited the lake in September 1971 and found it almost dry. "It was muddy; the weeds were overgrown, almost up to our shoulders," Bodman says. "But we walked out on the lake—we could have walked nearly all the way across it. That day I saw the first sedge and marsh wrens I had ever seen."

Access

From I-270 in north St. Louis County, exit on Dorsett Road. Drive west on Dorsett for 1.6 miles to Marine Avenue. (Don't turn at the entrance to Creve Coeur Memorial Park.) Turn right on Marine; drive a short distance to the lakeside park entrance. Turn left; drive to the Taco Bell Shelter, and park.

The trail system at this park is in the throes of change due to the construction of the nearby Page Avenue Extension into St. Charles County. Hikers will eventually be able to walk all the way around the lake as well as access the new Page Avenue bridge across the Missouri River.

Trail

Start your walk across from the Taco Bell Shelter near the falls at Dripping Springs. (Through donation cans in its national chain of stores, Taco Bell raised millions for the environment several years ago. Its charitable trust gave $100,000 to St. Louis County, and from this largess, Creve Coeur got a shelter and a boat dock.) The ancient springs are shrouded in myth. Some stories say that it was from the cliff at Dripping Springs that a brokenhearted Indian princess, Memetonwish, plunged to her death after a handsome Frenchman had rejected her love. "Baloney," says historian Esley Hamilton. "There were no Indians around here when the French had a settlement. Some late-19th-century promoter made up the princess story."

With the lake on your left, walk east on the asphalt trail with the yellow center stripe. Note the young bald cypress trees by the trail. They are among two hundred trees of various species planted along the trail after the ravaging 1993 and 1995 floods destroyed at least four hundred trees. According to Kent Thieling, county park arborist, "Most of the native trees that we have put in are conducive to low wetlands. Our policy is to plant at least one, and possibly two, new trees for every tree we remove, so we have much more planting to do. This is a massive reforestation project." This early section of the walk is referred to as Short Beach.

As you proceed, you'll pass two boat ramps, a fishing dock, and more fine, gravelly beach. The lake—an old

Footbridge over Creve Coeur Creek

oxbow of the Missouri River, which is 2 miles away—is stocked with fish by the Missouri Department of Conservation. In recent years, workers dropped around five hundred Christmas trees into the lake to serve as spawning beds for bluegill and crappie so that bass and other larger predators can't get at the eggs. "We tied the trees together in bundles of 8 or 10 with galvanized wire, then weighed them down with concrete," says Jim Kent, a county parks area manager. "We avoided shallow water because the treetops might stick out and hinder rowers and fishermen." The tree drops have stopped temoporarily because the lake faces a major dredging in 2003.

The trail bends to the left to parallel Marine Avenue along a half-mile stretch called Long Beach. Upcoming is the north beach parking area—which, Kent says, "customarily sees 25 or 30 cars parked in this lot at 5:30 or 6 AM"—another trailhead for hikers; it lies beyond the rest room facilities.

Continue ambling along the north shore, noting the Tremayne Shelter (named for Bertram W. Tremayne Jr., an advisory board chairman for the St. Louis County

Parks Department) and "finger docks" near Sailboat Cove, where boaters can float in and tie up their vessels. The Creve Coeur Sailing Association sponsors a dozen or so summertime races on Sunday afternoons commencing at Sailboat Cove. Keep walking west by the docks and past the PLEASE DO NOT HARASS THE WILDLIFE sign; then cross the new bridge over Creve Coeur Creek. Off to the right is the rowing pen shared by the Washington University Sailing Club and the St. Louis Rowing Club. Chartered in 1875, the St. Louis Rowing Club had members who participated in the 1904 Olympic rowing contest here at the lake. In the 1920s and 1930s, the club held regattas on the MIssissippi River between Eads Bridge and Poplar Street, then interest dwindled. In 1987 a revived club—currently ranked among the 10 best rowing groups in America—sponsored a regatta at the lake and has run it annually ever since. Head through some bottomland forest before you make a left at the old Missouri Pacific tracks, and hike by the lake to a trail intersection where there's an information board.

Hikers frequently see vintage biplanes circling over the park area. Based at Creve Coeur Airport, 0.5 mile off Creve Coeur Mill Road west of the park, the antique aircraft are part of the collection of the Historic Aircraft Restoration Museum. "For a $50 donation, you can take a ride in a World War II Stearman open-cockpit training plane," says manager Bob Cameron of the airport complex.

At the fork, walk to the right; proceed past soccer and polo fields on the left and farms and nurseries to the right off Creve Coeur Mill Road, which parallels the walkway. When you reach the west parking area, you must make a decision: Walk straight ahead on the long loop, which we choose to do, or take the short loop.

To complete the short route, turn left at the parking area, cut through it on the service road, and then pick up the lakeside main trail, turning left to follow your steps back to the Taco Bell Shelter and your car.

The long loop stays abreast of Creve Coeur Mill Road, stretching past leased cornfields on the left and more agricultural fields off to the right.

Before you swing left on the path to begin the part of the walk with the most forest shade, look south on Creve Coeur Mill Road toward the new Page Avenue overpass. Page Avenue in west St. Louis County is being extended westward into St. Charles County. The first phase involves construction of two eight-lane bridges, one over the southern tip of Creve Coeur Lake and the other over the Missouri River, plus the connecting roadways. Just south of the overpass a building on the left will be reconfigured to serve as a visitors center/trailhead for this park trail and for walkers and bicyclists seeking access onto the extension.

Shortly, the path swings left. Around the 3-mile marker you pick up the lake on the right, where there are some favorite corners for canoeists and fishermen and even a viewing board for a more focused look at visiting and resident waterfowl. Now you'll pass the point where the short loop intersects the long loop—by a lakeside parking area where great blue herons and egrets can frequently be seen and where you can walk right down to the water if you wish. As you continue, you'll see some benches, walk-in viewing spots, and a gazebo on your right where you can look out toward Sailboat Cove (and see sailboat races if you're lucky). After the trail intersection just ahead, the path will look familiar to you as you double back and return to your car by the Taco Bell Shelter.

4 · Cuivre River State Park: Blazing Star Trail

Location: Near Troy, Missouri
Hiking distance: Almost 2 miles
Hiking time: 2 hours
Bicycles: Not permitted

Cuivre River State Park is the major recreational destination of Lincoln County, which, by the way, is not named for Honest Abe. Major Christopher Clark, an original settler, hailed from Link Horn, North Carolina, and that's the name he wanted to give the area's broad sweep of hills and valleys. But according to a 1925 state publication *A Travelog of Missouri Counties*, "In some forgotten fashion, Link Horn through the years was modified into Lincoln and has so remained." So much for fragmented history!

In spite of the park's name, it is only partially beholden to the Cuivre River, which flows beneath bluffs along the park's southwest edge. It is much more indebted to Big Sugar Creek, which glides down the middle of the park for 8.5 miles, then empties a few miles later into the Cuivre River.

Cuivre River State Park possesses an array of endearing features such as glades, grasslands, woodlands, small springs and bluffs, and rock outcroppings. These features are unusual, since its overall landscape more closely resembles the Ozarks of southern Missouri than

it does the typical terrain of the northern part of the state. Nevertheless, the park's proximity to St. Louis, its 24 miles of quiet, meditative hiking trails, and three state natural and two state wilderness areas within its 6,400 acres stamp it as one of the state's most important and popular parks, drawing half a million visitors annually. The park houses rare and endangered species such as ringed and four-toed salamanders as well as plants such as the auriculate false foxglove, which appears only occasionally on prairie patches. Moreover, it's one of many state parks where restoration of the landscape back to an appearance that might resemble presettlement times is strongly encouraged through such tools as prescribed fires and thinning.

The park has a strong kinship to the New Deal-era Civilian Conservation Corps (CCC), which enrolled more than three million unmarried, unemployed men between the ages of 17 to 23 to engage in projects to demonstrate sound land use and build new recreational areas. In Missouri one of three such undertakings, under National Park Service guidance, was the Cuivre River Submarginal Land and Recreational Demonstration Project. The CCC assigned one major company to build bridges, roadways, culverts, picnic shelters, and four group camps to attract church and school groups, large families, and others seeking outdoor fun and exercise. Camp Sherwood Forest, with an incredible 48 CCC buildings, is the largest of three surviving camps. CCC workers were stationed at the park from 1934 to 1942, when the organization was disbanded so that many of its enrollees could join the U.S. armed forces and use their newfound skills to help win World War II. The National Register of Historic Places has designated two national historic districts in the park—one for Camp Sherwood Forest alone, the other for a collection of other CCC-related structures.

Access

From I-270 in west St. Louis County drive west on I-64/US 40, or on I-70, to Wentzville. Turn north on US 61 to MO 47 near Troy, Missouri, about 15 miles. Drive 3 miles east on MO 47 to MO 147, the roadway into the park. From the entrance, it's 2 miles to the visitors center, where you'll find up-to-date trail maps and park information. From the visitors center, drive north on Lincoln Hills Drive, the main park road, passing on the left Sugar Creek Valley observation platform (worth the stop) and then making a sharp left to continue the trip to the parking area near Blazing Star Trail.

Trail

From the parking lot, which also serves as trailhead for the comparatively short Sac Prairie Trail immediately to the west, walk downhill through a relatively open woodland where some hickories, but mostly white, northern red, black, post, and shingle oaks, reside. "As you go deeper into the woodland you'll see the predominance of white oak," says Bruce Schuette, park naturalist since 1978.

This woodland is an example of the state's intent to protect and restore whole ecosystems. "We don't manage this park to protect any particular species of plant or animal, we manage for the entire forest or prairie and everything in it," Schuette says—although exceptions are made for extremely rare species. Park staff members conduct prescribed burns in this woodland and at most other spots along the Blazing Star Trail. Among other benefits, burning helps clear the understory of bushes and fast-sprouting saplings so that woodland grasses and wildflowers can flourish. (Prescribed burns occur on all of the park's eight trails. No trail is closed more than a day or two when burns are being conducted.)

Historical accounts state that in such open woodland landscapes, settlers could spot a deer 500 yards away. "This woodland might resemble what the first settlers saw in the early 1800s, but of course we'll never know for sure," says Schuette, who adds that "some of the understory grasses here are the same species that would have been seen by the early settlers."

Walk left at the bottom of the hill, cross a dry creek bed, then up a cherty hillside. Here you may find woodland grasses such as wild rye, river oats, and bottlebrush. Once on the ridgetop, you'll find the first defined

A butterfly investigates a blazing star near Sherwood Prairie.

stretch of prairie. Each piece of prairie on this trail is part of Sherwood Prairie, the park's largest (of four main prairies) with around 50 total, but scattered, acres. On the woody edge of the prairie you may see some beautiful open woodland asters in season and one of two species of magenta to violet blazing stars that grow along the trail and within the prairie. The prairie blazing star, likely to be found in the middle of the prairie, is the more common of the species; it blooms from mid-July through early August. The rough blazing star, seen more routinely along the woodland edge, flowers in the fall. There are seven or eight additional blazing star species elsewhere in Missouri. Little bluestem, with characteristic silvery seed clusters, and plume-topped Indian grass seem to be the dominant grasses in this part of Sherwood Prairie. Birds such as field sparrows, eastern towhees, blue-winged warblers, and yellow-breasted chats are found here, especially in the spring and summer.

As you approach the second patch of prairie on the

trail, look at a sloping nearby hillside where, most probably, the land has not been plowed, and perennial wildflowers such as blazing stars, rattlesnake master, and wild indigo have root systems that can survive for decades.

Continue your hike through the prairie and the northernmost part of the trail where the prairie is at its brushiest. It's brushier here because this section of the trail had species such as sassafras bushes that had become more established, and more tenacious, before the park began its prairie-management program, according to the park naturalist. At a major fork, a green arrow on one of the trail's brown fiberglass signs points to your right. (If you walked straight ahead at the fork, you'd arrive at the park's overnight camping area.) Keep on to your right, proceeding through some valleylike terrain. In this open woodland you might find woodpeckers, summer tanagers, eastern wood-peewees, and indigo buntings—even barred owls.

Schuette has a pretty good idea about the presence of other wildlife in the park, which includes the Blazing Star and the other trails. "In the winter, we do helicopter deer counts after it snows," he says. "We fly low, about 50 feet above the treetops, so we can see the animals better. . . . [T]he herd size fluctuates annually—sometimes it is around 200; other times 500, once it was up to 750. Often the deer are bedded down in thickets. Sometimes the helicopter noise spooks them, so they come out into the open and help us facilitate the count. We also see wild turkeys, coyotes and foxes. Two years ago we saw a bobcat."

After following the winding trail through the valley and along the creek beds, turn left at another key trail intersection, and follow the signs to the parking area.

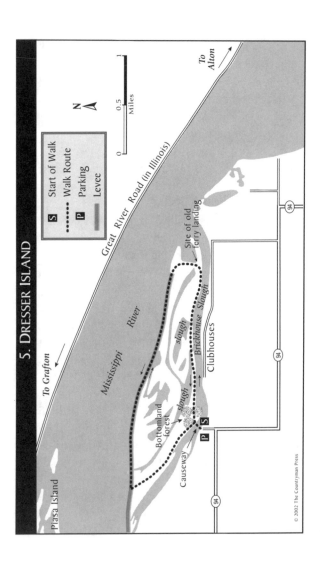

5. DRESSER ISLAND

To Grafton

To Alton

Mississippi River

Plasa Island

Great River Road (in Illinois)

S Start of Walk
••• Walk Route
P Parking
▬ Levee

N

0   0.5   1
Miles

Bottomland forest

Causeway

Slough

Slough

Brickhouse Slough

Clubhouses

Site of old ferry landing

94

94

94

5 · Dresser Island

Location: Near West Alton, Missouri
Hiking distance: 4 to 6 miles
Hiking time: 2 to 3 hours
Bicycles: Not permitted

If you were heading up the Mississippi River aboard one of the St. Louis-based Streckfus sternwheel passenger steamers in the 1930s, ship crew members would call out passing landmarks: the mouth of the Missouri River, the Piasa Thunder Bird, the Charles Lindbergh airmail navigation light (about 4 miles west of Alton on the Illinois side), the Palisades (one name for the great limestone bluffs), and Dresser Island.

Dresser Island was the least-known landmark to Streckfus travelers. Since first appearing on a 1797 map of Upper Louisiana, Dresser has been a floodplain fixture opposite the majestic white bluffs in Illinois. In his *Account of Upper Louisiana*, Nicholas de Finiels called the surrounding floodplain the "Grande Prairie." For years conventional wisdom held that most presettlement islands such as Dresser were blanketed with prairie. Not so, according to John Nelson, formerly of the Illinois Natural History Survey (INHS) in Brighton, Illinois. "Dresser was heavily forested back then," he says.

There is a presumption that Daniel Boone and a

party of 36 crossed the Mississippi River and entered Missouri at the eastern tip of Dresser Island in 1799, en route from Kentucky to resettlement in Missouri. "We're 99 percent sure that the Boone party forded the river on horses from Hop Hollow, which is west of Alton on the Great River Road," says Ken Kamper, a widely respected St. Louis-based Boone scholar. He and local historian Don Mincke came to this conclusion after carefully studying the topography in early 2001. After the crossing, the group probably accessed what Kamper calls "the Trail to the Village of the Missouris ... the main trail used for the migration movement to the lands west of the Mississippi River, and remained as such at least until the early 1820s." That crude road had started just north of the mouth of the Missouri River. Most likely, the Boone party and their stock animals walked through the nearby settlement of Portage des Sioux, then on to St. Charles on their way to establishing homesites near the Missouri River some 20 miles west of St. Charles.

Perhaps the first real inhabitant of the island was Toussaint Cerre of St. Louis, who was awarded a Spanish land grant around 1800, says Mincke, who wrote *The History of Portage des Sioux Township—The Land Between the Rivers.* Cerre named his place "Grand Isle of Pysa (Piasa)." In 1803, according to Mincke, Auguste Chouteau, a wealthy fur trader, adviser to Lewis and Clark, and perhaps the most powerful man in St. Louis, purchased the land, which locals began to call Chouteau's Island. Chouteau, who ran unsuccessfully as the first mayor of St. Louis in 1823, owned the island until his death in 1829. Thomas Dresser, an Alton farmer, bought the island for $511 at the courthouse steps in

1841. He kept the island until 1855, when a partnership bought into the acreage. Ownership changes occurred frequently in the late 1800s and into the 20th century. Mincke discovered that in 1892 a partnership divided the island into 16 lots for a proposed project entitled "Gibson and Reglemann's Subdivision of Pecan Grove Farm." It was never built, but the developer's plat map showed a dirt road circling the island and a 40-foot-wide central east-west road splitting it. Eight buildings were on the land.

Anyone standing on the shoreline of Dresser Island in July 1815 would have noticed some unusual movement on the river. It was in Portage des Sioux that a great council of peace and friendship, ordered by President James Madison, was held with Indian tribes of the region. To protect the 1,500 to 2,000 Indians who had come in white birch-bark canoes, pirogues, and on foot, the Americans brought in two fully armed gunboats and at least three hundred soldiers from nearby Fort Belle Fontaine. William Clark, governor of the Missouri Territory, opened the council and shared its leadership with Ninian Edwards, governor of Illinois Territory, and Auguste Chouteau, who was reported as being resplendent in a scarlet coat with gold braid and brass buttons. At the council's conclusion, treaties were signed with 13 tribes; the following year, 19 more treaties were finalized. The treaties paved the way for the "normal westward sweep of the American agricultural frontier, unhampered by foreign influence or Indian hostilities," Robert L. Fisher wrote in the *Missouri Historical Review* in 1933.

Ed Powers bought Dresser in the Prohibition days of the 1930s, ostensibly to farm but also—allegedly—to run a still. "Every now and then a big wooden barge would bring in a load of sugar so Powers could make hootch," recalls Marvin Little, a Portage des Sioux resident. "Back then, you could drive directly from Highway 94 onto the island to reach Mr. Powers's gate. He or one of his hands had to unlock the gate personally to let you in. He owned a couple of homes on the island and took kindly to people who wanted to hunt. My uncle used to hunt rabbits and squirrels here back then and also pick up 10 or 20 pounds of pecans. He knew where the pecan trees were. I also recall hearing that there were a few wolves left around here at the time. They say that the last timber wolf was killed in the 1940s on Island Road near here."

In the 1930s, when the Mississippi was not as channeled as it is today with the presence of Alton Lock and Dam 26, some adventurers elected to swim across the river. Around 1935 Eldon DeWan swam the Mississppi north of Alton—but not as far as Dresser Island—mainly to impress a young girl he was infatuated with. "I walked a mile upstream from downtown Alton... where there were trees and bushes so I could change my clothes," he recalls. In his swimsuit, the recent Alton High School graduate made it halfway across without any problem but then experienced fatigue. He made it to the Missouri shore by resorting to a sidestroke. After resting for a long while, he faced the return trip. "I looked around until I found a log that would keep me afloat. With the help of that log, I was able to get back across. However, the current carried me so far downstream that I was miles from where my clothes were. Once back on shore, I walked and walked until I reached my hidden clothes." Incidentally, the object of

A winter hiker on Dresser Island

DeWan's affection was not duly impressed with his feat. "She told me how foolish I was."

Today, the 950-acre island is a pleasantly walkable yet complex backwater with many braided and inter-connected sloughs and marshes and a low-profile levee installed by the U.S. Army Corps of Engineers, which owns the land.

"People around here don't understand how nice the island is to walk on," says Mincke, the historian.

Nelson says that Dresser Island's ecology, like that of many other river islands, is driven by flooding. The memorable flood of 1993 affected the island. "Now we have a less diverse forest because of damage to hickories and a wipeout of most of the pin and burr oaks. Because some of the nut-producing trees disappeared, there is less wildlife to partake of the acorns. Flood-tolerant silver maple trees have taken dominance of the forest," Nelson explains.

In 1991, the 5-mile, 5-foot levee along the river side of the island and part of Brickhouse Slough was completed by the Corps to control silt deposits during flooding and render Dresser's interior wetlands more palatable to wildlife. Before then, silt and sediment had nearly dried up the island's marshes and small ponds. With the dam in place, the Missouri Department of Conservation, which manages Dresser, has opened it to duck, deer, rabbit, and squirrel hunting, as well as fishing. (Hunting and fishing regulations change, so it's advisable to phone the conservation department at 314-441-4554 for up-to-date information.)

Dresser Island's survival contrasts with the demise of a much smaller, now-vanished, island several miles to the east. Fourteen-acre Sunflower Island was immediately across the river from Alton, just west of the present MO 367 bridge into Alton. In 1842 lawyer Abraham Lincoln was challenged to a duel by Illinois state auditor John Shields, who said Lincoln had made fun of him in some anonymous letters published in a newspaper. Lincoln apologized, but Shields persisted. So the two of them and their seconds rowed from Alton to the island. Lincoln was given his choice of weapons. "Swords," he said. Since Shields was 5'9" and Lincoln nearly 8 inches taller with longer arms, Lincoln had the obvious advantage. As the duel was about to begin, friends of both combatants pleaded for a stop. Both men shook hands, rowed back to Alton, and headed for a saloon. "The episode was one of Lincoln's most painful memories," wrote Pulitzer-prize winning author David Herbert Donald in *Lincoln*. "He was so ashamed of it that he and [wife] Mary 'mutually agreed—never to speak of it [again].'"

During the Civil War, Sunflower Island was the site of a hospital for smallpox victims among Confederate,

Union, and civilian prisoners of war who were housed in the crowded Alton Penitentiary—bunks stacked nine high in each cell. Hundreds of smallpox fatalities were buried on the island. As late as 1935 skulls and skeletons were discovered near the new federal dam that was to open in 1938. Untold numbers of buried victims were never accounted for. The approximate site of Sunflower Island now lies under today's Lincoln-Shields Recreation Area. The dam was removed more than a decade ago when the new Alton Lock and Dam 26 opened just south of Alton.

Access

From I-270 in north St. Louis County, drive north on US 367 to MO 94 near West Alton. Turn left on 94. Drive through West Alton, and continue farther west until you see the sign to Dresser Island. Turn right, and drive to the parking area by the causeway.

Trail

Cross the causeway, then walk straight ahead—northward to the Mississippi River. This walk takes you along a bottomland forest dominated by post-1993 silver maples, slippery elms, and cottonwoods—all strong enough to tolerate ravishing, unforgiving floodwaters.

According to Michael S. Arduser, regional natural history biologist for the Missouri Department of Conservation, for a year or two after the great flood, Dresser's understory was comparatively bare. But gradually the natural growth thickened. "Everything new has come in via seeds delivered by birds, wind, or floodwater," Arduser observes. One example of flourishing flora: the giant white-to-pinkish hibiscus plants that bloom lavishly by the trail in late summer. Mingling among the flora is a bumper crop of thick, tangling vines: poison ivy, wild grape, false grape, and pipevine. Hiking in late August, we saw a yellowish giant cloudless sulphur, a butterfly species that lays eggs on or hides in partridge peas and clover. A yellow-bellied cuckoo flew over us, heading into the forest to find a cottonwood roost.

Brickhouse Slough is the linear body of water to the right of the trail. Clubhouses, some inhabited year-round, line its bank on the far side. The slough is relatively shallow, attractive to dabbler ducks such as mallards, gadwalls, and wood ducks. Occasionally northern shovelers are seen floating in a flock of common coots. Herons and egrets are frequent sights. After 0.5 mile, the first observable slough appears on the left, bordered by buttonbushes, sedge, and wild millet, which is choice duck food.

On your tramp northward look for sunning turtles on logs by Brickhouse Slough. John Tucker, an INHS research scientist, says the slough has a good mix of turtles, including snapping, map, softshell, musk, painted, and red-eared—the latter two the most frequent baskers. "Turtles use the sun to process vitamin D for healthier bodies," explains Tucker. "They start [sunning] early in the morning, sit for several hours to let their body temperatures rise, then slip into the water to forage for aquatic plants and algae. When they finish, they climb back on the log to dry out. Most humans that Dresser and Brickhouse turtles see are walkers. If you get too close, they may slide off their basking platform. But if you walk by and don't stop, they may remain on their log."

Hikers are sometimes puzzled by rollers that lie

across the path by the slough. These were meant to accommodate duck hunters and fishermen, says Nelson. "If you were a fisherman, you'd aim your boat for the rollers along Brickhouse Slough, remove your motor, physically pull the boat over the rollers and into the interior water, then put the motor back in, and head into the island."

After a walk of 1.6 miles, you'll arrive at the Mississippi. Here you have an option: Turn around and return to your car or continue a full loop by walking west along the river toward the western tip of the island. Look for a trail sign that will direct you onto an interior forest path that leads back to the parking area. You should be forewarned that the river is not always in view from the walking path. For about 2 miles the river is partially obstructed by bottomland forest, although several narrow paths go to the river's edge, where you may see barges, sailboats, cabin cruisers, or water-skiers.

Near the tip of Brickhouse Slough was the approximate place that Boone and his party landed after crossing the Mississippi from Hop Hollow. About 1807, a river ferry started at Hop Hollow and by 1814 had its fourth owner, George Smeltzer, who supposedly imported bricks from Illinois to build a home on Dresser Island, hence the name Brickhouse Slough. Smeltzer's business faced competition from the much busier Fountain or Alton Ferry, located 3 miles downriver opposite Alton. (In an 1820 newspaper announcement, the Fountain ferry's owner said: "The owner keeps a TAVERN at the Ferry, for the accommodation of travellers.")

If you continue to hike toward the west along the river, it isn't unusual to see a large flock of swirling, soaring white pelicans out for a thermal ride on the Mississippi flyway, perhaps America's busiest "birdway." At other times you may observe six or seven hundred of these birds huddled in blurry masses on a sandbar out in the river.

Some hikers have reported finding snakes on this long section of the trail. Three species of water snake are about all that's around, says John Tucker, INHS research scientist. "Some neighbors think the place is loaded with cottontails and water moccasins, but there are none here since this is floodplain habitat. You'd have to climb some of the rocky bluffs over in Illinois to find snakes with venom. Water snakes aren't poisonous, but they'll bite you if you pick them up. So will a mouse."

In the river's main channel, at least 88 fish species can be found, an INHS survey says. But in the ponds and sloughs within the island's center, the species array is somewhat restricted to bluegill, crappie, spotted sunfish, shortnose and spotted gar, and channel and flathead catfish, says Fred Cronin, INHS fish biologist. Although the U.S. Army Corp of Engineers had hoped that fishermen would flock to Dresser, most people fish off the causeway, says Nelson. "Some of them throw their lines in the water, then return to their cars."

In the forest edge along the trail, Eurasian tree sparrows, found almost exclusively in the United States in the St. Louis region, dart among the cottonwoods and maples. Woodpeckers abound here, too, favoring trees left for dead after the 1993 flood. Bald eagles and ospreys are repeat visitors. Birders have come here for years. As far back as June 1934, *Nature Notes*, the bulletin of the Webster Groves Nature Study Society, announced that its ornithology group had visited the island the previous March, noting: "The feature display was the arrival of four Bald Eagles, circling low overhead with the grace and precision of a fleet of army planes."

The trail ends near the island's western tip within view of the Ameren UE Sioux power plant—with its 600-foot smokestacks—and nearby Piasa Island, where there are some clubhouses. The remaining segment (to be completed and signed in 2002) through the forest is about 1.5 miles. "This (trail) has been more or less a service road for the corps and the conservation department," says Tom Leitfeld, wildlife management biologist for the conservation department, "but we're finding that hikers enjoy it so much that we will develop it further to accommodate them."

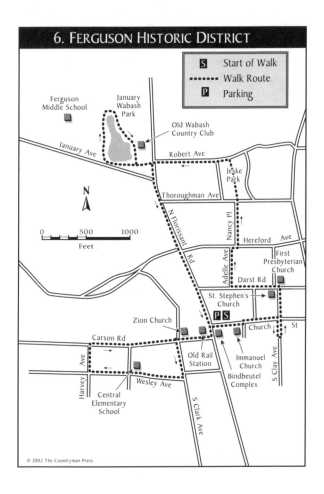

6. FERGUSON HISTORIC DISTRICT

S Start of Walk
••••••• Walk Route
P Parking

Ferguson Middle School

January Wabash Park

Old Wabash Country Club

January Ave

Robert Ave

Jeske Park

Thoroughman Ave

N Florissant Rd

Nancy Pl

Hereford Ave

Adelle Ave

First Presbyterian Church

N

0   500   1000
Feet

Darst Rd

St. Stephen's Church

P **S**

Zion Church

Carson Rd

Church St

S Clay Ave

Old Rail Station

Immanuel Church

Harvey Ave

Wesley Ave

Central Elementary School

Bindbeutel Complex

S Clark Ave

© 2002 The Countryman Press

6 · Ferguson Historic District

Location: Ferguson, Missouri
Hiking distance: 2.5 miles
Hiking time: 1.5 hours

Incorporated in 1894, Ferguson is one of St. Louis County's more genteel suburbs, with some peaceful Victorian-tinged neighborhoods that are comparable to sections of Webster Groves and Kirkwood in the southwest part of the county.

Ferguson is named for William B. Ferguson, who traveled to the area from Ohio in a covered wagon in 1845, pitched a tent, liked what he saw, and settled along a spring on what is now the south end of Elizabeth Avenue. He and his wife, Laura, eventually purchased 640 acres, built a log cabin, then two more substantial homes. Ferguson deeded a 9-acre right-of-way to the North Missouri Railroad so he could open a passenger depot in 1855 (which was accordingly named Ferguson Station). Today the successor depot exists as the Whistle Stop, a custard stand and history gallery. "This depot is the only 'cookie cutter' small trackside station left in Missouri," says Ruth Brown, one of Ferguson's foremost historians. Such stations once covered the Midwest, all built from the same company blueprint, she says. "Ferguson's station is from the 1870s plan of the Wabash Railroad, which featured nail-saving board and batten rather than horizontal siding." The old North Missouri road evolved into the Wabash Railway Company, which, under the red, blue, and gold flag of the "Banner Route," ran interstate and commuter trains for more than half a century. *The Blue Bird,* one of the two famous Wabash passenger trains (the St. Louis-to-Detroit *Cannon Ball* was the other) stopped at Ferguson daily en route to Kansas City. One old-timer remembers Wabash commuter trains that Fergusonians nicknamed "the works, the clerks, and the shirks" which, respectively, carried earlybirds, clerks and managers, and executives to work in St. Louis. In the late 1960s the station was used as a freight depot by the Norfolk & Southern, successor to the Wabash. "We were once known as 'the queen city of the Wabash,'" says Brown.

Until the 1930s Ferguson was considered a city of livable homes with little industry, save for the Universal Match Company. It was close to Lambert Field, the St. Louis airport, "with aircraft flying over us morning, noon, and night," wrote H. D. Condie, a civic leader, in 1933. Condie claimed that Ferguson was home base for "the Flying Haizlips: Jimmy, who set the new West-East transcontinental plane record, and his wife, Mae, who at Cleveland established the new speed mark for women flyers." A *Los Angeles Times* reporter wrote of the Haizlips: "They have taken their town [presumably Ferguson] off the map and written it across the sky."

Along with its handsome homes and quiet neighborhoods came a collection of churches. Mr. Ferguson helped established the Presbyterian church in town. For a while, the fledgling congregation met at the railroad station. The white-frame church, funded with money

On the path around January-Wabash Lake

procured by Ferguson, was dedicated in 1871 at the end of a new street that led directly from the railroad station—Church Street. The Presbyterians occupied their church until 1929, then built a newer building on Darst Road. Reminiscing in the Florissant Valley Historical Society bulletin in 1969, Ferguson resident E. R. Schmidt stated that the still-used logo or emblem of the St. Louis Cardinals baseball team originated at the Presbyterian church. At a dinner of the Goodfellowship Club in 1921 or 1922, main speaker Branch Rickey, then the Cardinal manager, spotted a place card illustration that depicted a baseball bat with a cardinal "perched there-on" prepared by Edna Mae Schmidt, E. R.'s sister. Rickey liked the bat concept so much, he had it adopted and restyled by his ball club. For her artful decoration, Edna Mae was awarded a lifetime pass to all Cardinal home games.

The National Register of Historic Places contains two Ferguson listings: Central School on Wesley Avenue and the Church Street Commercial district, where our walk ends. The hike includes a jaunt around the lake in January–Wabash Park, where the Wabash Railway maintained a "country club" and bathing beach for employees.

Access

In North St. Louis County, take I-70 to the Cool Valley exit. Turn north on Florissant Road. Take Florissant to Church Street in downtown Ferguson. Turn right onto Church Street, and park in the city hall lot on the left.

Trail

From City Hall, walk east on Church Street to Immanuel United Church of Christ on the southwest corner at Lewis Avenue. Once known as "the rooster church" because a metal rooster sat atop its steeple weathervane, the original church—replaced in 1930 by the present brick building—was established in 1888 by German-speaking Evangelicals. Its church bell was salvaged from the remains of an abandoned steamboat. (The retired rooster rests in a display case in the church basement.) Before automobiles, Immanuel members came to church in buggies and surreys, hitching up their mules and horses while at worship. One adventurous member rode his horse to church all the way from Bridgeton. It wasn't until 1941 that services in German were discontinued. In 1995, Immanuel opened the educational building on the northwest corner.

Across Lewis on the right is Vogt School, an architectural gem erected around 1930. The building materialized from the drawing board of William B. Ittner, a St. Louis-based architect who was nationally respected for his design of at least 430 schools over 38 years. Ittner, who died in 1936, told a local reporter in 1933 that consolidated buildings where children and adults would learn together were on the horizon. "The terms elementary, junior high, and senior high will most likely become misnomers," Ittner predicted. "The little folks and the big folks will all go together to the one school in the neighborhood." Traditional classrooms with fixed rows of seats will give way to larger rooms "more on the order of small assembly halls."

Turn right at South Clay. At 100 South Clay is the John Atwood residence, built in 1910 on the site of a frame home owned by William Ferguson. Much of the walnut timber from the original Ferguson home is used in this Tudor-style building. Across Clay at number 99 is the 1906 Sam Pryor home. Pryor gave a daughter in marriage to Lowell Thomas Jr., son of one of America's famous radio newscasters from the 1930s to the 1950s. Pryor's second home, in Hawaii, was next door to that of a close friend, Charles A. Lindbergh, according to *Ferguson: A City and its People* by Irene Smith. Between 99 and 117 South Clay is Allen Place, marked by brick entrance columns. The one-block street, which runs to South Maple, was never paved and retains a grassy boulevard appearance.

Turn around, and take South Clay back to Church; continue across Church to Darst Avenue. Turn left. The First Presbyterian and St. Stephen's Episcopal Churches are Clay and Darst neighbors. The 56-year-old original St. Stephen's edifice closed in 1955, replaced a year later by the present building. Cedar shingles have been added to evoke the original building. The Presbyterians have been in their church home on Darst since 1929.

Continue west on Darst to Almeda Place. The corner Italianate frame residence (built in 1869) at 42

Almeda was purchased in 1897 by the recently widowed Mrs. Almeda Menke, whose husband had been Ferguson's postmaster. Almeda was one of many German immigrants who came to Ferguson to work at the Section House hotel and restaurant on Florissant Road. She met and fell in love with Menke, then married him in his later years.

Turn right on Adelle Avenue, then right again on Hereford Avenue to Nancy Place. Adelle and Nancy were daughters of Dr. John Hereford, the city's first resident physician. Make a left on Nancy Place, and walk to Ferguson's first city park, named for Fred Jeske, mayor from 1939 to 1945. Walk through the grassy park, and then turn left on Robert Avenue. Walk two blocks west; cross North Florissant Road, and enter January-Wabash Park.

Ferguson-owned since 1947, the park contains a 5.5-acre lake and the building that was the Wabash Railway Club from around 1910 to the early 1940s—now the city parks and recreation office. Open to both Wabash employees and management, the club had a 9,000-square-foot dance hall with a hard white maple floor, a "Blue Bird" powder lounge, a dining room and bar, a screened porch facing the lake, and an adjoining boathouse, bathhouse, and dock. The club peaked around 1930 with nearly two thousand members. Summer weekends were aswarm with swimmers; handball, tennis, and baseball players; fishermen; boaters (the club had 24 all-steel rowboats); and picnickers. "You could rent a cotton bathing suit for a dollar," says historian Brown, although a firm club rule was that no one in a "bathing costume" could rent a rowboat. On some weekends special buses hauled swimmers and their guests from the rail depot or nearby streetcar loop to the club grounds, a distance of only several blocks.

From the parking area, begin the nearly half-mile clockwise loop of the lake and the old clubhouse. At left is Ferguson Middle School, on the site where Thomas January had a mansion built in 1842. The six-bedroom home, which burned down in the 1920s, faced the spring that has become the lake. January bred "blooded horses" and exercised them on his own nearby racetrack. January's son eventually sold part of the property to the Wabash. For years January's Pond—some called it "Death Pond," said Brown, since there were drownings over the years—was the favorite swimming hole for Ferguson youngsters.

Parts of the lake are up to 20 feet deep, says recreation superintendent Stan Kreitler. "We have our share of wildlife here," he adds, including the requisite Canada geese and mallard ducks as well as occasional tundra swans that drop in during migratory flights and snow geese with their trademark pink-orange bills and legs. As part of the urban fishing program sponsored with the Missouri Department of Conservation, catfish fishing is popular in the summer and rainbow trout angling from November through February. "I like to take in every scent and sound [of the park path]," writes Ferguson poet Pat Devine of her walks around January-Wabash Lake. "The smell of the cedars mingles with the smells of the fishy water, not an unpleasant odor, rather one that gives proof that primal life exists just yards away from the hustle and bustle of a busy thoroughfare." Thirty tree species, including nine oak species and even some rare scarlet oaks, have been reported along the lakeside walk.

You must hike most of the tree-rich loop before coming upon the former Wabash clubhouse, some of it covered with siding. Before you approach the clubhouse, you'll pass a 1983 picnic pavilion and a children's playground. In 1950, after the club closed, Ferguson built the swimming pool at the south tip of the lake. On the lakeshore across from the park office is an impressive grove of black locust trees whose bright white flowers dazzle in early to mid-May. An underground pipeline carried water from the lake to a tank near the depot to help run the steam locomotives when Ferguson was indeed "Queen City of the Wabash."

Leave January-Wabash Park. Walk south on North Florissant Road—pass the Ferguson public library—then walk under the railroad underpass. Turn right, and head up Carson Road. Once past the depot, note a handsome English-influence redbrick building at 107 Carson; it was the Zion Lutheran Church from 1927 to 1957 and is now a Zion-owned child development center. On the next corner, the new Zion church supports a congregation that organized in 1906 in a nearby cherry orchard. Services were conducted only in German in the church's early years.

Turn left on South Clark Avenue, and walk one block to Wesley Avenue. At 110 South Clark is a century home that served as a one-room school from 1867 to 1880. The building was first located on South Florissant Road, then moved here in 1877.

Walk west on Wesley to Central elementary school, which early on had two classrooms below and the village hall upstairs. With room additions, the building became a two-year, then (in 1903) a four-year high school, the first in St. Louis County. In 1930 the building reverted to its current elementary-school status. The original bell tower remains but doesn't ring much anymore. E. R. Schmidt, a longtime Fergusonian, recalled the school in 1892. "Each room was heated by a large pot-bellied stove. Drinking water was contained in two cedar buckets, one for boys, one for girls. On the boys' side of the building (there were separate entrances for both sexes) was a wooden shelter for the protection of horses or ponies that brought pupils who had come a long distance."

Continue west on Wesley. At 335 Wesley, at Georgia, is a home reputed to have been rented in the 1930s by the future World War II air legend General James H. (Jimmy) Doolittle. (My research places Doolittle in west St. Louis and University City residences in the 1930s, however.) The man who led the B-25 bombing raid on Tokyo in 1942 and who set flight speed records and won air races throughout the 1930s was aviation products manager for Shell Oil in St. Louis during part of his time here. At 425 is the home built by Dr. George Case in 1894 for his daughter, George (that's right—George). Louis Maull, who bought the place from Miss George Case, concocted Maull's Barbecue Sauce, still sold today. The longtime advertising slogan "Don't baste your barbecue, Maull it" may have been created in Maull's home or in the unique barn behind it. Maull's life wasn't all sauce—he once served as Ferguson police commissioner. Turn right on Harvey; walk one block to Carson Road, and turn right. At 502 Carson is the Case house, erected in 1927 with lumber salvaged from a larger and older 20-room home (built elsewhere in 1853 and moved to this location years later) at 420 Carson. Dr. Case, a physician who practiced medicine in

Baden, built the first streetcar line in St. Louis—from Baden to downtown—and is alleged to have brought in the first streetcar tracks west of the Mississippi River. Later, Case served Ferguson as both street and building commissioner.

Continue east on Carson to North Florissant Road. Cross North Florissant, and jog left to Church Street. On the southeast corner of Church and North Florissant is what some describe as the oldest existing commercial district in St. Louis County: a four-building group, some with cast-iron fronts. The gem of the group is the three-story corner structure built in 1895 as the Tiffin Building; it was sold in 1903 to Frederick Bindbeutel, whose family kept it for 81 years. Bindbeutel ran a butcher shop; his neighbors were a grocery, barbershop, and the town's first post office. Next to the Bindbeutel building is a smaller structure containing the Thyme Table restaurant. At 100 Church is Spencer's Bakery, which started life in 1909 as Dr. Walker's Drug Store. These buildings comprise the bulk of the Church Street Commercial District, which Ferguson historians describe as a "rare streetscape from the early part of the [20th] century." Once you've strolled past the commercial district and the nearby 1952 city hall, the walk ends.

7 · Fort Belle Fontaine County Park

Location: Bellefontaine Farms, Missouri
Hiking distance: 3.2 miles
Hiking time: 1.5 hours
Bicycles: Not permitted

One of the first arteries constructed west of the Mississippi River was Bellefontaine Road, marked out around 1811 on orders of road commissioners who sought a direct route from downtown St. Louis to the army post Cantonment Belle Fontaine—the predecessor of Fort Belle Fontaine—situated near the Missouri River 4 miles above its confluence with the Mississippi. The road supplanted parts of what had been known as the "Great Trail," which led from St. Louis "into the undeveloped northwest," wrote Henry G. Hertich in *History of Old Roads and Pioneer and Early Communities of St. Louis County.*

On its way to the fort, the first U.S. Army post west of the river, the road wound past "the Town of North St. Louis," "Central St. Louis," and settlements named Bremen, Baden, and Lowell. One pioneer resident along Bellefontaine Road was gentleman farmer Alexander McNair, who became Missouri's first governor (1820–1824). General Daniel Bissell purchased 2,300 acres of land and built a Federal-style home and started a farm

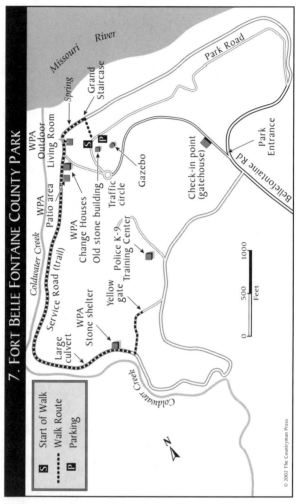

7. FORT BELLE FONTAINE COUNTY PARK

Missouri River

Park Road

Spring

Grand Staircase

WPA Outdoor Living Room

Park Entrance

S

P

Gazebo

Check-in point (gatehouse)

Coldwater Creek

WPA Patio area

Traffic circle

Bellefontaine Rd

WPA Change Houses

Old stone building

Service Road (trail)

Police K-9 Training Center

Yellow gate

Large culvert

WPA Stone shelter

Coldwater Creek

N

0   500   1000

Feet

© 2002 The Countryman Press

Start of Walk S

Walk Route

Parking P

at what is now 10225 Bellefontaine Road; he lived there until his death in 1833. On the National Register of Historic Places, the home is open for public tours. Bissell was military governor of Upper Louisiana, then commander of Cantonment Belle Fontaine in 1809. Later on he commanded one of the last battles of the War of 1812, at Lyon's Creek near Lake Erie. He retired to his farm in 1821. During his tenancy on Bellefontaine Road, there were charges that Bissell was more interested in using the soldiers from the fort to develop his farm then to have them perform their military duties, said Charles van Ravenswaay in *Saint Louis: An Informal History of the City and its People, 1764–1865*.

The military post was first developed in 1805 near a spring at the edge of the Missouri River close to the mouth of Coldwater Creek. Described as being on a "dry, narrow bottom of the Missouri, near a fountain [or spring] of pure water competent to supply 1,000 men daily," the installation was called Cantonment Belle Fontaine. The garrison, built under the supervision of Jacob Kingsbury and Major John Whistler, grandfather of the painter, James A. McNeil Whistler, included at least three companies of the First U. S. Infantry, log hut barracks, a magazine, a major Indian trading post or "factory," and officers' quarters. The trading post reflected President Thomas Jefferson's interest in "conciliation of Indians," Professor Kate L. Gregg told the Missouri Historical Society in 1935. "It was an important part of his policy of foreign relations. With the trading post went invariably the military protection"—as well as a chance for Indians to purchase goods at uncommonly fair prices. Hunters of the Sac and Fox tribes exchanged furs, curios, wild fowl, and fresh meat for cloth, beads, and whiskey. Unrelenting flooding and the threat of typhoid and cholera rendered the fort "unhealthful"; it was ordered atop the bluff in 1810. In its more permanent location—occupied today by the county park and the Missouri Hills Home—were some 30 buildings arranged in a rectangle around a parade ground.

"There was great excitement there [at the fort] in the stirring days of the war of 1812–1815," a *St. Louis Star* reporter wrote in 1932. "Time after time, maurauding bands of Indians, in the pay of the English, threatened to attack. Hundreds of redskins at one time were encamped across the Missouri. But the fact that the strong settlement of St. Louis was nearby deterred them from attacking." In July 1826 the fort was abandoned, its remaining four infantry companies transferred to the new Jefferson Barracks, a larger and more strategically located military tract in south St. Louis County. The old fort's forsaken acreage was sold and resold many times; at one time the land was platted as a subdivision called Belle Fontaine, but the plan evaporated. In 1913 the city of St. Louis bought the property for $62,000 so that it could replace the House of Refuge, an aging institution in south St. Louis that sheltered delinquent and homeless boys.

In the 1878 book *A Tour of St. Louis, or the Inside Life of a Great City*, the barred and grated House of Refuge is described as being hidden away behind a 20-foot stone wall. The inmates, both boys and girls, were compelled to spend three or four hours daily in a school classroom, then several more hours in vocational training. Once re-established in St. Louis County where there was plenty of space and a huge outdoors potential, the institution changed its name to Bellefontaine Farms and restricted its residents to boys. The new bluff-top campus consisted of nine two-story yellow brick cottages (five still are active), each with a husband-and-wife head and matron.

In every cottage was a dining hall, schoolroom, and dorm and about 30 boys. The boys' newspaper, *Belle Fontaine News*, explained in 1936 that the cottages observed "the rule of President Theodore Roosevelt: When you play, play hard—when you work don't play at all." The campus included a large Georgian Revival superintendent's home marked by four imposing Corinthian columns, a dairy barn, poultry house, shoe-maker's shop, greenhouse, gardens, and orchards. The boys soon were canning peaches, apples, and pears from their trees as part of their vocational training.

In 1939 the boys brought out a special "Mrs. Roosevelt" issue of their paper. FDR's wife had paid the campus a "surprise visit" accompanied by Mrs. Edna Gellhorn, a St. Louisan who had been national president of the League of Women Voters. (One year later, Mrs. Gellhorn's daughter, Martha, a foreign correspondent and novelist, would marry Ernest Hemingway.) "This is my idea of what every institution like it in the country should be," Eleanor Roosevelt told a school assembly. "Your boys sang 'God Bless America' much better than did the Kiwanis Club yesterday in Kansas City," she added. Another surprise visit came in 1952— this time a circuit court grand jury investigating complaints of leather strap beatings and excessive punishment at the school. One boy said he had been beaten on the head because he didn't know how to dress a chicken correctly. The upshot of the hearing was that the longtime superintendent was ousted, the place was reorganized and renamed the Missouri Hills Home for Boys, and the school's 64 prize cows were auctioned off so that a new machine shop could replace the out-moded dairy barn.

The boys boasted that their dairy barns contained the "national champion of Class B. "Though there's no indication as to what species of cow that champion was, this bovine, according to their publication, produced "17,000 pounds of milk and 717 pounds of butter in 365 consecutive days. The boys watch eagerly the production record of their cows. Each tries to have his cow produce more than the other fellow's." The boys worked their poultry operation to such an extent that they were able to furnish other St. Louis institutions with chickens and eggs. During its heyday, Bellefontaine Farms hosted out-of-town organizations that came on campus to learn the secret to its success. Even the dictatorship of Argentina's Juan Peron sent a delegation following World War II.

Around the time of Mrs. Roosevelt's visit, men from the Works Progress Administration (WPA) were building several formidable stone structures on or near the campus. The most imposing structure was the grand staircase and terraces, which led from the bluff down to the Missouri River. In its faded glory, the surviving structure still renders a commanding view of the bottomland between the Missouri and Mississippi rivers as well as the skyline of Alton, Illinois, less than 10 miles to the north. Other impressive WPA structures will also be found along the trail.

Not to be overlooked is the Lewis and Clark connection to our walk. The two explorers and their party camped directly across from the future site of the cantonment on May 21, 1804. "They camped that night [the first night out on their trip to the Pacific Northwest] on the head of an island on the starboard side," writes Stephen E. Ambrose in *Undaunted Courage: Meriwether*

In the foreground of this photo is the WPA grand staircase and terraces.

Lewis, Thomas Jefferson and the Opening of the American West. Now referred to as Cora Island (after a 215-ton merchant steamer, the *Cora,* that got snagged and sunk with no lives lost in August 1869), it was known as Chouteau Island in Lewis and Clark's day, says Ronald A. Brunnert, founder of the Fort Belle Fontaine Historical Society. On their return trip, the expedition stopped near the cantonment on September 22, 1806, their last night out. Ambrose writes that the two explorers and their party visited the fort, established during their trip west, and then the Corps of Discovery left early the next morning: "In less than an hour [the expedition] was swinging into the Mississippi River, past the old camp at Wood River, last seen twenty-eight months and eight thousand miles ago." (Another visitor to the cantonment was Aaron Burr. He arrived for a short stay in September 1805, about a year after he had defeated the first secretary of the treasury, Alexander Hamilton, in a duel, which Burr—bitter about Hamilton's support of Thomas Jefferson instead of him for president in 1800—had demanded. Hamilton would die from the injuries he sustained.)

Access

From I-270 in north St. Louis County, exit at Bellefontaine Road. Take Bellefontaine Road north 3.8 miles to the Missouri Hills Home gatehouse. After checking into the grounds, drive the narrow roadway straight ahead toward the flagpole circle, then veer right. Drive along the bluff top to the grand staircase area. Park on the side of the road opposite the staircase.

Trail

Before descending the staircase, note the remains of a WPA-erected gazebo across from the terrace as well as the abandoned caretaker's home from when the school was operated by the city of St. Louis. Walk west 200 feet or so to the small stone building that seems a relic of the past. Its lineage mystifies contemporary historians, one of whom speculates that the foundation may be constructed from stones salvaged from the fort's original buildings. Earlier writers said the building was an office for the fort or a powder house, or magazine. Others said it was an outbuilding in a farm operation from the mid-1800s or a pioneer home. An old photograph shows the present building attached to a larger frame residence that was razed by fire around 1940. Some think the building was an office for Bellefontaine Farms in its early days.

In 1895 a writer for the *Alton Evening Telegraph* toured both fort sites. He said he found the parade ground, ruins of the officer's quarters, the small stone-based building— which he called "an abandoned block house"—and a cemetery with the tombstone of an infant son of General Zebulon M. Pike. Pike figures in the site's history since in 1805 he departed from here with nearly two dozen men on a westward expedition into New Mexico and Colorado. While in Colorado he sighted, but didn't climb, the peak that bears his name. Pike had left his wife and infant son behind at their living quarters in the low-lying cantonment; there is no documentation as to how the infant died. Other major journeys into the west are also said to have begun at the cantonment, one being Stephen Long's scientific expedition. As to the site of the spring near the original cantonment, the reporter wrote: "The main channel of the Missouri River passes directly over the ancient fortress and barracks." One historian summarized in 1936: "The chocolate colored Missouri gnawed away steadily at the low land on which the trade building and the cantonment stood, until the flood of 1810 drove the establishment to the top of [the bluff]."

Return to the grand staircase area.

Lewis and Clark commemorative plaques and a

replica of a cannon from Jefferson Barracks are found on the top terrace of the staircase. Before you descend, orient yourself to the scene before you: the prominent wing dikes on the Missouri River, and the bottomland forest across the Missouri on Cora Island. Descend the stairs, broken up by terraces and landings and supported by stone retaining walls. All of the WPA building endeavors, including the staircase as masterpiece, were built in 1939 and 1940 to "improve Bellefontaine Farm . . . and open the property to citizens of St. Louis as a park" wrote Esley Hamilton, preservation historian for the St. Louis County Parks and Recreation Department, which acquired the site in 1986 and began restoring the staircase. When it was first constructed, the terrace extended to the river and part way to the mouth of Coldwater Creek. "People came here, walked down the stairs, admired the beauty, and then had a picnic," says Brunnert.

Walk left on the service road, which parallels the Missouri River. At about 200 feet on your right is a narrow path that heads to a picnic site by the river and the site of the original spring. "Across the river from here is Cora Island where Lewis and Clark made their first overnight campsite," points out Steve Tiemann, the park department's ranger supervisor for north St. Louis County. Near the picnic site is an unusual array of Kentucky coffee trees. "They're the largest concentration of Kentucky coffee trees I've ever seen," forest entomologist Ramon Gass noted one day as we hiked. Characterized by flaky gray bark, leathery mahogany-colored pods from 4 to 10 inches long, and, in summer, compound leaves up to 3 feet long with 100 or more leaflets, the trees in this area stand nearly 80 feet high and are generating fast-growing saplings. Neighboring cotton-woods and stately black willows are likewise growing unusually tall. The spring is near a typical wing dike, installed by the U.S. Army Corps of Engineers to help channel the river to make barge traffic easier.

Three splendid WPA-made stone assemblies, all within the first half mile of the hike, will soon appear on the left. The first is what Brunnert calls "the outdoor living room and barbecue pits." In the 1940s a waterfall originated atop the bluff and tumbled down the back stone wall into a kind of moat. "It was driven by an automatic pump," says Brunnert. "People would drive here from all over north St. Louis County on Sunday afternoons just to see the waterfall. It was probably shut off for good about 40 years ago." The Fort Belle Fontaine military cemetery stood on the bluff edge near the waterfall pump. Most of its burials were transferred to the military cemetery at Jefferson Barracks. Brunnert and other historians used ground-penetrating radar to find traces of remains from the old military cemetery— but to no avail, says Bob Emde, longtime park mainte-nance supervisor. Just beyond the waterfall area on the left is a wide swath that heads uphill." Some say that's the very end of Bellefontaine Road," says Emde.

Next in line up the trail are the WPA-era men's and women's changing houses and showers (their water pipes are still visible) and the skeletal remains of a large stone shelter, its surviving stone pillars suggesting a kind of Roman ruin. "Back in the 1940s, the change houses were set in an overhanging garden arrange-ment," says Brunnert, who has copies of the original blueprints. "Back then, people swam in the Missouri River, which was slower and more meandering. That was before the corps of engineers put in wing dikes to make it a trench."

Beyond the change houses on the left is a wide swath of open land, tilting downhill. Under this clearing is a 2.4-mile, 9-foot-diameter pipeline that tunnels effluent from the Metropolitan Sewer District Coldwater treatment plant to the Missouri River. According to the plant manager, the effluent pouring into the river at the rate of more than 30 million gallons a day is 95 percent pure.

Foaming effluent rushing into the river carries dissolved oxygen that seems to warm the water and possibly makes the river near here attractive to fish. "Catfish love it around here," says Tiemann. "One summer evening when I was patrolling, I saw two fishermen on the riverbank. I told them the park was closing and that they'd have to leave. Just then, the bell rang on one of their fishing lines. 'Oh, Mr. Ranger, look at that,' one of the fishermen said. 'Can't I stay until I reel it in?' I relented. He reeled in a 35-pound blue catfish. It was magnificent." Tiemann said that other catfish lurk in the water, including channel cats, bullheads, and flatheads.

To see the waterfall effect of the rushing effluent as it's piped into the Missouri, you can follow the wide swath—the tunnel clearing—to the right as it heads to the river. This is a good spot to see the mouth of Coldwater Creek on the left as well as an occasional eagle or osprey and more common creatures such as great blue herons and white egrets. Somewhere nearby was the first cantonment as well as Lewis and Clark's last campsite, both now washed away by the shifting river.

In the early 1800s frontier revivalists appeared in the vicinity and may have attracted the interest of some of the fort's soldiers. The two- or three-day camp meetings gave frontierspeople opportunities to visit their widely scattered neighbors and make new acquaintances—as well as politicians to electioneer and merchants to sell.

Return to the service road and continue to the right. Soon, the third large WPA structure, a 20-foot coarse-rubble fireplace set in an imposing stone patio area, comes into view on the left. "There were plenty of parties and picnics here," says Brunnert, "and lots of bonfires." The fireplace is situated on a onetime quarry site, one of four on the park grounds. WPA workers quarried stone from the property for most of their construction here.

After the third WPA site, the path settles into bottomland forest and becomes modestly hilly as it runs abreast of Coldwater Creek. On the right are some great views of the creek's natural landscape, abetted by limestone shale and ledges, and hillside truck roadways slicing the grounds of the Fort Bellefontaine Quarry across the creek. You'll see many of the 28 stone culverts put in by WPA workmen on the trail. At about the 1-mile mark, the largest culvert appears, providing an optimum place to view Coldwater Creek's valley and limestone ledges. All along the way you might well encounter deer, wild turkeys, coyotes, foxes, owls, and even an occasional eagle.

After passing another quarry site on the left, you'll come upon the ruins of an over-sized WPA stone shelter plus fireplace at the 1.5-mile point in the walk. Unfortunately, vandals have pretty much decimated the place, and some of the structure has already fallen into Coldwater Creek.

As you follow the roadway, the river bends westward, and you head up a hill. (Note a narrow grass path that heads right from the roadway, following the creek. Though it isn't maintained by the county parks department, the pathway can convey you all the way to MO 367 over a half mile away, passing the remains of an old brick railroad trestle.) At the top of the hill, stop at the yellow gate, look around at the leased farm field to the right, and then turn around and retrace the trail back to the grand staircase.

It's necessary to turn around at the gate because the St. Louis Police Department K9 training center, along with a K9 cemetery, lies about a quarter mile ahead on the roadway. Much of the time the German shepherds are penned up, but when they're working in their outside training area, it's not advisable to be walking in the vicinity. Eventually the hiking trail may follow the western perimeter of the field laid out to avoid the K9 center completely and finish the loop of the county park grounds.

8 • Historic Fulton Walk

Location: Fulton, Missouri
Hiking distance: 4 miles
Hiking time: 2 hours

Fulton is a small college town of nearly 10,000 and the seat—since 1825—of Callaway County. It is home to Westminster College and William Woods University as well as to Missouri State School for the Deaf and Fulton State Hospital, both said to be the first institutions of their kind west of the Mississippi. "The town is substantially built, mainly in the old Southern fashion, with here and there a fine specimen of modern architecture, and, with its fine old leisurely homes, noble collegiate and asylum buildings...impresses the visitor as an inviting city," crowed the *History of Callaway County* in 1884. Originally named Volney, the settlement was renamed Fulton around 1830 for Robert Fulton, "the first person who propelled a boat through water by steam," the 1884 history explained.

From 1825 to 1946 Fulton was not well-known outside of Missouri. When British Prime Minister Winston Churchill delivered his "Iron Curtain" speech in Fulton in March 1946, all anonymity ceased. Churchill, introduced to the Fulton audience by then President Harry S. Truman, left enduring legacies in the city. Among them: the Winston Churchill Memorial and

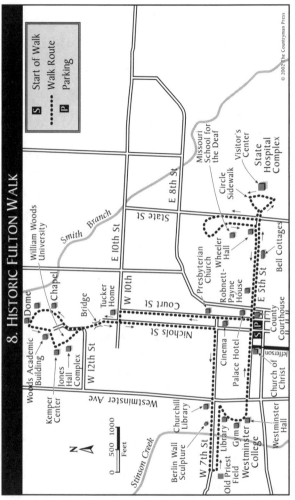

8. HISTORIC FULTON WALK

Legend
- **S** Start of Walk
- **····** Walk Route
- **P** Parking

© 2002 The Countryman Press

William Woods University

Smith Branch

E 8th St

State St

E 10th St

Missouri School for the Deaf

Circle Sidewalk

Visitor's Center

State Hospital Complex

Presbyterian Church

Robnett-Wheeler Hall

Bell Cottages

Dome

Chapel

Bridge

Tucker Home

W 10th St

Court St

Payne House

E 5th St

S P County Courthouse

Woods Academic Building

Jones Hall Complex

Kemper Center

W 12th St

Nichols St

Cinema

Palace Hotel

Jefferson

Church of Christ

Westminster Ave

Churchill Library

Berlin Wall Sculpture

W 7th St

Old Priest Field

Library

Gym

Westminster College

Westminster Hall

Stinson Creek

N

0 500 1000 Feet

Library, which reposes in the 17th-century Christopher Wren-designed Church of St. Mary the Virgin, Aldermanbury, brought to Fulton from London stone by stone and opened in 1969; an imposing bronze statue of Churchill by Czech-born sculptor Franta Belsky, known for his sculptures of the British royal family; the largest remnant of the Berlin Wall in the United States, sculpted by Edwina Sandys, Churchill's granddaughter; and a string of prominent speakers who enjoyed appearing on the same platform as Churchill: Lord Louis Mountbatten, Prime Minister Margaret Thatcher, Truman on several occasions; Gerald R. Ford, Ronald Reagan, Mikhail Gorbachev, and Poland's Lech Walesa.

Stories persist about Churchill in Fulton. On the 30-mile automobile trip from Jefferson City, the party halted at Fulton's outskirts to switch to an open car so that street crowds could get a better look at the world-famous guests. Once into the convertible, recalls John E. Marshall, former Westminster vice president, Churchill supposedly told the driver to stop again. "Churchill reached into his pocket for a cigar, then lit it. 'Now you can proceed. The people of Fulton will expect me to have a cigar.'" That day at lunch, Churchill was served country ham, which he enjoyed. "The pig has reached its highest form of evolution in this ham," Churchill is said to have told the president's wife, his hostess.

Six years before the Churchill visit, a hometown author, Henry Bellamann, published *King's Row,* "a novel that concerns itself with the continuous and varied flow of events that make up the life of a community," in the words of a *New York Times* book reviewer. "The book is a grand yarn, full of the sap of life." Bellamann denied that the book was written specifically about Fulton, but Westminster professor Jay Miles Karr, who republished the book in 1981, said he found Bellamann's original notes that referred to "the Fulton novel." Supposedly fictitious landmarks in the book include "Aberdeen College, the Presbyterian school for boys; [and] the State Asylum for the Insane east of town." Kings Row was the county seat in the Bellamann book. Many Fultonians objected to what they perceived as fairly true-to-life portrayals of themselves, and for years, says Marshall, "the books would be put on the local library shelf and one by one most of them would disappear." In 1942 *King's Row* the movie appeared. Robert Cummings, Ann Sheridan, Betty Field, Ronald Reagan, Claude Rains, Judith Anderson, and Charles Coburn were cast members. Cummings played Parris Mitchell, who aspired to be a great doctor. Mitchell's best friend was Drake McHugh, played by Reagan. Reagan's three-piece tweed suit worn in the film is on view in a display case in the Kingdom of Callaway Chamber of Commerce office on Court Street.

One prolific architect, M. Fred Bell (1849–1929), dominated early home and building designs in Fulton. A historic buildings inventory provided by architectural historian Vicki McDaniel calculates that nearly 70 Fulton structures designed by Bell remain. On the list are Westminster Hall; Dulany Auditorium, William Woods's oldest building; the local hospital; the downtown Palace Hotel; and numerous Queen Anne cottages and enduring larger residences that continue to give class to Fulton's main avenues. Bell designed Jesse Hall and most of the buildings around Francis Quadrangle at the University of Missouri-Columbia. In a booklet published in 1906, *Typical American Homes*, Bell said he could supply architectural references from every state. Beyond architecture, he opened the telephone office in Fulton in 1882, providing the first phone service in Missouri outside of St. Louis and Kansas City. In addition to many other activities—once serving as Missouri's state architect and, later, state adjutant general during the Spanish-American war—he was general manager of the phone office, under a direct license from Alexander Graham Bell, until his death. "My hobby has been the telephone since its invention," he told the *Fulton Daily Sun-Gazette*.

Access

From the intersection of I-270 and I-64/US 40 in west St. Louis County, drive 33 miles west to Wentzville. At Wentzville, ramp to the left onto I-70 west; drive 56 more miles to exit 155, accessing County Road Z and following it through Calwood (at the "Crossroads of the World" according to a sign) for about 7 miles to Business US 54 in Fulton. Take a left; follow the 54 sign into downtown Fulton. At the courthouse (East Fifth Street) turn right, and park.

Trail

Start the walk by visiting the Callaway County Courthouse. George Tutt, retired art department head at William Woods University, executed the colorful mural just inside the Fifth Street entrance to the 1938 WPA-built structure, which is the fifth courthouse since the county's founding. Tutt's canvases depict key events such as the 1815 ambush killing by Indians of county namesake Captain James Callaway, a grandson of Daniel Boone, as well as Boone's own appearance in the county as a hunter and surveyor of the old Boone's Lick road around 1801. There are scenes from the short-lived but well-remembered Kingdom of Callaway incident during the Civil War. In late 1861, the Kingdom story goes, six hundred Union troops stationed near the present town of Wellsville in Montgomery County, about 40 miles northeast, were poised to strike rebel-dominated Callaway County, defended in part by Colonel Jefferson F. Jones, commanding six hundred troops of his own. Spies of the Union commander, General John B. Henderson, found that Jones's troops were well dug in and could possibly annihilate Henderson's forces. Wary of potentially heavy losses among his soldiers, Henderson agreed to Jones's proposal that if Union forces cancelled their invasion of Callaway County, Jones would disband his army. Historians now say that this understanding allowed Callaway County to negotiate a treaty with the federal government in October 1861, granting the county a right to govern itself as a foreign state. Even after the Civil War ended in 1865, the county was slow in being reconstructed and governed by outside forces.

When leaving the courthouse by the same entrance, take a look at Boone's Rock by the courthouse steps. It bears the legend D. BOONE, 1801, with an arrow pointing west. The stone was found on a creek bluff close to I-70. Some historians believe that parts of the ancient Boone's Lick Road now intermingle with today's I-70. An impressive statue remembering Captain James Callaway sits beside the stone.

Walk left to Court Street. On the southwest corner of Fifth and Court is the 1890 three-story, high-Victorian Italianate Clapp Building, with an unusual cast-iron facade. Walk north on Court, where the bricks on this street were laid in the very early 1900s. At 508–10 Court is another high-Victorian Italianate structure. The building at 511 (which Bell may have designed) is the former Montgomery–Bell Dry Goods Company. The city

Winston Churchill Memorial and Library on the Westminster College campus

library once occupied the second floor of the building at 533–35.

Cross Sixth Street. On the left is the Fulton Cinema, where in 1990 former President Ronald Reagan visited the city to speak at Westminster. Reagan's costar in *King's Row*, Robert Cummings, was brought to town for the occasion. "While they were in town we drove both of them past the theater where *King's Row* was being specially shown," recalls John Marshall, who arranged the drive-by. "Both of them were amazed to see what was up on the marquee. Cummings was feeble," Marshall says. "The Fulton visit was one of his last appearances before he died."

At Court and Seventh is the 1911 neoclassical revival First Christian Church. Up Court is the 1884 First Presbyterian Church, designed by Bell, who was a member. An early pastor was William W. Robertson, who labored successfully in the early 1850s to get a Presbyterian-sponsored college for Fulton, then, as the college's founder, served for 30 years as board chairman. Many other early pastors of the church were Westminster professors, presidents, or board members. For decades it was the custom for baccalaureate services during Westminster College graduation weekends to be held at the church.

At 808 Court is an 1883 French Second Empire home that housed Westminster's Beta Theta Pi fraternity around 1915. William E. Parrish, a former history professor who has written *Westminster College—An Informal History, 1851–1999*, states that the Delta Delta chapter of Beta Theta Pi, now located on Westminster's fraternity row, was "the first chapter (in 1868) of any fraternity in the state of Missouri" and is reputedly the oldest fraternity chapter in continuous existence west of the Mississippi River. The home at 810 (another possible Bell design) was temporary home to Westminster's Kappa Alpha fraternity in its early days.

The home at 815 Court is listed on the 1936 Historic American Buildings survey. Vernacular and neoclassical in style, the place began as a log cabin around 1847, gradually evolving into its present appearance. At 915 is the former home (built in 1905) of two recent Westminster presidents, Franc McCluer, host to Churchill in 1946, and Dr. Robert L. D. Davidson, responsible for the Churchill Memorial Library and related projects. Bell designed the Queen Anne-style home at 917 at the corner of East Tenth; it was built in 1906 for J. Roy Tucker and his wife, Mattie, to move into upon their marriage. Once it had an impressive Bell-designed veranda, but it was razed. A new owner hopes to restore it someday.

Turn left on East Tenth by the one-time James Tucker home, a Georgian Revival building by Bell at One East Tenth. A block east on East Tenth is the onetime Seminole Hotel, a four-story building that was formerly the Synodical College for Presbyterian Women, thought of as an educational counterpart of the then all-male Westminster College. It operated from 1873 to 1928, when it ran out of money. Turn right on Nichols Street and walk over the curving bridge onto the William Woods University campus, keeping on the sidewalk as it bends right.

In the 1890s Kansas City banker William S. Woods, who had been an orphan, took an interest in the financial woes of the Female Orphans School of the Christian Church of Missouri. Located in a small town north of Kansas City, the school served orphaned daughters of Civil War soldiers. In 1890, the beleaguered school was moved to Fulton. It chose a new name—Daughters College—but couldn't escape its debts. Woods and his wife stepped in to pay off the mortgages. Grateful trustees changed the school's name again, this time to William Woods College. Although Woods ran a group of 18 banks, he took time to help hundreds of William Woods students financially until his death in 1917. His widow, Albina, later bequeathed funds to establish a William S. Woods academic building. It remains a vital part of the campus today.

Thurmond Chapel, designed in the Williamsburgh-Colonial tradition, is the first major building on the right as you begin your campus walk. Across the roadway is Senior Lake, once a place where only seniors could visit and now, with its concrete bridge, a nostalgic ceremonial spot. "Freshman at William Woods University cross the bridge joined by a chain of ivy; when they graduate, they cross the lake in the opposite direction, and the chain is cut, symbolizing the beginning of their new, independent life," Mary Ann Beahon, WWU director of public relations, explains. When the bridge was a wooden structure—before 1948—pranksterish Westminster men tried, sometimes successfully, to burn it, or to drain the lake. In retaliation, notes Marshall, William Woods students would sometimes travel over to the Westminster campus to soap fraternity house windows. Next building on the right is the John G. Burton Business and Economics Center; next door is a residence complex, and then comes the six-story "Dome," a silver geodesic structure that is the campus center. A 1,350-seat auditorium is housed within it. Beahon says that evangelist Oral Roberts visited the dome during its construction in 1970 and liked what he saw so much that he returned to Tulsa and ordered a similar building for Oral Roberts University.

Cross the roadway, and walk west on the sidewalk by the William S. Woods Academic Building, another Bell job. As the sidewalk loops southward, the Gladys Woods Kemper Center for the Arts, a 41,000-square-foot facility for students in the visual, performing, and communications arts, comes into view. Kemper was Woods's granddaughter, the first female trustee of the school. Next to the center is the much smaller Dulany Auditorium, another Bell building dating from 1907; it is a Missouri Historical Landmark. On the right as the sidewalk tour ends is the Jones Hall complex, once known as "the Main Building" and now a residence hall. It, too, was destroyed by fire—in 1956. A small newer section of the old building, Jones North, was rebuilt after the fire.

While leaving the main campus, look to the right along West Twelfth Street. Several buildings, notably Atkinson and Harmon Halls, once dormitories, are now sorority houses. Recross first the bridge, then East Tenth; continue south on Nichols. At 909 Nichols is the Herndon house, site of an original farmhouse. It was probably constructed before 1877, when Edward William Herndon was born. An undertaker, he lived in the Queen Anne-revival home for 67 years until his death in 1944. At 715 Nichols is the county YMCA, once a horse stable known as McIntire's Livery. Turn right on West Seventh Street and walk toward the Westminster campus. In Bellamann's *King's Row,* West Seventh was known as Federal Street and, wrote Bellamann, the street contained "people of consequence."

The circa-1885 home at 104 West Seventh was remodeled twice by Bell, although he didn't design the original building. He designed a Queen Anne-like front porch that faced Nichols. A lithograph of the house is included in his booklet, *Pleasant Homes and How to Make Them.* Cross Jefferson. The old Fulton Female Academy, long-gone 1850s predecessor of the Synodical college, was located to the right side in what is the present 300 block. At 300 West Seventh is the George-Dulany home that has two "log" rooms dating to 1853. The structures at 302, 304 and 315 West Seventh are all Bell homes. Cross Westminster Avenue, and enter the Westminster campus.

Fraternity houses line Westminster Avenue to the left. On the right is the Winston Churchill Memorial and Library, located in the ground-level "undercroft" of the restored Christopher Wren church.

One should not leave Fulton without a visit to the

remarkable museum, filled with Churchill-related memorabilia. Outside the Wren church, damaged by a Zeppelin bomb in World War I and left in near ruin by a Nazi bomb in World War II, is a powerful Churchill bronze statue executed by Franta Belsky, the Czech who sculpted the British royal family. Next to it is "Breakthrough," the largest section of the Berlin Wall in the United States. The structure was officially unveiled in Fulton in 1990 by Ronald Reagan. The Wall remnants were made into a sculpture by Edwina Sandys, Churchill's granddaughter, who symbolically carved outlines of a man and a woman escaping through the wall. The cut-out pieces (or "voids") are now displayed at the FDR Memorial Library in Hyde Park, New York. In 1992 Gorbachev spoke in front of the Berlin Wall sculpture in an appearance symbolically closing the Cold War—46 years after Churchill had come to Fulton to announce its start.

Continue walking west on West Seventh over the Stinson Creek Bridge to Hickman Avenue. Walk left to look around the former Priest Field, Westminster's traditional athletic ground. From the 1890s Westminster football teams played home games here. After intercollegiate football was discontinued in 1931, it wasn't until 65 years later that football was resumed on this vastly improved playing field. In an earlier incarnation, it was here in September 1875 that former Confederate president Jefferson Davis delivered a one-hour speech that pulled his largest postwar crowd, some 25,000 people. The place was filled with Confederate army veterans, including Brigadier General Francis Marion Cockrell, who was a U.S. senator from Missouri. "Davis spoke about how the Upper Mississippi Valley could lead

America to a new era of prosperity—and not a word about the Civil War," said Robert L. Hawkins III, executive director of Beauvoir, the Jefferson Davis Home and Presidential Library, in Biloxi, Mississippi. "As Davis approached Fulton, a group of Confederate veterans detached his [carriage] horses and personally pulled the carriage to the speaker's platform," adds Hawkins.

Turn around; walk east on West Seventh. Leave the sidewalk at Westminster's Hunter Activity Center and proceed onto the hilltop campus, which is classified as a National Historic District. Walk up the stairs between the activity center and Reeves Library on the left until you reach the main walkway, turning right. Next on the right is Washington West House, the administrative office of the college and once the president's official residence. When he spoke here in 1946, Churchill rested in a second-floor bedroom. After that heavy lunch of country ham, fried chicken, and mashed potatoes, Truman said to his chief of staff, Major General Harry Vaughan, a Westminster graduate and later trustee, "I know Mr. Churchill would like to have something [alcoholic] to drink before giving his speech." Vaughan, as Marshall relays it, sent out for whiskey from a downtown shop, prepared and iced the drink, put it on a tray, and carried it upstairs to the resting Churchill's room. Vaughan rapped on the door. "The president thought you'd like some liquid refreshment before your speech," Vaughan said. "Excellent," responded Churchill. "I was beginning to think Fulton was in the middle of the Sahara Desert."

Next to Washington West is the Westminster gymnasium where Churchill spoke; the facility is now a National Historic Landmark. Next door is the new

Westminster Hall, dedicated in 1911 two years after the first Westminster Hall was leveled by fire, with only its columns remaining. Nowadays Westminster seniors march through the columns on graduation day as a symbolic gesture of entering a new era in life. In 1971 one of the historic columns fell over. Several days later the college ordered the remaining five columns razed. Thanks to alumni, six new columns were installed, all topped by the original cast-iron Corinthian capitals. (Down the hill to the right is Truman Lake, once a clay pit at a firebrick refractory. It sits in the part of town formerly known as Hopkinsville, or "Jinktown" as it was dubbed in *King's Row*.) Last building on the circle is Newnham Hall of Science, erected in 1903 as the Hall of Science. A $4 million legacy from the estate of 1932 graduate Eugene Newnham brought about the new name for the building.

John Marshall recalls a 1960 incident on the Westminster front lawn when Homer G. Tomlinson, head bishop of the Church of God in the United States, came to crown himself "King of the World." "He attracted about 20 people," says Marshall, who was present. "He wore a Japanese kimono. On his head was a crown fashioned out of some kind of metal and painted gold. He sat on a folding lawn chair with gold fringes dangling from its arms. He held up to his shoulders an inflated balloon with the map of the world on it and made his proclamation. His immediate goal, he announced, was to travel to China and march atop the Great Wall until it tumbled down like Jericho. I never heard about him again."

Continue east on West Fifth Street, passing several fraternity houses. At Jefferson is the Fulton United

Church of Christ, once the German Christian Church, which dropped the word "German" during World War I. "I am suspicious that this church is a Bell, but I have no proof," says architectural historian McDaniel. "To me it looks similar to the First Presbyterian on Court St, another Bell Gothic revival." Walk past the old post office at 100 West Fifth, now a bar and grill. Pass the courthouse again, and then cross Market Street. On the left is the old Palace Hotel (Bell designed the building plus an addition) and its still-in-business Tap Room, a traditional watering hole for Westminster students. "We nearly lost the hotel building for a county prison a few years back," says McDaniel. Next door to the east is Bell's 1912 *Fulton Sun-Gazette* building.

On the left at Fifth and Bluff Streets is the Greek Revival Robnett-Payne House (1858). Until 2000, the white-frame home was located on West Seventh Street near Priest Field. Westminster wanted to raze the home, but architecture buff McDaniel and her husband purchased it, then moved it here. Nominated to the National Register for Historic Places, the home was highlighted in a 1941 feature piece in *House and Garden* magazine. Across East Fifth at Bluff are the three "Bell Cottages" (from 306 to 302). The Queen Annes at 302 and 304 are both on the National Register of Historic Places. "A fourth Bell cottage was removed to allow Bluff St. to cross Stinson Creek," McDaniel says. Bell designed and resided in the home (from 1882 to 1929) at 308 East Fifth, boasting that the place was constructed over eight years for less than $66 a month. Bell made this a truly eclectic masterpiece with examples of French Second Empire, Queen Anne Revival, and Neoclassical Revival styles—plus the striking octagonal gazebo. Lore has it that Bell staggered the sites of the three cottages immediately to the west so that he could have a better view of downtown Fulton. Bell thought that his "prize" cottage was across East Fifth at 305, a place he built for his daughter around 1902.

Fifth Street ends at the gates to Fulton State Hospital, the city's largest employer. To explore the grounds, get on the Fifth Street Circle sidewalk. Forty-two buildings, most connected by underground tunnels, are on the property, originally known as State Lunatic Asylum #1, but most are hidden from casual view. In 1881 a building for the criminally insane was opened. The first major building on the right was the acute-care hospital, now used for storage and offices. In the redbrick visitors center/administrative offices structure, site of the original Bell-influenced administration building that burned in 1956, are lobby exhibits open to the public. After examining the exhibits and exiting back to Fifth Street Circle, look behind the building. On the near horizon is the 100-foot brick smokestack, now used only twice a year to burn off excess diesel fuel, and the hospital water tower, now owned by the City of Fulton. In the hospital's peak years between the 1950s and the 1970s when 2,500 patients were in its care, the hospital was totally self-sufficient. In those critical years the hospital had its own water and electricity supply, tailoring shop, machine shop, and dairy barn. (Its cemetery, long closed to burials, has 723 interments; it is located behind the water tower. It opens to the public two weeks before each Memorial Day. Most graves have no names because of the stigma once associated with mental illness.) Completing the short walk, notice the Hyde and Hadley buildings to the right. Hyde was a patient dormitory with about 100 beds; Hadley was a complete tuberculosis sanitarium.

Walk off the hospital grounds, and then take a right on State Street, the north-south artery that splits the Missouri School for the Deaf campus. For seven years Bell was the chief cabinetmaker for the school before starting his architectural career. On your left fronting Fifth Street is the large redbrick Wheeler Hall, which contains the high school and administrative offices; fronting Sixth Street on the left is Ingle Auditorium and Harrison Gymnasium. On the right as you continue north on State Street is the Shipman Building, originally the gym but now a field house, canteen, and garage. Ernest Shipman was an MSD football hero from the early 20th century. Behind Shipman is McClure Athletic Field for football and track events. Continue on to the parking lot on the left.

In the parking lot area is the site of the school's original administrative building, which was completed in 1854. It was renovated (by Bell) and expanded in 1884, burned down in 1888, rebuilt with the help of Bell from 1888 to 1890, and finally torn down in 1957, reports Richard D. Reed in *Historic MSD: The Story of the Missouri School for the Deaf*. Bell designed an ornate clock tower for the 1890 addition; it immediately became a Fulton landmark. A 1927 tornado damaged Bell's tower, making it necessary to remove the top third but leaving the functioning clock. In 1935 this tower and the towers of two other campus buildings were completely removed. By 1957 all the campus's original buildings had been razed.

Look around the parking lot area. To the south is McKee Dining Hall and two dormitories. To the north are the central-supply building, the health center, and the 1996 Stark school, MSD's primary department. Return to State Street; turn right, and walk back to Wheeler Hall. Walk right onto the curving sidewalk that leads past Wheeler and the superintendent's home to the entrance gates at Fifth Street. Follow Fifth back to the courthouse square to end your Fulton journey.

9 · Greensfelder County Park: Beulah Trail

Location: Wildwood, Missouri
Hiking distance: 2 miles
Hiking time: 1 hour
Bicycles: Not permitted

Albert P. Greensfelder, a St. Louis construction magnate who died in 1955, is the namesake of this county park. The *P* in Albert's name stands for Preston. His father obviously had pleasant memories of Preston Place in the Lafayette Square neighborhood, the tree-lined street on which the family once lived. Those memories were apparently so enduring that he added the street name to Albert's identity.

Greensfelder Park opened in 1964 with 16 miles of hiking trails and 25 miles of equestrian trails. Its master plan in 1970 advised that since poisonous snakes were in the park, "hikers should carry sticks and wear high leather shoes if possible." (Copperheads and other venomous snakes are occasionally reported, so be alert.) The 2-mile Beulah Trail on which we'll hike is a typical Ozark forest trail. "You're only 40 minutes from downtown St. Louis, but here we are in an Ozark forest," Steve Tiemann, a county parks ranger supervisor, likes to tell hikers.

St. Louis County Supervisor James H. J. McNary had

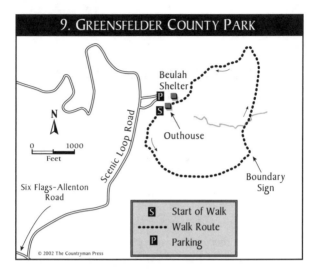

9. GREENSFELDER COUNTY PARK

Beulah Shelter

Scenic Loop Road

N

0   1000
Feet

Six Flags–Allenton Road

Outhouse

Boundary Sign

S   Start of Walk
•••••••   Walk Route
P   Parking

© 2002 The Countryman Press

noted in 1963 that Greensfelder's gift to the county of 1,600 acres made the park "larger than any other park in the metropolitan area, exceeding Forest Park (in St. Louis) by 200 acres. It is enhanced by numerous springs, caves, and a wealth of virgin timber, botanical specimens, and wildlife." Today Greensfelder has 1,734 acres and is the largest park in St. Louis County.

Greensfelder, who left a trust fund that financed the land acquisition, was conservation minded all of his life. At his death he was chairman of the St. Louis County Park Board and before that both the University City and St. Louis County Planning Commissions. He is said to have helped develop the Missouri state forest system as well as Creve Coeur Lake Memorial Park and Rockwoods Reservation in St. Louis County.

Greensfelder was a civil engineer with one main hobby, said the *St. Louis Star-Times* in 1947: "Civic improvement." He liked to stroll in the woods with a walking cane, recalls Sonya Glassberg, whose late husband, Myron, was Greensfelder's nephew. "I enjoy taking in the beauty of Missouri's trees and flowers and taking snappy photographs," Greensfelder told a reporter. He referred to the inspirational power of "glorious fields and forests. They invigorate the languid, recuperate the sick, and refresh the weary."

(The Glassberg Shelter, a large picnic pavilion named for Myron Glassberg, is located within a mile of the Beulah Shelter toward the end of Scenic Loop Drive. Its architectural antecedent is the Round House, the circular weekend country home that Greensfelder and his wife, Blanche, built on the grounds in 1928 and which fire destroyed in 1969. Its stone foundation survives— it's worth the 750-yard walk in from the main park road. Curiously, more than halfway to the memorial, the roadway takes you into Rockwoods Range, a Missouri Department of Conservation tract. Briefly, you will walk on the Green Rock Trail, a well-known 10-mile Boy Scout trail from Rockwoods Range to Rockwoods Reservation.)

As a member of the Mississippi River Parkway Commission, Greensfelder espoused "a green river parkway" for St. Louis County nearly 50 years ago. Such a network would correspond with much of the thinking behind today's greenway networks around the area. An unfulfilled passion of his in the late 1940s was a 6-mile walking trail—"a memorial fairway"—to run from Washington University east to the St. Louis riverfront.

Of the six trails in the park, Beulah Trail captured our attention simply because it was named for a mule. Beulah the mule was owned by Ed Bright, a local horsemen, businessman, and one-time co-owner of St. Louis's

Bright and Free Laundry. When he decided to retire, he said, "I've been in business all my life, and now I want to become a character." He converted to a wardrobe that included a 10-gallon campaign hat, leather vest, buckskin trousers, and a necklace of jackass teeth. He rode Beulah mostly in and around Greensfelder Park, up to 3,000 miles annually. Bright usually threw an old McClellan army saddle on Beulah, once augmenting it with battery-operated brake lights for better navigating at dusk. Bright's fox terrier, Button, often sat behind him on the saddle. To Bright's delight, Beulah was named the world's champion riding mule in 1971 by the National Donkey and Mule Society. He would describe Beulah as "the most publicized mule in the world—" almost as famous as Francis, the Talking Mule.

Bright, who had been a cavalry soldier searching for Francisco (Pancho) Villa on the Mexican border with the American Expeditionary Force, donated $1,000 to the county to erect a shelter in honor of his mule. With hitching posts, cooking facilities, and an outhouse, the Beulah shelter was built in 1972 as a stopover or picnic place for equestrians. Bright said that so far as he knew, the shelter was the only public building in America dedicated to a mule. He died in 1979 at 86, leaving Beulah to the St. Louis County Parks and Recreation Department, which promised to care for her until her death. Beulah died in 1998 at Suson County Park. Her shoes are embedded near the fireplace at her namesake shelter.

Access

From I-270 in southwest St. Louis County, take I-44 west to exit 261, about 15 miles. From the exit, drive north 1.5 miles on Six Flags-Allenton Road to the Scenic

Loop turnoff inside the park. Drive 0.8 mile to the Beulah Area. Turn right into the parking lot. Walk down to the shelter for a look around.

Trail

From the shelter, walk back to the red outhouse with the half-moon on the door. To reach the official Beulah Trail, you must walk south about 800 feet on a narrow leaf-blanketed rutted path, or take the blacktop Scenic Loop Drive until you see the red-and-white squares on trees that denote the trail. When you arrive at the Beulah Trail, swing to the left. For the first 0.5 mile, you'll be walking on a ridge through the upland Ozark-type forest, sharing the trail with friendly equestrians.

Early on the trail one day, we encountered John Henry III of Troy, Missouri, riding his mule, Penny, in an equestrian party of four. "I love the ups and downs of this trail, the steepness of the valley," Henry said. "Of course, my mule can walk anywhere, down any straight embankment. A mule is so smart. On the trail, he walks faster than a horse, who usually just pokes along. When the mule stops to rest, he's all business—he'll never move. A horse will be agitated when he's at rest. Did you ever notice that a mule can position its head to see all four feet at one time? Horses can't do that. I'll never ride a horse again." Brandy, the mule owned by John Henry III's father, was declared world champion riding mule in 1997.

The long entrance into the heart of the valley is filled with oaks and hickories, some old logs on the path, and stunted cedars here and there in the woods. The leaf-covered trail gradually swings north, then comes to a wooden park-boundary sign, where you turn left and begin a long meander down to the valley floor. On the descent the trail gets rockier and in stretches is more a gully than a trail. (Directional signs are few as you approach the valley and walk its floor, so you must be prepared to intuitively follow your nose at times. Faded red-and-white marks or red splotches on trees, predecessors of the new red-and-white squares, can be useful, as well. Additional signs for the trail are promised.) A usually dry streambed lies at the bottom of the hill where spring wildflowers can be rich and abundant in late April and early May. Walk for a quarter mile or so on the valley floor, crossing the stream—wet or dry—at least three times before starting uphill on the gullied, leafy south slope path. After a short climb the path dips back into the valley bottom, recrosses the stream, and then shoots upward in earnest.

The terrain's ruggedness lends itself to local history. Around 1915 and 1916 cavalry troops from the Jefferson Barracks army post in south St. Louis County brought their horses to this valley—it reminded some of them of the New Mexico-Texas-Mexican border—to train for eventual maneuvers in the Southwest with Brigadier General John J. Pershing in the early years of the Mexican Revolution. Ed Bright was among those who trained in the future Greensfelder Park; later he was deployed to the New Mexico border to help chase the revolutionary Pancho Villa's cavalry forces.

In the earliest survey of the area—around 1820—the land around this part of the property appeared to be open oak-hickory savannah, says county parks ranger Dennis Hogan. "Even as late as 1936, aerial photos show what is now Greensfelder as open, with forested

The Beulah Trail in autumn

areas only in the valleys." Redbuds, hickory saplings, and blackberry and spice bushes are part of the understory in this now densely canopied section that you see as you move up the trail.

Some years back an elderly neighbor told Hogan that before World War II, area farmers would get together to burn many of Greensfelder's hills so that their cattle could graze more freely. "All of that burning has helped to perpetuate many of the prairie grasses and forbs in the park today," says Hogan.

The future park was 90 percent savannah in 1936. Nowadays, 10 percent is open, and the rest is what we see on the Beulah Trail: uplands Ozark oak-hickory forest. Nevertheless, says Hogan, who continues to oversee prescribed burns to keep some of the park's key hillsides open, "We have plants here that aren't found in our other parks, especially on southwest-facing slopes."

The botany group from Webster Groves Nature Study Society has identified scarlet, post, red, white and black oaks on the Beulah and other trails. Summertime botanists have spotted wildflowers such as coral root orchids, purple prairie clover, Engelmann's adder's tongue, and wild petunia.

The trail continues winding up the sometimes rocky, dry slope. At a barbed-wire fence that denotes the property line, veer left to continue the long climb out, the deep ravine sitting close by on the left. You reach the top of the slope at the 1.75-mile spot on the walk. The final upland lap of the walk is on what looks like a wide boulevard compared to the narrow stretches in and out of the valley. The entire walk, basically a trip around the bowl that constitutes the valley, is a near-perfect loop—*if* the trail signs are followed closely.

10 · Lafayette Park and Square

Location: South St. Louis, Missouri
Hiking distance: 2 miles
Hiking time: 1.5 hours

At 30 acres and carved from undulating prairie, Lafayette Park was the city's first public park. Dating from around 1836, the place was first used as a public parade ground where home guard militia trained and drilled. It wasn't until the 1850s that the city sold bonds to develop the park and encourage home building on its four surrounding streets.

To enhance the new park, thousands of trees were planted, a lake and a miniature pond were created, a superintendent's cottage was erected, and Sunday concerts were staged that drew hundreds to this "gem of all suburban retreats," as a writer called it. Later additions included a bandstand, playground, Chinese pagoda, rockery, grotto, rustic bridges, waterfalls, fountains, and formal gardens.

In 1868 nearly forty thousand people came to the park for the unveiling of a 10-foot statue of one of Missouri's first U.S. senators, Thomas Hart Benton, by sculptress Harriet Hosmer, also known as the first woman admitted to an American medical school. That Benton was sculpted wearing a Roman toga—he usually strolled St. Louis streets in a black suit and white

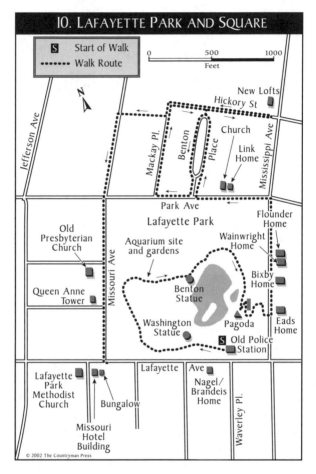

10. LAFAYETTE PARK AND SQUARE

S Start of Walk
••••• Walk Route

0   500   1000
Feet

Jefferson Ave

New Lofts

Hickory St

Mackay Pl.

Benton Place

Church

Link Home

Mississippi Ave

Park Ave

Lafayette Park

Flounder Home

Old Presbyterian Church

Aquarium site and gardens

Wainwright Home

Missouri Ave

Queen Anne Tower

Benton Statue

Bixby Home

Washington Statue

Pagoda

Eads Home

S Old Police Station

Lafayette Park Methodist Church

Bungalow

Lafayette Ave

Nagel/ Brandeis Home

Waverley Pl.

Missouri Hotel Building

© 2002 The Countryman Press

shirt—raised eyebrows among the gentry. A year later a bronze replica of Houdan's marble statue of George Washington, which sits in the statehouse rotunda in Richmond, Virginia, was dedicated. Both statues remain as vital features of the park. Shortly after the 1904 St. Louis World's Fair, a statue of Gilbert du Marquis de

Lafayette was transferred from Forest Park to Lafayette Park, but its plaster-of-paris infrastructure soon withered away.

In 1870 some two dozen European tree sparrows, imported by a local bird dealer from Germany, were released in the park and were next seen about a year later in Tower Grove Park, several miles to the west. Area birders know that the tree sparrows have not spread much farther than metropolitan St. Louis—it's an "exclusive St. Louis bird," the Webster Groves Nature Study Society declares. However, the birds were forced from the city to the suburbs by fiesty and pugnacious house sparrows and have colonized in several locations here and in nearby Illinois. The brown-capped birds with black ear spots have had a scientific name change since their first flight in Lafayette Park—they're now known as Eurasian tree sparrows.

In later years the park erected a ten-tank aquarium, covered with what looked like rock outcroppings, so that fresh and saltwater specimens could "disport themselves," and added as ornaments three cannons that had been on the deck of a British warship in Charleston, South Carolina, harbor in the Revolutionary War. Mule-drawn trolleys pulled in daily from downtown St. Louis with hundreds of visitors. For a nickel visitors could ride three times around the lake in a boat with a swan's head etched on its bow, followed by live swans hoping for food morsels tossed overboard. When the lake froze in the winter, skaters abounded. "No description can adequately portray Lafayette Park. It must be seen, and then the words become useless," gushed a commentator in 1878. In its flush period—the late 1800s—visitors paid 15 cents to enter the park and walk its grounds.

Park police enforced a dress code, and anyone walking on the grass was hauled off to the stationhouse, notes historian Ruth Kamphoefer in *Lafayette Comes Back*. In 1896 a powerful tornado swept through the park, smashing the bandstand, destroying hundreds of trees, and knocking the George Washington statue slightly off its base. "The trees were uprooted and prostrated to the earth like the frailest herbage," commented William Hyde and Howard L. Conard in their 1899 *Encyclopedia of the History of St. Louis*. "Boats were blown out of the water, some landing 200 feet from the lakeshore."

The first homes were built around Lafayette Square in the 1850s, though several country places from the 1830s were already in the neighborhood. Lafayette Street accommodated the square's first homes, and then a subdivision appeared along Mississippi Avenue on the east side. Missouri's best known 19th-century architect, George I. Barnett, designed two residences on Park Avenue in the early 1870s: at 2107 and 2115. Lots were first sold for Benton Place, between Park and Hickory, in 1867. Benton Place was platted by Montgomery Blair, who was then U.S. postmaster general.

Access

From I-64/US 40 in St. Louis, take Jefferson Avenue south to Lafayette Avenue. Turn left on Lafayette. Drive east to Mississippi Avenue. Park by the old police station on the southeast corner of Lafayette, and enter the park grounds.

Trail

Start the walk at the old police station, which serves as both a St. Louis Police Department substation and headquarters of the impressive 750-member Lafayette Square Restoration Committee (LSRC), untiring volunteers who work to preserve and redevelop Lafayette Square, with the park as a focal point. Shaded by a spreading white pine tree, the station was built in 1867 and thoroughly rehabilitated in the early 1990s by the LSRC. The late Elinor Coyle, a longtime chronicler of area buildings, considered the station a miniature edition—"built to perfect scale—of the stylish Victorian manor of this period." It's "a composite of Second Empire with Italianate tower," commented George McCue in *The Building Art in St. Louis: Two Centuries*. Inside the building is a bust of Gilbert du Marquis de Lafayette, presented to the city by the French government in 1976. A member of the French aristocracy, Lafayette, a hero of the American Revolution, had impressed St. Louis leaders on his visit here in 1825. Two years after his death in 1834, writes Ruth Kamphoefner of LSRC, "Saint Louisans who were grateful for his unselfish and heroic support throughout the revolution, commissioned what was to become an elegant memorial: Lafayette Park—the first official park west of the Mississippi River." LSRC's tabloid newspaper is called *The Lafayette Square Marquis*.

Walk west on the path that parallels Lafayette Avenue. The black wrought-iron fence that encloses the park was installed in 1869; its spearheads have been fixed and fresh black paint applied by LSRC volunteers. Up ahead is the bronze statue of George Washington that has been in the same spot since 1869, though it was jostled somewhat by the 1896 tornado. In this area are some of the park's most majestic trees—sweetgums, sycamores, even some bald cypresses. The gate to the left, opposite Waverly Place, is one of eight formal gates and several minor entrances to the park.

Continue walking west, and then veer to the right at the park's western edge that runs abreast of Missouri Avenue. Turn right into an area marked by a sign that says GARDEN IN PROGRESS. This is the site of the park aquarium, long vanished except for the stairs to the east. As to progress, a volunteer recently raised funds to lay down the flagstone walkway that bisects the site. Walk up the stairs; continue east. On the left is the foundation for the park bandstand that is still in ruins from the devastating tornado but is on LSCR's restoration list. Straight ahead is the Hosmer statue of Senator Thomas Hart Benton. Benton, who was senator from 1820 to 1850, advocated a transcontinental railroad that would somehow provide a connection with India. "There is east, there is India," he declared in his memorable "Westward the Course of Empire" speech in St. Louis in 1849.

Walk toward the left to view the three cannons that have been fixtures in the park since 1897. They had been salvaged from a British ship, the *Acteon*, sunk in Charleston Bay in June 1776 in the Revolutionary War. Walk over to the old boathouse/picnic pavilion, erected on the site of the first superintendent's cottage. Next, walk toward the park's east side, noting sculptor Robert Cassilly's whimsical turtle and frogs within the A. P. Greensfelder Creative Play area.

Walk over to Lafayette Park Lake, comanaged by the city and the Missouri Conservation Department. The lake has an average depth of 3 feet and contains mostly channel catfish—stocked by the department from May through October—and common carp, which are stocked in April. Green sunfish are additional lake dwellers. The lake, kept filled mainly by rainwater, is part of the St. Louis Urban Fishing Program, the nation's oldest and among its most successful.

Notice the small island in the lake with the duck house. This relatively new duck house, built in memory of LSRC member Allen Doede, is a replica of an 1880s duck house on the island as revealed in old photographs. Mallards are the main occupants. Turn around and walk to the Chinese pagoda. From the pagoda, look east toward the park's rockery/lagoon area. In the early days a double-cascaded waterfall was located behind the pagoda, emptying its spill into the lagoon. Walk over the 1859 footbridge, built by Koken Iron Works in St. Louis. This bridge was once pretty ornate—it had mammoth ornamental urns, decorative railings, and gaslights. (When gaslights were first installed in the park, neighbors worried that a sudden jolt might set off an explosion that would shake the area.) Ruth Kamphoefner and her partners are uncovering rocks and planting flowers in the mostly dry lagoon area, which was covered with clay, gravel, and rubble in the 1960s, when the city couldn't afford maintenance costs. Many of the rocks in the park are lava or igneous types, nearly 70 carloads of which were shipped in by neighborhood railroad magnates in the late 1800s. Walk through the lagoon area, then stroll over to the entrance gate opposite Kennett Place and exit the park.

Kennett Place is where Adolphus Busch, founder of Anheuser-Busch, had a home (now restored with a gazebo) at 1838. At 1554 Mississippi is one of the square's tallest structures. Erected in the early 1870s, it

Lafayette Park's old police station

was once the home of Josephine Eads (a daughter of Captain James Eads, designer of Eads Bridge in downtown St. Louis; Eads built homes facing the park for each of his five daughters) and her husband, Estill McHenry, as well as Dr. William Taussig, a business partner of Captain Eads. Standing watch up in the third-floor window since 1994 is an ex-Denver department store mannequin named Tallulah—holding a candle that lights up come dark. "We dress her up seasonally," says Melanie Smythe, who currently owns the home with her husband. To the right, on what is now the Gateway Christian School playground, was the site of Stephen D. Barlow's three-story 1858 mansion. Barlow, president of the Iron Mountain Railroad Company, is thought to have platted the first subdivision on the soon-to-be square. Shortly after the Barlow mansion was razed to make room for the playground, the Lafayette Square Restoration Committee formed, vowing to block any further destruction of the irreplaceable collection of Victorian and period homes in the area.

Walk north on Mississippi. The home at 1532 with the lavender-bluish facade was once the residence of Mark Twain's navigation instructor and a central figure of his *Life on the Mississippi*, Horace Bixby. "Bixby married a Shepley. They were steamboat owners who lived at Mississippi and Park," says Kamphoefner, who restored the home at 1526. Ellis Wainwright, who owned St. Louis's Wainwright Building, which some hold to be America's first skyscraper, lived at 1516 Mississippi for a while. Nearby at 1512 is a so-called flounder home (some say it resembles the bottom-dwelling flatfish, which swims on its side). Flounder homes were said to be half the size of other homes so needed to pay only half the taxes. This four-room home has a dizzying spiral staircase, reports Kamphoefner.

Turn left on Park Avenue. Look to the right down Park at the Lafayette Square business district that was developed in the gilded age of the 1880s and 1890s. At the corner, the building that houses Arcelia's Mexican Restaurant contained saloons years ago. At 2031 Park is the gray stone mansion designed in 1895 by Edmund Jungenfeld, mainly a brewery architect, for Ernst and Magdalena Link. In the mid-20th century, the building became a light-housekeeping apartment building with 15 rental units, then it was restored. (Local legend says that Theodore Link, architect for St. Louis Union Station, designed the home, since its gray facade evoked the station. But Jungenfeld's name was found on the building permit by the Landmarks Association of St. Louis.)

At 2035 is the Apostolic Church of Jesus Christ of St. Louis. This was the original home of St. Louis mayor

James S. Thomas (1864–1869), followed by a girls' boarding school, then a long spell as the William Reed boarding home. The building has a flat roof because its top two stories were destroyed by a long-ago fire. The largest structure bordering the square is said to be the building at 2051 Park, now divided into town houses. Before its conversion, the building had been a Bible college and the Calvary Assembly of God Church. In the early 1900s members of grain merchant Charles F. Orthwein's family occupied the mansion.

Turn right into Benton Place, passing the stone watering trough by the east sidewalk. Benton Place, thought to be one of the first private streets in America, was designed by Julius Pitzman in 1867 around an oval common ground. At #10 is a home once occupied by Frederick Lehmann, the U.S. solicitor general under President William Howard Taft. President Theodore Roosevelt attended a funeral at #22 for the owner's son, who was killed in the Spanish-American war. At the end of the cul-de-sac, the home at #38 is rather new, built to emulate the prevailing Victorian styles on the block. South on Benton Place is #21, the one-time home of architect John Albury Bryan whose 1969 monograph, *Lafayette Square*, is credited with triggering the restoration movement following decades of vandalism and deterioration. A good example of a Second Empire mansard roof is seen in the restored home at #9. Mrs. Firmin Desloge bought the home at #5 in 1870. For decades, what is now St. Louis University Hospital was known as Firmin Desloge Hospital.

Turn right at Park Avenue. On the corner at 2043 (formerly known as 1 Benton Place) is the 20-room French/Italianate mansion that Timothy G. Conley in his illuminating book, *Lafayette Square: An Urban Renaissance* called "the most splendid home on the square." Probably the most photographed building around, it was designed by George I. Barnett in 1878 for William L. Huse, proprietor of a large ice and fuel company. In effect, the Huse edifice tripled the size of the home of Montgomery Blair on the same site—a place that Barnett had initially designed for Blair, who went on to become Lincoln's postmaster general as well as owner of Blair House across from the White House in Washington, D.C. Conley moved into the home and restored it to unparalleled beauty. The pre-Conley building, which resembles the Barnett-designed Missouri governor's mansion in Jefferson City, had languished for 70 years as an unseemly rooming house. Farther west on Park, at 2107, was the home of Congressman Anthony Ittner, whose son, William, would become one of America's leading school architects in the early-20th century.

Turn right on Mackay Place, named for Mackay Wherry, an old-time land surveyor; walk one block north to Hickory (which, reveals William B. Magnan in the 1994 guidebook *Streets of St. Louis*, is named for the tree!) Another flounder house is at 1231 Mackay Place. Turn right on Hickory to view the massive stone retaining wall that is 30 feet below Benton Place. The huge brick structure on the north side of Hickory at Mississippi once was an International Shoe Company factory and, much earlier, Schneider's brewery and adjacent beer garden. Parts of it are now being transformed into residential lofts. Turn around, and walk west on Hickory to Missouri Avenue. Turn left on Missouri, and walk to Park Avenue.

Cross Park. At Albion Place is the old Lafayette Square Presbyterian Church, a building badly stricken by the 1896 tornado. The damage amounted to $13,000, but "a society of ladies, the King's Daughters, undertook alone to wipe out this indebtedness," say archival papers kept by the Presbyterian Historical Society in Philadelphia. At its peak—in the early 1900s—the church was said to have the city's largest Sunday school. Organized in 1878, the building was designed by John H. Maurice, who was the architect for many of the nearby mansions. In the 1940s the church merged with the Tyler Place Presbyterian Church in St. Louis. In more recent years the church was known as the Glad Tidings Temple. A local man has purchased the building to convert it into artist studios. At 1525 Missouri—at Whittemore Place—is a 27-room restored home with a Queen Anne-style tower. The town houses from 1616 to 1623 Missouri Avenue have been elegantly restored over the years. On the corner at Lafayette is the 32-room McLaughlin Funeral Home. Built in 1873, the house has been a mortuary since 1909. Its original mansard roof was blown away by the 1896 tornado, then replaced with so-called German Baroque architectural adornments.

Cross Lafayette. Note on your right the Lafayette Park United Methodist Church at 2300 Lafayette. Here since 1889 the church has a century-old Kilgen pipe organ; mostly cherry pews arranged in theater-style, with four balconies—and four 1950s-era bowling alleys in the basement. Walk east on Lafayette. The Missouri Hotel once occupied the building at 2166 Lafayette, but now it is empty, its checkered history of prostitution, gambling, and illegal drinking now a blur. The hotel was

connected by a covered walkway to the small bungalow next door at 2164 where the owner lived for 30
years "in plausible deniability...about what went on in
her own hotel a few feet away," says an LSRC house tour
guidebook. The home at 2156, now a bed-and-breakfast, was a gift from Captain James Eads to his daughter,
as was a home next door to the east. Eads's funeral was
held at 2156 in 1887. Charles Nagel, U.S. labor secretary under president William Howard Taft, resided at
2044; in the late 1870s, his brother-in-law, Louis D.
Brandeis, lived in the home while establishing himself
in the practice of law. Brandeis went on to become an
eminent jurist on the U.S. Supreme Court.

Cross Waverly Place. The sandstone-faced building at
2018 Lafayette also contends as tallest structure on the
square. Its "windowed roof structure," as the American
Institute of Arts calls it, "provides 'chimney effect' cooling by circulating hot air out when cool air is admitted
on the first floor." The home at 2012 is erected on the
site of a mansion built by David Nicholson, a wealthy
wine and food importer/retailer and purportedly the
city's leading seller of bourbon and rye. He created
"David Nicholson's Liquid Bread, a substitute for all
alcoholic abuse...used by invalids with the most beautiful results." If you wish, you can remember Nicholson today by purchasing a bottle of David Nicholson
1843 brand Kentucky straight bourbon whiskey at your
package store. Here the walk ends since you're close to
the old police station and your parked automobile.

II · Meramec State Park Wilderness Trail: South Loop

Location: Near Sullivan, Missouri
Hiking distance: 6 miles
Hiking time: 3 hours
Bicycles: Not permitted

Old attendance and use records tell us that in the busy summer of 1938, when Meramec State Park, then Missouri's largest, was only nine years old, visitors were coming in droves. From mid-June through October, 63,550 visitors were counted. Ranking as the number-one activity for visitors was picnicking, followed by day camping, then "auto riding." Nearly five thousand swimmers and bathers were counted on or near the Meramec River, which flows for 8 miles along park borders. Even waders were registered by the vigilant counters; there were 144 of them riverside.

Since the Missouri state park system was relatively new, as were many of our state and county roads, Missourians were prone to sightsee in prodigious numbers. The Missouri State Park Board in 1938 reported that in all the state parks combined sightseeing was the primary activity (47 percent of all visitors were classified as sightseers.) Hiking and nature study were combined by

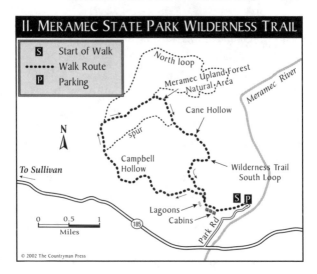

statisticians; nearly 8 percent of park users fell into that category.

In the year 2000, visitors to Meramec totaled more than half a million. "You'd be surprised what people come here looking for," says Daniel Drees, until recently a park naturalist here for more than 20 years. Among the quarries: spring wildflowers, mushrooms, deer, dogwood and redbud in bloom (this draws travelers from northern Illinois and Minnesota, where there are few such trees), the banana-like fruit of pawpaw trees, yellow lady's slippers, and caves (the park reportedly has more caves than any other state park in America). "We have inventoried 48 caves of all sizes in the park," reports Drees. "There's never a week in the year when there aren't cave explorers down here."

One cave, Fisher, is a showpiece. "It has many miles of passageways with numerous stalagtites and stalagmites that are a wonder of the first magnitude," stated *A*

Century Passes but Memory Lingers On: The Centennial History of Sullivan, Missouri. Fisher was known as one of the state's party caves between 1890 and 1910. These parties "attracted large numbers of participants from St. Louis and were advertised by the railroads," writes H. Dwight Weaver in *Missouri: The Cave State.* Events in the caves included meals, singing, dancing, swimming, and cave exploration. In 1867 Missouri Governor Thomas Fletcher invited his cronies in for a dance in the cave's largest room. Today, reminds Drees, Fisher "is a sanctuary for cave life only visited by guided tours—as it should be."

For St. Louisans, Meramec has been a crowd drawer since it opened in 1927, when a Mrs. Holman Hinchcliffe sang the "Star Spangled Banner" and Governor Sam A. Baker gave a speech. In the late 1920s and early 1930s, members of the Webster Groves Nature Study Society (WGNSS) would pile into cars and drive down Route 66 to reach the park. Some members practiced the novel sport of "birding by automobile." This was achievable when you drove about 40 miles an hour and trained your binoculars in the right places, members claimed. Of course, the driver was prohibited from birdwatching. In June 1935 its newsletter said that a WGNSS group "parked under the trees and began their hike without a trail." What they saw back then is still pretty viewable today, at least on the Wilderness Trail.

While some WGNSS members hiked on that June day, others stayed behind to pick blueberries. When the hikers returned, they found the berry pickers in a "rapt circle" around a nighthawk, "which remained unmoved upon the ground with one downy chick under her wing and the other 2 inches away. While cameras clicked away, the bird permitted her head to be stroked, her chick to be petted, and her wing to be spread. After seeing that display, nothing which occurred thereafter seemed eventful," reported a WGNSS bulletin.

Today's park infrastructure is supported in part by a collection of stone buildings and structures built by members of Company 2604 of the Civilian Conservation Corps (CCC). They were among the one hundred thousand Missourians in 41 state camps who planted trees, erected fire towers, dug out lakes and irrigation projects, laid out roads and campgrounds, and constructed lodges, shelters and other buildings. At Meramec, CCCers put up the dining lodge, cabins (now extensively altered), recreational hall and dance floor (now a park storage place), picnic shelters and concession building, plus some of the trails. Three CCC buildings—an octagonal trail shelter near the Bluffview Trail (used as a prototype for National Park Service shelters built in the 1930s and 1940s), a pump house south of the dining lodge, and a handsome stone picnic shelter with flagstone floors on the south side of the MO 185 bridge—are on the National Register of Historic Places.

Deer are abundant in the park, says Drees, but this has not always been so. Early in the 19th century, from 345,000 to 690,000 deer were in Missouri, according to Charles and Elizabeth Schwartz in *Wild Mammals of Missouri*. But deer habitat dwindled as land was cultivated. By 1925 only some 395 deer remained in the state. So Missouri was forced to import deer from other states, notably Michigan, to "restock vacant habitat." Imported deer were brought to Meramec and a few other parks, and released. The program was very successful. With turkeys also in short supply in 1925 the conservation department began a program of importing what it termed "semiwild" turkeys. In 1932, one report says, the department purchased 600 "semiwilds" for release in Meramec and other parks.

Access

From I-70 in south St. Louis County, drive 48 miles on I-44 to exit 226 at Sullivan, Missouri. Drive left on MO 185 for about 3 miles to the park visitors center. Follow the park road from the visitors center to the Wilderness Trail sign in a parking lot, nearly 1 mile away.

Trail

From the trailhead parking lot, cross a wooden footbridge, and then proceed uphill to walk past the CCC-era cabins (20 are in the park) into the oak-hickory upland forest that prevails through most of the Wilderness Trail. The rocky path passes the park's three-lagoon sewage treatment system, which is down the hill to the left (hard to see in warm months because of thickened vegetation) as well as what Dan Drees, the naturalist, calls a "necklace of glades" on the right.

The series of glades that stretches along the hill on the right is loaded with plants and small trees that thrive in arid soil. "These are what I call low-integrity glades," says Drees, "because they are overgrown in red cedar trees." In the spring one sees bright-red Indian paintbrush in full flower and later on other glade favorites: prairie dock, purple coneflowers, and, of course, big and little bluestem. Managing the park's 48 distinct glades is a nonending task, says Drees. When he takes to the trail, he carries a pair of long-handled pruning sheers to snip invasive plants or a can of herbicide spray to block the growth of non-native plants, such as bush honeysuckle or autumn olive. Left to themselves, invaders can overtake and change the natural character of the land. "We don't do proactive trail maintenance here because our staff is stretched too thin," Drees says. "The trail pretty much manages itself. If there is a problem with a tree down or a boulder on the path, hikers usually report it, and we follow up." The same procedure is followed at most parks and conservation areas.

The trail continues through the length of Campbell Hollow, plunging into some of the park's most mature, remote, and densest parts. Here birders find Kentucky warblers, ovenbirds, and wood thrushes in the May and June migratory and breeding seasons. Here, too, are Bewick's wrens, great-crested flycatchers, and tanagers. By late June, Drees observes, the melodic singing of some of the birds falls off as they establish territories and start producing families. "They still will sing at sunrise or if the weather is cool, but there is usually not much intense singing since they are busy raising their young near their nesting sites."

After noting a sign pointing to backcountry Camp A—Meramec has seven similar backpack camps—you will cross Campbell Hollow Creek (something you will do often over the next 2 miles). Chunks of iron ore—including a huge moss-covered piece wedged next to a sycamore tree root—are exposed. "In the 1870s an iron smelting operation was located in Hamilton Hollow, about 5 miles away. The abundance of these surface iron deposits made the smelter feasible," says Drees.

When you spot the sign to Camp B, follow it over a creek bed to the campsite. Whatever the time of year, a pool of water can usually be found in the creek bed,

Along the Wilderness Trail in Cane Hollow

observes Drees. He spots some sculpin, a dark and wrinkled prehistoric fish species, scooting around the pool surface. Close by are orange-throated darters and red-bellied dace—named for the vibrant-red stomach of the male during breeding season—so resourceful that they can live in apparently dry creeks by burrowing deep until they find a trickle of water to tide them over until the next big rain. Drees says that in the early 1900s this valley, or hollow, was owned by poor families on small farms where corn was raised on cherty fields, and hogs and goats ranged openly. "Many of those hardy people ate possum or raccoons. If it fit into a stew pot, they ate it. And, as the saying goes, if it was green, they either ate it or their livestock ate it," Drees says. "This once-depleted land is testimony to the resiliency of Mother Nature if you save all the pieces."

Before the fourth creek bed crossing, look to the right and slightly uphill to find the first cave on this trail. Drees, who has explored most of the park's caves, says that this one may double as a bobcat den. After a snow bobcat tracks are visible near and inside the cave entrance. Ordinarily nocturnal animals, bobcats can also relish the sunlight. "Many of them are surprisingly comfortable being seen by people," says Drees, who adds that active bobcat dens are close to the trail but are purposely not identified to the public. "Too much disturbance at the entrance of their den might cause the dens to be abandoned," Drees explains. On the left side of the trail opposite the first cave, a walk uphill will bring you to the site of an abandoned small quarry that may have yielded foundation stones for the CCC cabins. On ahead and still off the trail is the second cave in the area with a tight entrance but a half-mile passage for experienced cavers. No one is allowed inside without a permit, obtainable at the visitors center.

Continue on the main trail; cross and recross the Campbell Hollow creek bed several more times as you troop through the deep forest interior. On a rare occasion a hiker may see a black bear roaming the hillside. "We have had substantial bear activity in the park for more than a decade," reports Drees. All of the sightings, including one in the camping area by the Meramec River, have been single bears only. "A while ago, however, a female with cubs was spotted upstream from the park. We were excited by this." Bears don't use the caves to hibernate, adds Drees. "The caves are too tarnished with human scent for them, so they dig their dens elsewhere." (In earlier days bears were common in Missouri woodlands, state Charles and Elizabeth Schwartz. "Both settlement and sport hunting caused the disappearance [after 1880] of this large mammal from Missouri." It was around 1950 that bears began reappearing in the state.)

In the forest depths pileated woodpeckers and wood thrushes visit often when fruit from the serviceberry and other trees and bushes ripen in June. That brings out birders, as well, of course. In late April and early May, dogwoods and redbuds put on phenomenal color displays here. Dogwood, Missouri's official state tree, is the dominant understory tree in the forest. As the trail proceeds, moss appears on the path, a suggestion that the trail is not used often enough to stamp out the moss. "This is also testimony to the privacy of the Wilderness Trail," says Drees of the park's least used walkway.

Between the mossy section of the trail and an upcoming Missouri shortleaf pine plantation you will cross the Spur 185 blacktop road, at about the 2-mile mark of the walk, and take a right at a trail fork. The pines were put in as 16-inch seedlings by CCC workers in the 1930s. Cross an abandoned forest road and walk into the section of the park called Cane Hollow. This area is burned every five years or so mostly to protect the protein- and fat-rich oak and hickory trees. "All of Cane is a prescribed burn unit. In the burning, most of our understory dogwoods and redbuds are thinned or eliminated so we have a more open, sun-filled understory," explains Drees, who was the park's burn boss and chief fire starter. "This is the type of open woodland that early settlers described," he says. And due to its openness, scarlet tanagers and indigo buntings consider it choice territory in their active seasons.

Soon a trail sign announces your entry into the Meramec Upland Forest Natural Area where there are off-trail caves, sinkholes, and glades. "This area remains pretty natural," says Drees. "It has never been farmed, has no pine plantation, quarries, or old logging roads. It has a superlative natural integrity."

Another trail sign soon signals that the north loop is rejoining the south loop; at the sign, walk to your right. In this vicinity—beyond the creek bed—at least 100 yellow lady's slipper plants are sought out by orchid aficionados each mid-May. After the walk along the creek bed, you must climb a hearty hill on top of which are major sinkholes where salamanders and frogs reside. In the first warm, wet days of spring, the mating calls of the frogs can be overwhelming, says Drees. A CCC-installed white pine plantation lies ahead, where some trees reach 100 feet, though the average is around 75 feet.

After 4 miles of hiking, cross Spur 185 again to enter Deer Hollow, where the conservation department released imported deer from Michigan 70 years ago. This part of the trail is the place to find—and pick—orange- or yellow-capped chanterelle mushrooms, "the most delectable of all mushrooms, including morels," declares Drees, who harvests them with family members after midsummer rains. Guidebooks warn, however, that inexperienced mushroomers should not casually pick and eat chanterelles since they resemble Jack-o'-lantern and other poisonous species. Better bring a mushroom expert along with you!

When the sign to Camp H appears, fork right to hike up another tough hill. Then cross a gravel service road, and re-enter Campbell Hollow. From here on it's mostly a downhill walk on a gravelly and dry south-facing slope. When the familiar necklace of glades pops up on your right, you'll know that the hike is nearing an end. Soon you'll rejoin the main path where you must turn left for the short hike back to the parking area.

12 · Overland Estates Trail

Location: Overland, Missouri
Hiking distance: 4 miles
Hiking time: 1.5 hours

According to Robert E. Parkin's 1956 *Overland Trails and Trials and Your Community Today*, the area of northwest St. Louis County known as Overland was settled first by Mr. and Mrs. William Walton from Virginia around 1792. The Walton homestead was supposedly near present-day Midland Boulevard and Woodson Road, close to Overland's central business district.

The Waltons seemed to have bred well. Slaveholders until at least the early 1850s, they continued to own property—minus slaves— in the northwest county. James Walton, William's grandson, owned land at Page and Woodson in 1878. His daughter, Cyrene, married Martin F. Hanley, whose family had settled in Clayton. A son Charles married Sarah Ann McCausland, whose family owned much of what is now Richmond Heights. Another pioneer, Rufus J. Lackland, built a plantation-style home around 1844. He later became president of Boatmen's Savings Bank in St. Louis.

During the Gilded Age of the late-19th century, some fairly large estates appeared in the Overland area. Henry D. Laughlin had an estate that included a deer park and fish pond at Brown and Lackland Roads. In 1894 his

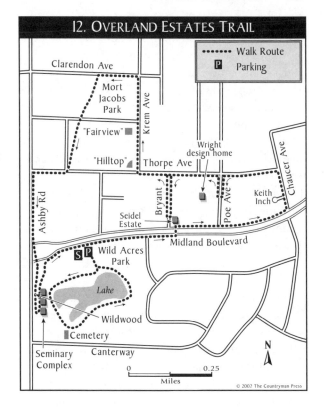

12. OVERLAND ESTATES TRAIL

•••••• Walk Route

P Parking

Clarendon Ave

Mort Jacobs Park

Krem Ave

"Fairview"

Wright design home

"Hilltop"

Thorpe Ave

Chaucer Ave

Ashby Rd

Bryant

Poe Ave

Keith Inch

Seidel Estate

Midland Boulevard

S P Wild Acres Park

Lake

Wildwood

Cemetery

Seminary Complex

Canterway

N

0   0.25

Miles

© 2002 The Countryman Press

daughter, Hester Bates Laughlin, was named the Veiled Prophet queen in St. Louis. His son, Randolph, owned Loch-Lin, where fox hunts with some 50 hunters wearing bright red coats were held regularly.

In the early-20th century, Overland's boundaries had been defined, although no legal entity known as Overland existed until the town's latter-day incorporation in 1939. An early real-estate leader was Edward Gocke, credited with developing from 30 to 35 subdivisions in Overland and neighboring communities. In 1914 he helped organize the Midland Valley (Meadowbrook) Country Club on Midland Boulevard. Meadowbrook moved to west St. Louis County long ago; a pleasant ranch-home subdivision called Midland Valley Estates occupies the club's old grounds. Gocke built the home on Poe Avenue near Midland known as the Frank Lloyd Wright home. In 1936, says Parkin, Gocke was named Missouri's "safest driver in recognition of his driving an estimated 279,270 miles in 26 years without an accident." The mileage total included both horse and buggy and automobile miles, Parkin explained. When Overland incorporated, Gocke was president of the local Businessmen's Association. Some homes on our walk were erected on Gocke-developed land.

Access

From North Lindbergh Boulevard in north St. Louis County, take the Midland Boulevard exit. Drive east on Midland for about 1 mile to the Ashby Road off-ramp. Follow the ramp; drive straight ahead at the stoplight (do not turn onto Ashby Road), and then turn into the parking lot at Wild Acres Park on the right. Begin your Overland hike by walking around the park lake.

Trail

Walk into the 25-acre Wild Acres Park, passing both a DO NOT FEED THE GEESE sign and a flourishing demonstration prairie. Turn right onto an asphalt path that rings the 2.5 -acre lake. This property was owned by the Holy Family Seminary for nearly 50 years until dwindling enrollment forced the seminary's closing in 1994. In the 1950s the seminarians doubled the size of the lake, making it a great fishing hole, according to Chuck

Boone, assistant public works director for Overland. Nowadays, the Missouri Department of Conservation partners with Overland to stock the lake with large-mouth bass, bluegill, channel catfish, green sunfish, and trout.

As the evergreen-lined path swings left, an imposing collection of buildings appears on the right. This is the former Holy Family Seminary complex, centered around a large home built in 1903 for paper manufacturer Charles D. Garnett, who called the place Wildwood. The *St. Louis Post-Dispatch* said in 1908 that Garnett's estate at 2500 Ashby Road was in the vanguard of homes being erected by wealthy St. Louisans who want-ed to escape the "smoke and din" of the big city. "[As the] automobile became an everyday affair, rich men began to realize that, if they moved a few miles further away and dwelt in the open country, the long distance would be immaterial. They could reach their offices quickly in the swift touring car." Garnett was said to be the first prominent St. Louisan to adapt "the elaborate country estate idea."

The *Post-Dispatch* described the buff brick Roman home as situated "on a knoll overlooking the county in every direction and surrounded by about 30 acres of magnificent old-growth forest. The grounds, naturally beautiful, are laid out with drives, bridges, granitoid walks, ornamental shade trees, and shrubbery. There is also a fine lake on the place and an extensive orchard and garden." The lake remains, as do some of the shade trees and shrubs; the old forest is gone. Architecturally, the mansion was described as renaissance revival. Con-crete was apparently a Garnett passion. "All of his foun-dations are built of that material and in some cases

At 2615 Poe is a Frank Lloyd Wright–designed home.

entire buildings are made of it. [Many ancillary buildings were on the grounds.] Upwards of 35 cars of cement, sand and crushed rock alone have been used in various building operations on the place," the newspaper reported.

Once a partner in a prominent paper company that faced bankruptcy, the 49-year-old Garnett had recently been summoned to a hearing to determine the whereabouts of $160,000 missing from the partnership. He made the decision to travel to New York City, where he was found shot to death by his own hand. After Garnett's death the home was sold to Louis A. Cella, the racetrack and theater owner who lived there from 1909 to 1918. At the time he moved in, says Esley Hamilton, preservation historian for the St. Louis County Parks and Recreation Department, Cella was reputed to be the wealthiest man in St. Louis. The *St. Louis Globe-Democrat* said that Cella's estate included "a $75,000 garage, said to be the finest private auto storehouse in America." As the half-mile lake walk bends to the left, note a crumbling concrete bridge on the right. Some speculate that the bridge (earmarked for future restoration by park officials) was a fixture on the 1904 St. Louis World's Fair grounds, but that notion has been quashed by historians who believe it was built in 1907 along with other concrete structures on the Garnett estate. Continue walking past several small buildings that were once garages. One of them, St. Joseph's Hall, was used as a kind of rec room by the seminarians. At the east end of the walkway is a gate leading into Holy Family Cemetery. Closed to burials in 1986, there are 46 known interments in the small plot. Most of the burials were religious brothers associated with the seminary. Return to the walkway, which leads you down a stretch by the steep lake banks where fishermen, including fly casters, can usually be seen in action.

Boone reveals that there are 2-pound goldfish carp in the lake "just like some of those you see in aquariums in Chinese restaurants." The park is home to several species of wild animals, he says. "I have seen a family of red foxes, several coyotes, some deer, beavers, and groundhogs."

Exit the park through its front entrance. Walk to the right along a chain-link fence. When Midland Boulevard is clear of traffic, hurry across it, and continue east to Chaucer Avenue. Walk left on Chaucer to Keith Inch Court, a cul de sac. Take a look at the large home at 10500, a timbered Tudor structure erected in 1905 by William Sutherland, a Scottish architect. The "inch" in Keith Inch is apparently derived from the Gaelic word *innis*, meaning island. In 1911 the family of John A. Harrison bought the home. "Water was funneled from a backyard pump house to a huge water tank on our third floor and from there piped down throughout the home," wrote one surviving Harrison grandniece recently. "I remember other families who owned large tracts of land across from the Meadowbrook golf course. And I remember Mother telling me about the wonderful streetcar parties. Friends would gather and get on the Creve Coeur Lake line . . . young and old, singing all along the way."

Continue walking on Chaucer to Thorpe Avenue. Walk left on Thorpe to Poe. Walk left to view the Frank Lloyd Wright home at 2615 Poe Avenue. Edward Gocke paid $500, ten percent of the building cost, for the Wright floor plans, which had been published in the *Ladies' Home Journal*. A St. Louis architect executed Wright's blueprints. Constructed in 1910 mainly of concrete, steel, and tile, the home features the signature Wright roof slab overhangs that protect the walls from the sun. "The house has been designed four sides alike in order to simplify the making of these forms," stated a promotional blurb, prepared by Wright, that accompanied the plans. "A structure of this type is more enduring than if carved intact from solid stone, for it is not only a masonry monolith but interlaced with steel fibres as well," the promo continued.

Retrace your steps to Thorpe; turn left again, and head for Bryant. Walk left to see the handsome gray stone home at 2612 Bryant with its BEWARE OF THE DOG sign prominently displayed on the front fence. This home was built in 1902 and is referred to now as the Seidel estate. Seidel was an office- and bank-equipment distributor. "For the benefit of the servants possibly, a small stone waiting station was built at the corner streetcar stop from the same stone as on the Seidel house," says Pat Westhoff, registrar/curator of the Overland Historical Society. The home overlooked Midland Boulevard and the Creve Coeur Lake trolley line.

Return to Thorpe, and this time take a left and walk to Krem Avenue, turning right. The corner home at 10305 Thorpe was built in the early 1900s on a parcel of land released from the next-door Von Maur estate at 2815 Krem. Mildred Zoering, who manages the historic Hanley House in Clayton, lived with her parents in the Thorpe home, called Hilltop, in the mid-1920s. "I remember the stone streetcar stop at the Seidel's house. We used to call him 'Commodore' Seidel. Whatever he did, he must have done it well," says Zoering. She recalls the Gocke house that Frank Lloyd Wright designed. "Inside the house it was all concrete and was considered a little odd. I guess we didn't appreciate Frank Lloyd Wright that much back then."

The home on Krem, which overlooks Mort Jacobs Park on its north side, dates from 1907. Designed by a New York architect for business executive Robert Von Maur, the estate was named Farview. "To this day the home is on such high ground that you can look out a third-floor window and see the St. Louis airport," says Westhoff. The estate encompassed at least 10 acres of orchard on land that is now Mort Jacobs Park. (Jacobs was Overland's seventh mayor, serving in the 1950s.) Mrs. Zoering says that the name Krem was derived from some neighbors named Kremer. "They didn't want their full name used, so they just called the street Krem."

Walk north on Krem, then left on Clarendon Avenue to the park's asphalt fitness trail, the only walkway through the grounds. Take the fitness trail about ½ mile south through the park, stopping to exercise if you feel the need. Leave the park through a gate in its south-west corner along Thorpe Avenue. Take Thorpe to the right to reach Ashby Road.

To complete your walk, make a left on Ashby, cross with extreme caution at Midland—obeying the stop-light—and walk to 2500 Ashby to view the front section of the pioneering Garnett home and estate. Reverse your steps, taking Ashby back to Midland and making a right on the sidewalk along Midland that leads to the parking lot at Wild Acres Park.

13 · Powder Valley Conservation Nature Center

Location: Kirkwood and Sunset Hills,
  Missouri
Hiking distance: 3 miles
Hiking time: 1 hour
Bicycles: Not permitted

Powder Valley Conservation Nature Center—42 acres in Kirkwood and 70 acres in Sunset Hills—is the largest of Missouri's four conservation education centers; others are in Jefferson City, Kansas City, and Springfield. The centers were assembled "to initiate understanding and enjoyment of Missouri's natural world and its fish, forest and wildlife resources," the Missouri Department of Conservation maintains. Powder Valley is situated in an Ozark border oak-hickory forest, marked by several major ridges, thin, rocky soils, and a network of drainages and streams. Three walking trails and an attractive educational complex are the main features on the site. Back in the 1930s and 1940s, St. Louisans would refer to the Powder Valley area as "foothills of the Ozarks" because the valley was 10 miles out of St. Louis—quite a distance back then.

During World War I, E. I. DuPont de Nemours is said to have manufactured and stored explosives in caves off South Geyer Road; a guardhouse stood on South Geyer by the one lane rock road (now Cragwold Road)

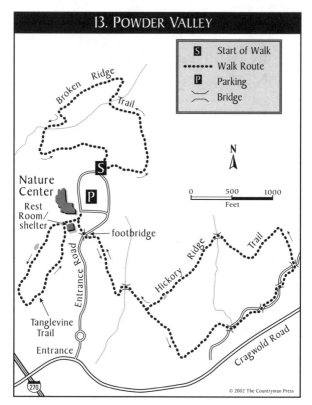

13. POWDER VALLEY

S	Start of Walk
••••••	Walk Route
P	Parking
⟩⟨	Bridge

Broken Ridge

Trail

Nature Center

Rest Room/ shelter

footbridge

Entrance Road

Hickory Ridge

Trail

Tanglevine Trail

Entrance

Cragwold Road

270

N

0   500   1000
Feet

© 2002 The Countryman Press

that led to the DuPont site. At least that's what the neighbors told Howard and Julia Sell, who purchased around 7 acres in the vicinity in 1943. The Sells claimed to have found storage sites and foundation stones near their property, which had allegedly been vacant since the end of World War I. Sell, who maintained that he named the area Powder Valley, erected a hilltop "show-place house filled with many Powder Valley originals . . . with a large red stone fireplace built with stones taken from our own creeks. It [the area] has century old oaks, sycamores, maples, and walnut trees which fill the valley and the hillsides." Later Alwal Moore purchased 112 acres, including, presumably, the Sell property, and in 1986 sold it all to the conservation department.

Before the Sells, Moores, and DuPonts, there were tales of how caves near the Meramec River had been used by Union militiamen to store blasting powder for blowing up the strategic Meramec bridge in Fenton if Confederate forces under General Sterling Price approached. As it turned out, Price, 80 miles south in September 1864, heard of the battle-tested Union forces massed in Kirkwood and decided to turn west to Kansas City to avert probable defeat here.

Even though Sell said he found a DuPont sign near his property, no evidence of stored explosives by the Union troops or by DuPont has been uncovered. DuPont corporate archivists in Delaware deny that there was an explosives plant during World War I (though DuPont had an ammonia plant elsewhere in St. Louis County). No clues seem to exist in Kirkwood Historical Society archives, either. So the "Powder" in the Powder Valley may be more legend than fact.

Headquarters for the nature center, which opened in 1991, is an attractive 22,000-square foot stone-and-cedar building that contains two levels of nature exhibits, a bird/wildlife viewing area embellished by outdoor bird feeders and a marsh—and speakers to pick up birdsongs and notes, a 3,000-gallon aquarium filled with Missouri fish, a 250-seat auditorium, a library, meeting rooms, a gift shop, information desk, and conservation department offices. Trained volunteers are on call to accommodate the more than 125,000 annual visitors, nearly 75 percent of whom use the trails.

Access

The nature center is situated at the northeast corner of the I-270/I-44 intersection in south St. Louis County. From I-270, take I-44 east toward St. Louis to the Watson Road exit. At the first stoplight, take a left on South Geyer Road, drive over the I-44 bridge, and turn left on Cragwold Road. Drive 1 mile or so to the Powder Valley Nature Center entrance. Park in the lot near the headquarters building.

Veteran hikers here usually walk all three trails, starting at any of the three. My preference is to start at the Broken Ridge Trail, 0.66 mile long followed by the 1.5-mile Hickory Ridge Trail, and ending with a lap or two around the shortest loop, the 0.3 mile Tanglevine Trail.

Trail

Broken Ridge Trail

Walk counterclockwise to the right on the flat and then gradually descending asphalt path. The asphalt was criticized by woodland purists when the nature center opened. But as a PV staff member explained, "Asphalt is safe and secure for walkers, and for us it's easy to maintain. Any kind of storm around here would wash away wood chips if they were on the paths." One birder, praising the trail surface, noted: "Asphalt doesn't make a noise like gravel or chips; we can get much closer to the birds on the blacktop."

Signs on trees early in the walk point out mockernut hickory, black cherry, post and black oak, and sassafras trees. Ubiquitous shrub honeysuckle is part of a fairly dense understory. As you plunge downward and near the first footbridge, you'll pass a north-facing slope

A footbridge on the Broken Ridge Trail

where white and northern red oaks compete for sunlight. Near the bridge, where there has been recent thinning of damaged trees, some relatively ancient stumps seem to indicate that not much cutting had been done in the woods in the previous 75 to 90 years.

After we crossed the bridge over the typically dry, rocky streambed on a February walk in 1999, we spotted two gray animals that, from the distance, appeared to be wolves. Quickly stopping, we reasoned that since wolves are unknown in Missouri, the animals 100 yards ahead of us must be coyotes. Indeed they were. The nonchalant pair looked back at us, then turned to drift into the woods. (Naturalists estimate that from four to six coyotes live on or near the Powder Valley grounds. Coyote scat is frequently seen on the asphalt paths.) With or without coyotes, the walk winds and rolls around the ridgetop, then takes a right and heads downhill into a canyonlike area and a footbridge over a stream edged with aged tree roots and packed with rocks and rock shelving.

This canyonesque area with its relatively wide streambed provides an optimum corridor for whitetail deer as they traverse the valley, especially in the winter months. You're apt to spot deer if you are a regular Broken Ridge trail user. (Between 15 and 20 deer may reside around Powder Valley.) Once you cross the bridge, make a left by the bench, and walk up through more oaks and hickories to trail's end.

Hickory Ridge Trail (long loop)

The trail—with seven bridges and nine benches—begins off the south parking area near the stone comfort stations and "staging area" (for large groups who come by bus) behind them. A 125-foot long footbridge that staff members call Old Rusty spans the entrance roadway, carrying hikers into the uplands forest. This self-weathering steel structure with a wooden deck was prefabricated in Minnesota, hauled to Kirkwood on two flatbed trucks, splice-bolted together, then lowered into place with a crane. Turn right onto the first path on the right.

Oak, hickory, and lots of white ash trees reside in these upper parts. According to naturalist Colleen Scott, so do box turtles, five-lined skinks with distinctive blue tails, and harmless rat snakes that search the hillside for rodents and birds' eggs. In sunny hillside openings or along the path you may observe, in the proper season, orange butterfly weed, pokeweed, lavender-whitish horsemint, and Indian physic, a 3-foot plant with five white petals that likes to sprawl over Ozark hills. And be on guard: These woods are littered with poison ivy.

Pass the first bench; then at a patch of pawpaw trees, turn left down the hill to the observation deck. Deck viewers sometimes see deer roaming the streambed nearby. Though the deck offers no sweeping vistas, it's a decent place to view scattered dolomite outcroppings—including a cavelike one that may contain a coyote den, Scott surmises—and tall trees reaching up for a share of sunlight. Forest vines can be studied closely from the deck, especially grapevines, which are customarily bald and hang loosely, and poison ivy vines, which appear hairy and cling closely to trees.

Past the deck are scores of maple trees, another footbridge, another spread of pawpaw, and the oft-dry stream. "This trail was first called the Trail of Many Creeks," says Scott, "but the Metropolitan Sewer District made changes somewhere above us, so the creeks are not so wet anymore. That's why we changed the trail name to Hickory Ridge." Several years ago an old steel leghold for trapping red foxes was found nearby—as was the DuPont explosives sign. Now the trail takes you up a respectable hill and by a trail intersection, where you should walk straight ahead to pursue the long loop.

The automobile, truck, and siren noise from I-44 can

be loud and unrelenting at times in this southern end of the nature center, but some people covet the distraction. "We have found that many trail users tolerate the noise because it keeps them in touch with the city," says Ramon Gass, the former conservation department forester and entomologist. One manager told us that the trails were laid out in circular, asphalt loops to accommodate some users' fears of getting lost in the woods!

At the next bench, swing left and walk downhill again. By a flat footbridge over a dry watercourse with a chair carved from a large white oak by its side, your hike through the bottomland begins. Scott calls this part of Powder Valley "the world's best classroom." In the spring clusters of Virginia bluebells—personally planted by the late Edgar Denison, a Kirkwood resident and author of *Missouri Wildflowers*—bellworts, and trout lilies line some of the banks as the asphalt trail parallels the stream. Among bottomland trees are sugar maples; swamp white oaks; burr oaks, and green ashes. (Green ashes are more inclined to moist bottomland; white ashes prefer upland forest.) Sycamores live along the riparian corridors by the trail, as do colonies of jewel-weed and pinkish smartweed. There's much honey-suckle, pawpaw, and dogwood within the understory. "You'll see lots of fallen oaks in the woods," points out Scott. "The trees will break down or decompose to pro-vide food for wildlife. We like to leave everything for animals and the little critters."

After the valley you climb a precipitous hill. Pass another bench (an oasis for out-of-breath walkers), turn left, and head toward a savanna, then a glade, both on the right. The conservation department has been developing what it calls a presettlement-type savanna, a place where trees such as oaks and hickories are given plenty of space and sunlight by removing non-native species that otherwise would crowd them and stymie their natural growth. To the west of the savanna is a gladelike piece of land where shorter trees like gum bumelias and chinquapin oaks live on thin, rocky soil and where glade wildflowers like the orange hoary puccoon pop life into the glade each spring. The trail now dips down, then heads over a footbridge where you'll see thorny-stemmed greenbrier vines entangled by the stream to the right. Up the hill on the left is a fishless rainwater-dependent pond that contains amphibians: primarily frogs, salamanders, and tadpoles. Smartweed and white snakeroot are neighboring flora. Scott sees chipmunk holes on the pond's north bank. "They burrow in to possibly rest or sleep," she explains. "Raccoons may be eating some of our frogs. Frogs are out at night, so they may be vulnerable."

Keep walking straight ahead at the pond. When the path dead ends, walk right to retrace your steps past the observation deck and back up the hill to the rusty footbridge.

Tanglevine Trail

Powder Valley's shortest and flattest loop—very suitable for wheelchairs and the handicapped—begins west of the rest rooms near the south parking area. Walk counterclockwise. Just as the trail starts, find the packed dirt path—originally trampled by deer—to the right that heads toward the bird-feeding area behind the nature center building. Hike in until you can see feeding activity—if you're lucky you'll encounter a turkey hen or two and a clutch of juveniles, known as poults, scratching the ground for nuts, insects, and seeds. Some 20 turkeys, only about three of them toms, are Powder Valley regulars. For the most part the feeding station belongs to common backyard birds and squirrels, with the exception of a few surprise visitors such as yellow-bellied sapsuckers, fox sparrows, or pine siskins. Return to the Tanglevine Trail, and pick up the path to the right. You'd better look over your shoulder to make sure that some of the turkeys aren't following you—they like to run and walk on the asphalt trails since even short flights through the woods are difficult for them.

Until a few years ago, the turkeys were often seen in the company of a lone fallow, or Sitka, deer, possibly a descendant of hooved animals kept in a nearby game preserve 60 or 70 years ago. The farm was run as a St. Louis Zoo annex by brewer Edwin A. Lemp, who resided in a spectacular home overlooking the Meramec River. In 1971 he sold his acreage to Russell Emmenegger, who donated his grounds to Kirkwood, which created a nature park in his name. The conservation department manages the park.

The fallow deer, which ran between Emmenegger and Powder Valley via culverts under I-270, was dubbed "the deer who follows the turkeys" because it was seen feeding with the turkeys under the bird feeders as well as in and around the Tanglevine Trail and elsewhere on the property. Ordinarily in the wild, fallow deer are found in herds of 150 to 175 in Asia and eastern Mediterranean regions.

Your walk through this forest with its thick understory will take you by all of the trees you've seen elsewhere in Powder Valley—pawpaw in great abundance;

hackberry; shagbark hickory; northern red, black, and white oak; black cherry; slippery elm; white ash, and sassafras among them. Information posts along the trail may inspire you to make backyard brush piles, construct birdhouses (a screech owl house nearby serves as a backyard possibility), think of your backyard as a café with acorns and berries as key entrées, and identify vines more clearly—for instance, poison ivy has white berries while wild grapes produce purplish, sour fruit.

Another fishless amphibian pond comes into view as you work leftward around the short trail. This pond, compared to the pond at the Hickory Ridge Trail, is normally spread evenly with pond scum. Even a mass feeding by white-tailed deer at the edges of the pond probably won't disturb for long its distinctive green lid. Deer and raccoon tracks are usually visible around the pond.

As you make the short Tanglevine walk—some regular hikers and even mothers pushing strollers may walk this trail three or more times in a row—note the specially made benches to accommodate the handicapped. (Those educational signs on the trail were also constructed to make them easier to read, especially for those in wheelchairs.) Because the trail introduces people to various aspects of nature and the variety of trees at Powder Valley, and because it is so short, it has become the center's most heavily used trail.

Before leaving Powder Valley, we suggest you visit the nature center building with its strong summertime collection of native wildflowers out front. Once inside and before you examine the replica of the keelboat used by explorers Lewis and Clark on their historic westward journey from 1804 to 1806, the windows by the bird-feeding area, or the very imaginative interactive nature sites and viewing areas, check out the phenology board by the library. (Phenology is the science of relations between climate and "periodic biologic phenomena" such as bird and animal migrations or the seasonal flowering or fruiting of plants.) "Maybe the best thing of all that the conservation department does is to connect hikers and other visitors to learning," says my wife, Lynn, a regular trail user and nature center enthusiast.

14 · DeMun-40 Thieves Walk

Location: Clayton and Richmond Heights,
Missouri
Hiking distance: 4 miles
Hiking time: 2 hours

This walk takes off down DeMun Avenue in Clayton
to explore one of America's largest and handsomest
seminary campuses, then continues on to view the
grounds of St. Mary's Health Center and its Convent of
St. Mary of the Angels. After crossing I-64/US 40 on
Highland Terrace, the walk takes in the hilly part of
Richmond Heights and spots a few of the so-called
Forty Thieves—homes that were built with salvaged
wood and metals left over from torn down buildings
of the 1904 St. Louis World's Fair.

A highlight of the walk is the 72-acre campus of Concordia Seminary, described in 1926, the year it began
operations in Clayton, as "the largest Lutheran seminary [Missouri synod] in the world," although "[a] person could live in Clayton and never know [the seminary]
was there," wrote Dickson Terry in his 1976 *Clayton: A
History*. "We have an open campus here," says the Reverend Glen Thomas, vice–president of community relations. "People walk and jog here all the time. We don't
want the campus to be a walled-off fortress." Eugene J.
Mackey III, a leading St. Louis architect whose firm has

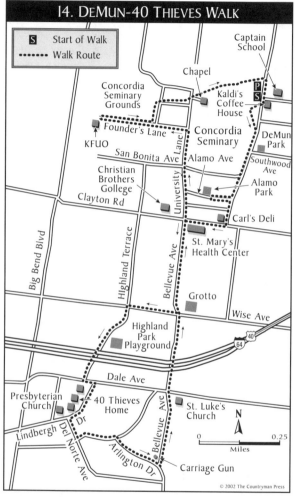

14. DeMun-40 Thieves Walk

S Start of Walk
•••••• Walk Route

Captain School

Chapel

Concordia Seminary Grounds

Kaldi's Coffee House

P S

Founder's Lane

KFUO

Concordia Seminary

DeMun Park

San Bonita Ave

Alamo Ave

Southwood Ave

Christian Brothers Gollege

University Lane

Alamo Park

Clayton Rd

Carl's Deli

St. Mary's Health Center

Highland Terrace

Big Bend Blvd

Bellevue Ave

Grotto

Wise Ave

Highland Park Playground

40
64

Dale Ave

Presbyterian Church

40 Thieves Home

Del Norte Dr

Bellevue Ave

St. Luke's Church

N

Lindbergh

Del Norte Ave

Arlington Dr

Carriage Gun

0   0.25
Miles

© 2002 The Countryman Press

drawn a new master plan for Concordia, notes, "For an architect, seeing this campus is a four-star event. If you are interested in regional collegiate architectural design, you *must* see Concordia along with Washington University and Principia College in Elsah, Illinois." At least 19 of the original Concordia buildings were designed in collegiate Gothic style by architect Charles Klauder, who ranks among "the great campus builders," says Thomas A. Gaines in *The Campus as a Work of Art*. Gaines includes Klauder, who designed major buildings at Princeton University, Penn State, Cornell, and Wellesley College, with other architectural notables like I. M. Pei, Cass Gilbert, and Stanford White. "At the time of his death [in 1938], he left the stamp of a great Gothicist on his buildings," states the *Bibliographic Dictionary of American Architects*.

St. Mary's Health Center, another focus on the walk, lies on 18 acres in Richmond Heights formerly known as Campbell's Forest, a property that once held a roadhouse/gambling joint. In 1919 the city decided to annex the Campbell property to get rid of the gambling and the troublemaking gypsies who camped there during the winter; ironically, a mysterious fiery blast leveled the place before annexation could occur. Some schoolchildren who witnessed the fire said the rising, powerful flames were shaped like a cross. The Sisters of St. Mary purchased the land the following year.

The 40 homes that a developer erected with scavenged World's Fair material were built on 10 streets in Richmond Heights. One home on Arlington was torn down in 1974, but the rest—mostly two-story frame structures with brick facades—survive. "Because of their dubious beginnings, the 40 homes were dubbed the Forty Thieves, and the name stuck," Joellen McDonald of the Richmond Heights Historical Society explained.

Charles Lindbergh resided in 1925 in Richmond Heights prior to his celebrated 1927 transatlantic flight in the *Spirit of St. Louis*. While flying for Robertson Aircraft Company, Lindbergh rented a room on Maryland Avenue (now called Lindbergh) near present Big Bend Boulevard. The home has since been razed. Tennis great Arthur Ashe lived in Richmond Heights while in training with his coach, Richard Hudlin. No one remembers who named the city Richmond Heights, but legend has it that Robert E. Lee, in St. Louis with the U.S. Army Corps of Engineers to work on the Mississippi River channel, enjoyed hiking and horseback riding in his time off. Apparently the future Confederate general sensed some similarity between the high ground in what is now Forest Park and the land to its southwest and his home territory around Richmond, Virginia—hence Richmond Heights.

Access

From I-64/US 40 east, make a right at the Bellevue Avenue ramp, then left on Bellevue to Clayton Road. Drive right on Clayton Road for one block, then left on DeMun Avenue. At the end of DeMun, park on the street by Kaldi's Coffee House.

Trail

Start the walk by Kaldi's at DeMun and Northwoods Avenues. Tiny Concordia Park, directly across DeMun, is leased to the city of Clayton as an official city park. Cross DeMun and stroll onto the grounds of Concordia Park, then up to the seminary campus, heading toward the nine-foot bronze Luther statue, which rests on a 12-foot marble pedestal.

In place since the campus opened, the statue of Martin Luther is a replica of the masterpiece at Wurms, Germany, which Ernst Rietschel executed in 1833. On June 13, 1926, one hundred thousand people were on hand for the campus dedication, which included the statue (it had been a focal point of Concordia's previous location on South Jefferson Avenue in St. Louis) and the Luther Tower, directly west of the statue and behind the Walther Arch. "People came in special excursion trains from the old centers of Midwestern Lutheranism," wrote Carl S. Meyer in *Log Cabin to Lutheran Tower* in 1965. At the dedication, the tower was only half finished; it finally opened—a Swiss chapel sits in its base—in 1966. Its 1920s planners envisioned the tower and its 49-bell carillon as dominating "the entire west end of the city of St. Louis," Meyer wrote without further comment. If you wish, you can proceed west from the tower to explore the seminary's main quadrangle. But then you must return to the Luther statue and walk back to DeMun Avenue.

Continuing south on DeMun, you'll see DeMun Park at the corner of Southwood Avenue. A synagogue once occupied this double playground area owned by Clayton. At Alamo Avenue, make a quick right to see the third Clayton park in the neighborhood, Alamo Park, which lies tranquilly among apartment units. Turn around, and walk to DeMun, going right. By Carl's Deli, cross Clayton Road, turning right on the sidewalk in front of St. Mary's Medical Center.

Dedicated in 1924, with a new entrance and building addition dating from 1987, St. Mary's is a 620-bed hospital. Turn left on Bellevue Avenue, and hike past the emergency room, the convent—which includes several additions including the sisters' retirement home, Our Lady of Victories—and the sisters' administration building, which is closest to the entrance driveway. (In a Richmond Heights 75th anniversary booklet, an old-timer remembered "nuns who would roller skate through the grounds with their habits flying behind them.") A grotto, at the south tip of the property at Wise Avenue, is a private space for sisters to pray and meditate. Dedicated to Our Lady of Lourdes, the grotto was unveiled in 1932. Four years later a rock garden, lying below an illuminated crucifix, was introduced. For years the sisters joined May and Corpus Christi processions to the grotto.

Walk right on Wise Avenue, where Richmond Height's first commercial stores were located. The building at 7357 Wise once housed an early grocery store, local historians point out. Walk to Highland Terrace, turning left. In the early-20th century, this section was known as Sunset Hills, the city's first subdivision. The home at 1319 was supposedly constructed with material from the wing of a World's Fair art gallery. Walk the curving street, noting the Highland Park playground on the left. Cross the I-64/US 40 bridge, and walk to Dale Avenue. Turn left, and then make a right at Lindbergh Drive.

The Market streetcar line, which later became the Forest Park line, operated cars along what is now Lindbergh Drive starting around 1910. The line also traveled along Bellevue and Wise Avenues and made loops at both Wise and Arlington Drive. Four of the Forty Thieves homes—all sharing similar floor plans and a couple with transoms above oval glass-front doors and arched bricks over windows—are located on Lindbergh at 7303, 7311, 7319, and 7327. Before you turn left on Del Norte Avenue, you'll see the Richmond Heights Presbyterian Church, the city's first chartered church.

The Luther tower at Concordia Seminary

The present building was opened in 1949, up the street from the long-vanished home where Charles Lindbergh rented a room. The corner home at 1504 Del Norte, extensively remodeled, is another of the Forty Thieves.

From Del Norte, make a left onto Arlington Drive, where six Forty Thieves homes exist, though none are on the stretch we're taking, which veers southeasterly up the hill to Bellevue, site of the streetcar loop and a 1941 75-millimeter carriage gun. Turn left on Bellevue. In the 19th century several lakes and springs were located east of Bellevue, historians say.

Walk north to Dale Avenue, where the Norman Gothic St. Luke's Catholic Church, which opened in 1929, is on the right. A rectory and school are part of the church complex. The city's first known resident, F. E. Niesen, searching for a decent place to settle, put up a three-story white-frame mansion near the northeast Dale-Bellevue intersection in 1892. Some of the Niesen land now belongs to St. Luke's.

Walk over the highway bridge and north to Clayton Road. Cross Clayton, and continue north on University Lane. At left is Christian Brothers College, a high school that opened here in 1922. In 1934 the school brought in U.S. Army Junior Reserve Corps personnel to operate the institution as a kind of military school. The military presence, complete with uniforms, pomp, and parades, lasted until 1993. In its pre-1922 location in St. Louis, CBC had been a Catholic college, even a seminary. For a while in the 1890s, the college's teams played schools like Notre Dame and the University of Missouri. The first CBC opened along the St. Louis riverfront in 1849, its archives state. (The school will move its campus to west St. Louis county in a year or two; its eight buildings have been purchased by Concordia Seminary.) Follow University Lane back onto the Concordia Seminary campus. The first building on the left is Concordia Historical Institute, archivist and historian to the Lutheran Church Missouri Synod.

At Founder's Lane, turn left. Walk past Loeber Hall,

where the student lounge and bookstore are situated. Behind it is the Log Cabin, a replica of the 1839 facility that housed the first Concordia school in Altenberg, Missouri. Farther along on the left is what has been called "the only Gothic smokestack in America," the signature feature of Concordia's powerhouse. When you reach Founder's Way, look left toward the Eldon E. Pederson field house (once an aircraft hangar, says architect Mackey) and, to its east, the tennis courts named in memory of Ted Drewes Sr., the school's first athletic director. Continue straight ahead on Founder's Lane to the KFUO-AM and FM studio on the left. Its broadcasting director, Dennis Stortz, says the facility, which started in 1924, is the world's longest continuously operating religious radio station. Furthermore, says Stortz, "[t]he National Association of Broadcasters credits us as having the country's longest continuously operating broadcast facility in the same building—for either radio or television." In 1999 KFUO-FM won the Marconi Award from the National Association of Broadcasters as the classical music station of the year. The station's call letters are etched over the front door of the building, which has been on campus since 1927.

Turn around, and walk back to South Seminary Terrace, going left. On the right is the heart of the campus, including the Chapel of St. Timothy and St. Titus immediately on the right. Dedicated in 1992, the chapel is the newest Concordia building, continuing the Collegiate-Gothic style of Charles Klauder. From this point you can wander back through the quadrangle area where you'll see integrated archways, slate roofs, four courtyards, cloisters, leaded and stained-glass windows, and dormitories and classroom buildings that incorporate five kinds of stone: red Colorado sandstone and four limestone varieties. Continue walking through the campus back toward Kaldi's Coffee House and the end of the trail. Stop in at Kaldi's for a well-deserved cup of their famous organic coffee, to be savored in the warmer months at one of the sidewalk tables while watching neighbors practicing yoga positions on the slopes of Concordia Park across the street.

15 · Riverlands Environmental Demonstration Area Missouri to Illinois Walk

Location: Near West Alton, Missouri
Hiking distance: 3.5 miles
Hiking time: 1.5 hours

There are many reasons to drive to the 1,200-acre U.S. Army Corps of Engineer Riverlands area on the Missouri side of the Mississippi River by the new bridge into Alton, Illinois. Among the reasons: to see rare birds such as the smew or Ross's gull (if you're lucky); to welcome annual visitors such as bald eagles, white pelicans, and trumpeter swans; to fish near the new locks and dam; to explore the nature trail that winds through tallgrass prairie, and, if you're like me, to walk from Missouri into Illinois without having to cross the Mississippi River.

This hike leaves from the trailhead parking area of the Two Pecan Nature Trail and heads east on Riverlands Way, the main artery on the property, to the Maple Island fishing/parking area. On your way, you literally enter the state of Illinois, and then continue walking north to the Mississippi River on a road relatively few hikers travel. (The nature trail, which you can take at your option, is named for the only two pecan trees

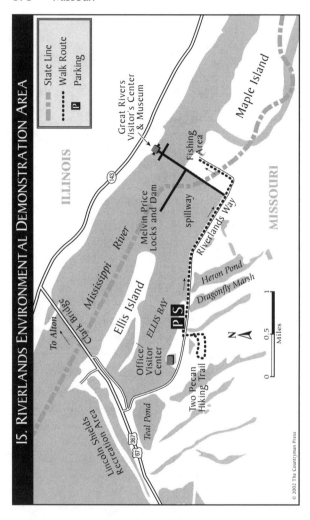

15. RIVERLANDS ENVIRONMENTAL DEMONSTRATION AREA

State Line
Walk Route
P Parking

ILLINOIS

Great Rivers
Visitor's Center
& Museum

Maple Island

Fishing
Area

143

Melvin Price
Locks and Dam

spillway

Riverlands Way

MISSOURI

Mississippi River

Ellis Island

Heron Pond

Dragonfly Marsh

To Alton

Clark Bridge

ELLIS BAY

P S

N

0   0.5   1
Miles

Office/
Visitor Center

Two Pecan
Hiking Trail

Teal Pond

Lincoln Shields
Recreation Area

67 367

© 2002 The Countryman Press

at Riverlands; both are circa 1880 and appear in full leaf on the trail.)

First, however, a few notes about Riverlands, an environmental demonstration project on former cropland converted into prairie habitat and wetlands as part of the new Melvin Price Locks and Dam #26 installation next door to the east. Riverlands sits beside 500-acre Ellis Bay, once a modest backwater slough but now a backwater bay, or "slack-water pool," and an important waterfowl refuge. Between the bay and the river is 360-acre Ellis Island, where eagles rest in midwinter—often by the dozens—high in bankside trees. Two small lakes and a least tern breeding area are included within Ellis Island. Parts of the island are walkable, but not from November 15 to April 15, when waterfowl start to fill the bay and use it as a true refuge. "During refuge season, we close all trails and walking areas south of Riverlands Way so the birds can rest freely," advises Erin Connett, a park ranger for the Corps of Engineers. She points south to a row of trees on the horizon, on the other side of which is the Missouri River. Riverlands' location beneath the migratory flyway between America's two greatest rivers makes the sanctuary a major destination for birds and birders. Eventually Riverlands may connect via a hiking trail to the new Missouri state park under development at the confluence on the north bank of the Missouri River.

"Riverlands is probably the best location in the area for finding species from all the main groups of water-related birds," reports *Birds of the St. Louis Area: Where and When to Find Them* (Webster Groves Nature Study Society, 1995). Most of the birds stop by Ellis Bay or nearby on the river channel or in sloughs and ponds. And most people watch birds along Riverlands Way through scopes, binoculars, and car windows.

In January 2001 perhaps the rarest bird ever spotted at Riverlands was seen afloat on Ellis Bay—a male

Riverlands Way by Ellis Bay

smew, described as a Eurasian sea duck and a member of the merganser family of diving ducks. Smews are commonly found in Siberia, the northern Pacific, and the Arctic; occasionally, they visit the Pacific islands of western Alaska, but midwestern Missouri is surely out of their range. Thus the appearance of this solitary all-white male with a black mask and black wing markings was sufficient to activate all the bird hotlines. "The smew was spotted at 10 AM; by 3 PM we had birders here from Chicago and Kansas City," recalls Connett.

During the few days of his stopover, the smew was seen by nearly 28,500 people from 31 states and 5 foreign countries. "In 1992 we had a rare Ross's gull for two days," says Connett. "During that time we had 14,000 visitors, even birders from Brazil." In the last decade Riverlands birders have spotted other exotic birds, such as Barrow's goldeneye ducks from the Pacific Northwest, red-throated loons, harlequin ducks, piping plovers, black-necked stilts, and red-necked phalaropes.

Access

From I-270 in north St. Louis County, exit at US 367 north. Drive 10 miles north on US 367, almost to the new bridge into Alton. Before the bridge, turn right by a service station, and drive east, accessing Riverlands Way. The busiest part of Ellis Bay is on the immediate left. As you drive on, the visitors center, with a conference room where you can view birds through scopes, is also on the left. Farther ahead is the parking lot for the Two Pecan Nature Trail. Park here.

Trail

From the parking lot, walk east along Riverlands Way toward the dam area. On the right is the re-created tallgrass prairie that contains Two Pecan Nature Trail. The large tract is heavily planted in big bluestem, once the dominant grass of the renowned Upper Midwest prairie. Each March the prairie is burned to fend off exotic plants such as thistle, which, if left alone, would crowd out the natural prairie grasses. "The week after we burn, the whole place is char black; the following week, it's green again," says Connett. Hidden from view in the prairie are several drainage ditches and ponds that the Corps of Engineers drains or floods periodically to help sustain wildlife.

Ducks, geese, pelicans, and swans come to Ellis Bay—on your left—to forage and rest. "We've had trumpeter swans [North America's largest waterfowl] who have visited us every year since 1992, when the first one was spotted here," says Connett. The first swan was banded by the Wisconsin Department of Natural Resources, so it was easier to identify. He has returned every year, bringing several more with him. On the right as you continue your walk are Dragonfly Marsh, then Heron Pond, both designed to attract waterfowl. "At Heron Pond, we might see—depending on the season—herons, egrets, ducks, and swans, but not pelicans. It's not deep enough for them," Connett explains.

Out in the usually shallow bay—average depth about 5 feet—are buoys that warn boaters to make no wake and sandbars that pop up to create floor space for bundling white pelicans, sometimes in the hundreds. Looking out into the open river—Ellis Island ends at about the half-mile point in your walk—you can see the Illinois side of the river and the berm on IL 143. Atop the berm, or levee, is a trail that heads west through Alton to Pere Marquette State Park and east to the old Chain of Rocks Bridge in north St. Louis, part of the 40-mile Confluence Greenway. Nearby is a regional visitors center operated by the Corps of Engineers and other state and regional environmental organizations. Still in development, the center is open weekends and, on a limited basis, weekdays until its extensive educational exhibits are fully installed by late 2002 or early 2003.

As your walk continues, a Corps storage warehouse and parking area will appear on your right. On the left is an observation platform, then a spillway that is useful during high-water times. The spillway, when dry, is not open to hiking. A stop sign and gate mark the end of the blacktop, and your walkway converts into gravel. After about 1.4 miles, make a sharp left turn. (Straight ahead is private farmland, although the Corps owns the levee that trails off to the left.) Down on your right is a fishing slough rimmed with willows. Behind the slough is Maple Island, another 360-acre island that is forested in mixed hardwoods.

Now, 1.5 miles into your walk, let me—and the white sign on your right (if it happens to be standing)—be the first to welcome you to Illinois. Yes, you are no longer in Missouri! "The old river channel once came through around here," explains Connett to a befuddled walker. "With the new dam in place, the channel has changed, but the old state line has been kept. It would take an act of Congress to put the state line where it should be: somewhere in the middle of the river." Connett says fisherman come to the visitors center to make sure their state licenses are applicable; tourists ask if the Illinois state line sign is a practical joke. "The Alton [Illinois] police department and the Madison County [Illinois] sheriff's department and the St. Charles County [Missouri] sheriff's office all patrol this area," says Stan Ebersohl, Rivers Project manager for the Corps. Before the new Alton dam was constructed, Kaskaskia Island, located south of St. Genevieve, Missouri, was the only part of Illinois situated west of the Mississippi. (The Rivers Project manages 416 miles of navigation channels on the upper Mississippi, Illinois, and Kaskaskia Rivers. This includes 110,000 acres of public lands and waters, five dams, and seven locks.)

Now that you're in Illinois, walk down to Maple

Island parking lot, which constitutes the most popular fishing spot at Riverlands. "This area gets year-round usage," says Connett. "Catfish is big here and so is paddlefish, which you must snag." Connett says eagles sometimes feed on stunned or dead shad by the dam; in the spring ospreys may hover about. Nearby, ring-billed and herring gulls are viewable much of the year.

Now you must turn around here in Illinois, and retrace your walk to the parking area at Two Pecan Nature Trail back in the Show-Me state. Before you start back, however, look out at the mammoth dam and the wall of its largest lock. Beyond the lock is the river; beyond the river is the real Illinois.

Once on your way back, you'll soon see a sign that may help you get realigned. It says: WELCOME TO MISSOURI.

16 · Ruth Park Woods

Location: University City, Missouri
Hiking distance: 3 miles
Hiking time: 1.5 hours

Eugene D. Ruth Jr., the University City mayor (1926–1933) for whom Ruth Park is named, was an energetic, at times controversial, yet extremely neighborly person. While in office, he built a spacious swimming pool at his home on Waterman Avenue, issuing a blanket invitation to neighbors to come by any time for a dip. They did!

The pool soon became the neighborhood gathering place. Ruth generously built locker rooms, then lit the yard for night swimming. "[He] took each Friday during that summer as a holiday and spent it in his backyard swimming with his neighbors," writes NiNi Harris in her meticulously researched history of University City, *Legacy of Lions.*

During his administration, Ruth added a nine-hole municipal golf course called University City Golf Course—later renamed Ruth Park Golf Course, stretched city boundaries, chaired a failed effort to annex St. Louis County to the city of St. Louis, battled aldermen, and acquired as a new city hall one of the area's most illustrious buildings. The new city hall was—and remains—the domed five-story octagonal tower at 6801 Delmar

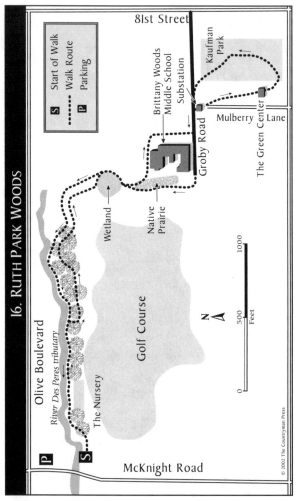

16. Ruth Park Woods

Boulevard that had been headquarters of a magazine empire operated by E. G. Lewis, who was appointed the city's first mayor in 1906, the year the city incorporated. Lewis recognized the purchasing power of out-of-town visitors to the 1904 St. Louis World's Fair. He set up a fee-based tent city—with boardwalks—in a field next to his building. And each night during the fair an 8-ton searchlight was raised through an opening in his building's dome. "The giant light of two million candle power lit up the sky," Harris wrote. In fact, until World War II Lewis's searchlight was the world's most powerful.

In 1931 the Ruth Park Golf Course was opened. One of its codesigners was Robert Foulis, a Scottish native who once worked at Scotland's St. Andrews golf course, one of the world's celebrated greens. Foulis had already designed—on his own—the Glen Echo, Normandy, Sunset Hills, and Algonquin Country Club courses in the St. Louis area as well as the first links in Forest Park.

In the late 1960s the University City School District arranged a new use for the woods north of the golf course. "The district used the woods for four years or so for outdoor education," recalls Henry J. Kaltenthaler III, a longtime biology teacher at University City high school. "Before then, the woods had been kept closed because the city used it for a nursery. It was a place where golfers would go in and retrieve golf balls."

It was the formation of the Green Center, a half-mile away in Kaufman Park, that brought the Ruth Park Woods back to life in the late 1990s. Housed in the large brick home once owned by Aubrey Green, a banker who operated a 7-acre nursery as an avocation, the nonprofit Green Center includes the restoration of 26-acre Ruth Park Woods as one of its main objectives.

"We treasure Ruth Park Woods because it is the last remaining green space in University City, and we want to use it well," says Irv Logan, a Missouri Conservation Department manager who is copresident of the Green

Center. (The state conservation department, through its now-disbanded urban wild acres program, awarded the city $5,000 to launch the restoration activities in the woods.) Eventually city officials hope that through its trail system, Ruth Park Woods can connect with a trail coming in from Olivette on the west. Officials also envision the trail from Ruth and Kaufman Parks connecting with Heman Park in University City, then continuing into St. Louis, finally meeting up with the Confluence Greenway by the St. Louis waterfront.

Access

Take I-170 to Olive Boulevard. Drive east on Olive to McKnight Road. Turn south on McKnight, and park in the strip shopping center at McKnight and Olive or on Mayflower Court off McKnight. Walk across McKnight to the Ruth Park Woods trailhead. (Don't walk into the woods via the yellow gate to the south, however. That's the service road into the city's leaf recycling center and isn't open to the public.)

Trail

Black locust trees are prevalent in the first section of the woods as are silver maples, indicators of nearby wetlands. They indicate well, since a tributary of the River des Peres is close by. Some insist that it is the River des Peres itself that borders the north side of the woods, but others like Logan and John Solodar, an officer of the St. Louis Audubon Society and veteran University City birder, view the stream as a River des Peres branch only. "The water here is polluted," says Solodar, "so there are few fish for the birds. A while ago, for example, a migrating kingfisher came through. He rested here for a couple of weeks, looked for food and found little, so he flew on."

Walkers will find "older woods" a block or so into the park where fallen trees and cottonwoods abound, and pokeweed is thick. Mallard ducks, green herons, and, during spring migration, Louisiana water thrushes and warblers can be attracted to the stream on the left. "All the bramble and the water combined is a draw for migrating birds," says Solodar.

At the first footbridge, look to your right at the University City leaf recycling operation. "We still call this place 'The Nursery,'" says Art Texier, superintendent of streets. "We pile leaves and some yard waste into windrows, then turn them over several times a month," adds James J. Crowe, city forester. "When we're busy we can have up to six rows of leaves that are composting." (The city picks up leaves four times a year, hauls them here, runs them through a grinder and separator, starts the composting, then trucks the mulch, or "black gold," to Heman Park for citizen pickup.)

"We are probably the largest mulcher in the metropolitan area," Texier said. "Other cities have been phoning us and scheduling visits to see how we recycle our leaves." Solodar scans the treetops—in vain—for a great horned owl, last seen in the late 1990s. "We had the owls nesting here in 1996 and 1997," he says. "One forestry department employee has stories of the owls looking down at him from their nest while he worked in the park below. At about the same time, a pair of foxes set up housekeeping in a den near the compost piles. The foxes had four babies—I saw them outside their den area. It was just like a photograph from *National Geographic!* We think that the foxes ate so much of the available food supply, such as rabbits, voles, mice, and other small animals, that the owls were deprived of food and left the area. We may have them back, however."

The path through the woods continues. Occasional bare spots or natural overlooks by the stream keep birders coming back to Ruth Park Woods. At one small bend in the stream—just off the path—Solodar says song sparrows and goldfinches are seen in great swarms. Several years ago he spotted a nesting Louisiana waterthrush in a quiet corner near the bend. The waterthrushes—shy brown warblers with signature white eyebrows—prefer the forest shade while remaining near the water. "I remember walking in here when a storm was coming on," says Solodar, as we pass one of three benches on the path. "I saw a raccoon up in a tree. As the storm got near, he walked halfway down from the top of the tree and tucked himself safely into a hole in the tree to wait out the storm."

Once you cross the trail's second footbridge and see another of the park's massive old cottonwood trees and much of the forest floor blanketed in dark-green myrtle, you must walk to the right and head uphill. In this hillside area to the left of the trail, a retired biomedical engineer, Daniel Talonn, has supervised the clearing of at least 10 acres of wildly invasive Japanese honeysuckle so that other plants, bushes, and trees can grow healthily.

"Originally, I had a lot of help," Talonn says. "The clearing work was first done through University City in Bloom. We had Saturday workdays. Scouts, students, community volunteers all showed up. The parks department supplied three men with chain saws and a chip-

Strolling the path through Ruth Park Woods

per. We dragged honeysuckle bushes over to the chipper and painted the stumps with Roundup, which killed the roots. After a while, few volunteers showed up, so I have kept at it with a manual bow saw since I don't trust chain saws when I am in the woods alone. This project may never be completed [he has some six acres to go], but I'll keep at it. I love these woods. What keeps me going is when I clear a section up to and surrounding one of the old trees, like a cottonwood that's 4 feet in diameter. I stand by the tree and admire it and say how happy I am that they are here." The city has been planting oak, hickory, black gum, dogwood, and persimmon saplings in the eastern end of the park that Talonn has cleared—aiming to prevent the area from becoming, in the words of the city forester, "a honeysuckle forest."

Solodar said that the great horned owls roosted in an oak tree within the circular hillside forest that includes maples, ashes, wild cherries, and hickories—whose understory Talonn has cleared with his four- to six-hour a day riddance effort. "I was hiking through here one day and heard the owls calling behind me," Solodar says. In former years the golf course crept into the woods here some 10 to 15 feet. Our walk in this eastern part of the trail runs parallel to the second and third holes of the golf course.

As the walk continues east, an unattractive surviving picnic shelter frame remains standing on the left, an outdoors education relic from decades past.

Soon you'll arrive at a T intersection with a long footbridge to your right. Walk across the bridge, recently built by the city over runoff from the golf course. "I find this area good for seeing spring migrating warblers," Solodar, the unstoppable birder, advises. Head up a hill by the golf course edge; the hilltop is abreast of the first hole. Walk along the far northern edge of the course—Swarthmore Drive is on the left. Brittany Woods Middle School appears on the right. As the golf course ends, cut down the hill, and go south toward the school. On a low area to the right is a half-acre wetland being restored by the Green Center with the help of a grant from the National Fish and Wildlife Foundation. Its mix of plant, aquatic, and insect life is a boon to elementary- and middle-school science and biology classes in the area.

Walk east behind the school to 81st Street, turning right. At the corner, walk left on Groby Road, then right again on Mulberry Lane. A redbrick ranch-style structure at the southeast corner of Mulberry and Groby appears to be a well-kept residence that fits the neighborhood. But, surprise! Constructed in the mid-1950s, this "home" with its "attached two-car garage" is in fact an Ameren UE substation with two sets of switch gears and two transformers within its aesthetic shell. There are few structures like it in the metropolitan area.

Walk south on Groby. On the right is a 1940s subdivision with one-car garages and stub-nosed redbrick homes. To the left is the city's 8-acre Kaufman Park, named after Nathan B. Kaufman, mayor from 1958 to 1978. Walk up to the Green Center headquarters, which occupies the Tudor-revival home and nearby carriage house/garage built for Aubrey Green and his wife on Blackberry Avenue in 1932 for about $10,000. In 1972 the Greens sold the property to the city but reserved the right to live there until they died. In 1996, with the home vacated, the city sought ideas for the property's use. Community artists, environmentalists, scientists, educators, and volunteers joined together and proposed the Green Center.

"When we arrived here about five years ago, you could hardly see the home for all the trees and weeds," Irv Logan, the Green Center officer, explains. "This was an agriculture center when the Greens were here." Adds Kay Drey, an active board member of the Center, "We didn't name the Green Center for Mr. Green, ironically, but for our interest in greenery and the environment. This place provides us a natural laboratory and cultural gathering place. We like performing and visual arts and outdoor experiences. We are right in the middle of a city with 26 acres of woods. Kids around here like to hike in the Ruth Park Woods, whose name I insisted on because I wanted the word 'park' in there so it would be treated gently.... [S]ome of those kids hike over in the woods, then retreat to Mr. Green's old garage to write poetry."

Walk around the Green Center—out front are volunteer-planted prairie, herb, and vegetable gardens and day-lily beds, called collectively "demonstration/learning gardens"—then head north through the playground area of Kaufman Park and downhill to Groby Road. Walk west on Groby. From the west side of Brittany Woods Middle School, walk to the right to see the half-acre prairie that was first planted by Brittany students in 1992 and is now under the stewardship of the Green Center. Walk down the driveway by the school bus parking lot and northward by the Green Center's wetland area to the end of the school property. Walk left back up the hill by the north edge of the golf course.

Once you're back in Ruth Park Woods and across the footbridge, continue to the T intersection, and veer right to re-enter Daniel Talonn's honeysuckle-clear forest. Off to the right is a gravel bar at a river bend that is usually a good place to see eastern phoebes, ducks, and maybe herons. After some more hills and turns, the path heads back past the mulch pile to the McKnight road trailhead.

17 · North Lake/Sunfish Lake Trail at Spanish Lake County Park

Location: Spanish Lake, Missouri
Hiking distance: 2 miles
Hiking time: 1.5 hours
Bicycles: Not permitted

Spanish Lake, up Spanish Pond Road from the confluence of the Missouri and Mississippi Rivers, is a natural lake of long duration. The lake and its surroundings date back at least to Spanish ownership (the Spanish were said to use the lake as a rest haven), then to French, then American. Around 1900 a supposed "Lady of the Lake" was sighted. The ghost was a maiden who threw herself into the lake for the usual legendary reason: unrequited love. Some say the ghost is viewable in evenings around Halloween. Please contact the park superintendent if you see it.

In 1971 St. Louis County acquired Spanish Lake and its two neighboring waterholes, North and Sunfish lakes. In the ensuing three decades, its managers have stocked the lakes, laid out hiking paths, and encouraged thousands of people to come for picnics, walks, fairs, flea markets, birding, and nature study.

In the decades before the county bought the land, it

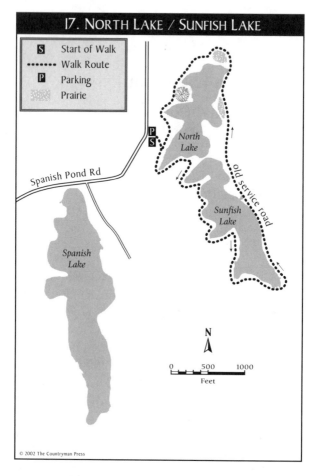

17. NORTH LAKE / SUNFISH LAKE

S Start of Walk
••••• Walk Route
P Parking
    Prairie

Spanish Pond Rd

North Lake

Sunfish Lake

old service road

Spanish Lake

N

0   500   1000
Feet

© 2002 The Countryman Press

was owned by the Heckmann family; from the 1950s to 1971, it was owned by a consortium of contractors. "When Bill Heckmann had the place, which he inherited from his father, they charged fishermen 50 cents to use the lake; the contractors did the same thing," recalls Virgil Wiegand, a retired ironworker who for nearly 65 years has resided in the home his father built across Spanish Pond Road from the park. (After the county purchased the property, it continued the fee fishing program. However, when the cost of trucking in the catfish to stock the lake ended up costing more than was earned in fishing fees, the county subsequently discontinued fee fishing.)

"In the old days, once you paid your fee, you could drive all around the lake," says Wiegand. "I remember one day a Model A Ford got parked on a lake bank. The driver must not have put his brakes on very tight because his car rolled into the lake. We had to use a team of mules and some strong people to pull the car out." Wiegand says there was a wooden footbridge across the lake in the 1920s, when the Heckmanns had a rowboat-rental operation. Some fishermen who fished Spanish Lake regularly kept lockers in the lakeside trees for tackle and clothing changes. Few people hiked in the area back then.

When it was thriving under private owners, the Spanish Lake property had a caretaker who lived in the small brick building inside the park grounds alongside Spanish Pond Road. Until 2001 the building was used as the office of the Spanish Lake Historical Society. "One caretaker I knew raised five kids there," says Wiegand. "At one time the place had a breezeway on its south side that connected with a wooden frame building where you could buy soda, tackle, and bait. The caretaker was the guy who took the fees at the gate."

Wiegand says that the enterprising Heckmanns dug five hatching ponds across Spanish Pond Road. Those ponds, still there but mostly hidden by vegetation, spawned the fish that Heckmann used to stock Spanish Lake. "Heckmann also owned what we called Lard's Pond [the Lards were early landowners hereabouts, starting in 1798], a sizeable body of water south of and to the west of Spanish Lake—where the Columbia Hills subdivision is now. In World War II the army would bring in amphibian vehicles called Ducks and unload them by Spanish Lake, then run them down through the hills and into Lard's Pond as part of their training. They drained Lord's Pond when they built the subdivision."

"When I was a boy," adds Wiegand, "there was what we called 'the black dog tree' right along Spanish Pond Road east of the park entrance. If you passed the tree late at night, the black dog was supposed to come out and scare your horses. Everybody talked about it and the pot of gold that was supposedly buried under the tree. Whatever tree that was probably doesn't exist anymore. The whole thing was pretty much a myth or a legend, but I believed it then."

In early 1942 two sinkholes east of the lake on property that the truck farming Ruthman brothers used as tomato and pepper patches suddenly filled with water and have stayed intermittently filled ever since. Those sinkholes are now North and Sunfish Lakes, major fishing destinations along with Spanish Lake itself. Sunfish is known as one of the best bass lakes around, according to Bob Emde, park supervisor at both Spanish Lake and Fort Belle Fontaine County Parks.

North and Sunfish Lakes are attractive to birders, says Paul Bauer, a coauthor of the *Birds of the St. Louis Area*. Warblers are found in many spots, and Carolina wrens savor the underbrush. "We once spotted a black-throated blue warbler in the underbrush," he says. "That's a bird we see only every few years. People rushed out to see it."

Access

From I-270 in north St. Louis County, exit at Belle-fontaine Road. Drive north 3 miles on Bellefontaine Road to Spanish Pond Road. Turn right on Spanish Pond Road and drive about 1 mile, passing the main entrance to Spanish Lake County Park and several other entranceways, to the parking lot at North and Sunfish Lakes.

Trail

From the parking area, walk to the right to pick up the dirt path alongside North Lake. The path works its way through a vine-covered mature-oak bottomland, then heads left at the first fork. After your turn, note a frog pond on the right.

Walk over a Boy Scout-built footbridge and up the eroded bank of North Lake. "This is a good place to see little green herons, blue herons, cattle egrets, even bald eagles on occasion," Emde advises. At the next trail fork, take a right, and make your way through another oak forest that includes a dogwood and redbud understory and, unfortunately, some very aggressive Japanese honeysuckle. "We've had some big owls in here," says Emde. "I've seen barred and great horned and screech owls here—they love mature forests. There are plenty of deer and foxes in here, too. Funny, though—I've never seen a wild turkey in all the 18 years I've been here."

As you walk, Sunfish Lake comes into focus to the left. Keep walking straight ahead, ignoring the first spur

North and Sunfish (foreground) Lakes

to the left but taking the second spur, marked by a tree
sign that features a red arrow on a white background. By
this time, you're nearly 0.5 mile into the hike. Walk
south to Sunfish Lake on the spur that cross-country
runners who use this and other side trails call "primitive
paths." Once you arrive at Sunfish Lake, take a right.
This crooked and meandering stretch of the walk takes
you through a scrub forest thickened with vines, honeysuckle, mulberries, and persimmons. Emde says that
common garter and water snakes are sometimes found
in this lakeside section; neither is venomous.

At the west end of Sunfish, the trail bends to the left,
heads uphill, and provides a sharp perspective on the
lake below. Quite often you'll see fishermen in their
boats, hoping to land a prize bass. (Fishermen routinely catch bass over 20 inches long at Sunfish; over at
Spanish Lake, by comparison, the bass average is 11 to
14 inches. And catfish taken from these lakes have
weighed as much as 50 pounds.) After a long woodsy

walk, take a left on an old service road at the southwest corner of the lake; it descends to a greenish bottom-land where cattails and bald cypress trees are among the residents. A chain-link fence put up by the neighbors, Pipefitters Local 562, demarcating their nearly 300-acre facility, soon appears on the right and helps define the trail as it takes a swing to the north. The Pipefitters operate an 18-hole golf course by the fence, as well as a large swimming pool, clubhouse, retirement center, and training facility on its nearly 300 acres. In the spring migration, warblers have been observed feeding close to the fence.

The trail starts uphill and connects with a restored and expansive prairie that emerges on the left, as does the northern tip of North Lake, which is often completely dry. Walk by a dam that's obviously infrequently in operation, since the lakes are seldom full. "The lakes haven't been full since I started to work here in 1985," says Bob Emde. (Paul Bauer, the serious birder, says he has seen both North and Sunfish Lakes completely dried up. "On North Lake I found 4-inch clam shells when I walked across it.")

As the path approaches the park's northern boundary at Spanish Pond Road, it veers to the left, still bordering the impressive prairie re-creation. To the right, several rows of trees mark the location of the old St. Vrain Road, which once headed downhill to the confluence area. "We called it Breakneck Road when I was a boy," says Wiegand. "The story was that a fellow took some horses along the road one night, and one of the horses broke its neck somehow. When the Pipefitters bought the ground, they fenced the road off." (Much of the present county park is located on the former estate of James De St. Vrain, stepbrother of Charles De Lassus, last colonial governor of Louisiana territory.)

Hike the prairie edge until you see the mowed path to the left. Take the path down through the prairie among summertime black-eyed Susan, wild hydrangea, purple vetch, bull thistle, and other forbs. The grass path flattens out, veers right among more prairie and wetland plants, then reaches an arm of North Lake. Stay close to the shore, following it all the way back to the boat ramp area where your hike began.

If you have time, drive over to Spanish Lake and walk around it on the blacktop. Begin your walk near the rest room area just south of the main parking lot. The counterclockwise hike takes you by fishing docks, majestic lakeshore trees, many bankside fishermen (on good days), side paths to subdivisions, picnic shelters, ball fields, and, toward the end of the loop, the redbrick building by Spanish Pond road that once was the caretaker's residence. End the loop walk by hiking out to "the Point," the narrow strip of land containing the handicapped fishing dock. Years ago old-timers say, there was a honky-tonk bar on the Point.

Spanish Lake is probably the most popular walking park in north St. Louis County. One walker we met, retired Hazelwood schoolteacher Adair Andrew, had an extraordinary goal: "I plan to walk 100 miles around Spanish Lake on my birthday in August." That meant getting permission to camp there overnight since, as he pointed out, "I can't do all 100 miles in one day."

18 · Tilles County Park

Location: Ladue, Missouri
Hiking distance: 1.8 miles
Hiking time: 1 hour
Bicycles: Not permitted

In 1932 Charles Andrew (Cap) Tilles, a wealthy investor in real estate and racetracks (including Churchill Downs in Louisville), donated 68 mostly virgin acres at Lay (now McKnight) and Litzinger Roads in Ladue to the city of St. Louis as a park for poor children. Tilles had purchased "Rest Haven" in 1912 from a group that wanted to establish a country club there but desisted because of poor access roads. Tilles built a modest log bungalow and a crude roadway; cultivated apple and pear orchards, trimmed his trees, and raised roses, which he clipped and took to hospital wards to cheer the sick.

Tilles stipulated that the city name the new park in memory of his mother, Rosalie, who succumbed to a heart attack at age 35 when Cap was 7 years old. (In 1926 Tilles had set aside more than one million dollars for a foundation in her name.) In accepting the gift, civic leaders said it would provide the first of many "outer" parks to accommodate a heavy population influx projected for St. Louis County. The leaders advised that the outer park system start soon before land prices

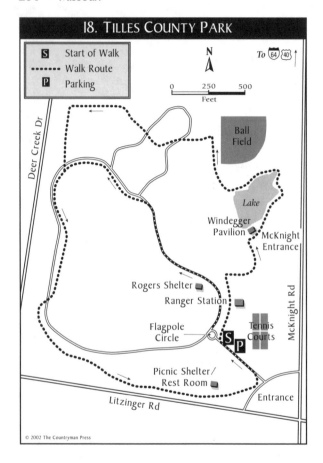

18. TILLES COUNTY PARK

Legend:
- **S** Start of Walk
- **····** Walk Route
- **P** Parking

N

To 64 40

0   250   500
Feet

Deer Creek Dr

Ball Field

Lake

Windegger Pavilion

McKnight Entrance

Rogers Shelter

Ranger Station

McKnight Rd

Flagpole Circle

Tennis Courts

S **P**

Picnic Shelter/ Rest Room

Litzinger Rd

Entrance

© 2002 The Countryman Press

became prohibitive. "In 1874 St. Louis bought Forest Park for $620 an acre, but 30 years later, [the city] was forced to pay $5,426 an acre for Fairgrounds Park," stated the *St. Louis Post-Dispatch* in a 1932 editorial. "There are any number of beautiful park sites along the Missouri, Mississippi, and Meramec Rivers available now for a song, and the city could not make a better investment."

Tilles had been a partner with Louis A. Cella, who later built the American Theatre in downtown St. Louis. Their firm was called Cella, Adler, and Tilles; it was known as "the Big Three" in racetrack operations in such cities as Cincinnati, Little Rock, Hot Springs, Memphis, Detroit, Buffalo, and Louisville. The firm was said to own at least half the racetracks in America at the time. The partners opened America's first night track near the site of the present McKinley High School on South Grand Boulevard in St. Louis as well as Delmar Race Track in University City.

Tilles spent the warm months in the home he built on his acreage. In 1915 he put in an artificial lake that still exists in about the same dimensions. His lake had a boathouse, canoe, sand beach, and water toboggan. Satisfying his passion for horses, he constructed a sizeable stable (razed in 1977) as well as an impressive rock garden (some remnants remain) and putting green. Tilles usually retreated in cold months to an apartment on Lindell Boulevard.

After the city took over the land in the 1930s, it brought in Works Progress Administration (WPA) workers to develop the outer park. On the premises for at least two and a half years, WPA people assembled the park infrastructure: two stone entrance gates, each requiring 110 tons of rock; three pedestrian gates (one remains); 10 stone comfort stations with dark-slate roofs; picnic shelters hewn of native stone; 10 "rock camp" fireplaces with adjoining fire hydrants; a wading pool; and a cyclone fence that surrounded the property. A yellow-brick cottage and garage for the park keeper were put up (they survive as a ranger station compound near the tennis courts), and a multitude of evergreens

A WPA-constructed rest facility at Tilles County Park

and shrubs were planted to enhance the woodsy appearance of the site. The WPA had to work around the 10 to 15 sinkholes on the land (they're still here). "During heavy rain, some of our sinkholes begin filling up," says Bob Taylor, park maintenance supervisor. "We have to plug them quickly, or we'll have small lakes we don't want." A circular roadway of gravel-coated bituminous macadam was put down by the WPA. It was nearly 1 mile long and survives, much repaved.

Tilles died in 1951 at age 85, leaving the heftiest bequest in his will to Mrs. Jeannette Windegger, described as a longtime friend. She was the daughter of a St. Louis philanthropist and in her later years was extremely generous in her contributions to St. Louis charities. According to Tilles's will—which bequeathed her his household goods, the stable, automobiles, livestock, and crops—she had the use of his country home until her death. Before she died in 1991 at 97, she had been persuaded by park officials to deed her property to them. In her final years she was driven from a nursing

home to the park, where she sat on a lake dock, a nurse
and social worker nearby, looking wistfully toward her
vacated home.

Access

At I-64/US 40 in St. Louis County, take the McKnight
Road exit, and drive south on McKnight—about 0.75
mile—to the park entrance. Park by the tennis courts.

Trail

Since the circular roadway around the park is less than
1 mile, we suggest that you do the walk twice, taking in
the lake and pavilion and some other points of interest
the second time around.

Start your walk by the flagpole near the plaque that
relates the park's history. Near the front entrance are the
oldest pine trees in the park, planted in WPA days. All
the other pines—there are plenty of them—were planted about 30 years ago. Walk on the left side of the circular roadway. On the right is the county park ranger's
station, the former caretaker's residence from the 1930s.
On the left is the Gloria Rogers Shelter, recognizing a
former St. Louis County Parks recreation manager and
Brentwood parks director. On the right is the Skow
Shelter, named for Charles R. Skow, St. Louis County
commissioner of parks and recreation from 1957 to
1962. Skow had been a mayor of Brentwood, then
chairman of the St. Louis County Council in 1953.
Soon to appear on the left by a major sinkhole is one
of the park's larger WPA-made comfort stations.

Another stone comfort station appears as you round
the bend, heading for the picnic grove, which sits in a
small plantation of Missouri shortleaf pines. It's our

thought that this park has more comfort stations per mile than any park we've hiked—here and abroad. In 1936 the WPA deployed 500 workers to convert the old wooded tract to an up-to-date park. WPA archives don't state exactly why all the comfort stations were required. Some of the stations were built exclusively for men, others for women. Most had red-tile or slate roofs and fancy stone motifs near their entrances. The St. Louis Parks and Recreation Department said in its 1940 annual report that Tilles officially opened January 7, 1939, in a complex that included the comfort stations, four hard-surfaced tennis courts, 11 camp stoves, and a full-time superintendent.

Keep walking around the bend; then leave the road, and head east on an asphalt path by still another rest room, this time ambling toward the chain-link fence that borders Litzinger Road. On the way to the massive stone entrance gate at Litzinger, you'll pass the park's largest rest room, the one that's specially outfitted for the handicapped. (Years ago, this facility contained change houses for youngsters using the park's wading pool plus an office for day-camp counselors. Nowadays, part of the building is used to store equipment for the annual Winter Wonderland event in the park, a drive-through Christmas decoration spectacle from Thanksgiving to New Year's that uses the main park roadway.)

Walk around the flagpole to begin your second lap of Tilles. Head for the Jeanette Windegger Pavilion and lake to your right. Begin a counterclockwise 1,500-foot walk around the lake. You must walk on the grass since there's no official lake trail. Be sure to give a wide berth to the dozens of Canada geese and Mallard ducks that may be lazing or grazing on the banks—and possibly territorially testy. Occasionally some wood ducks visit, and a pair of white egrets have been seen, but the place is pretty much the sole reserve of the wild ducks and geese. Incidentally, the fountain geyser in midlake can shoot a plume of water 50 feet in the air when the pressure is strong. Fisherman use the lake constantly; catfish, bluegill, bass, and trout are among the usual catches.

Check out the unadorned park entrance at McKnight Road; it's used mainly by neighbors. Near the gate is the site of the one-story frame Windegger residence. Park staff discovered what may have been the original log cabin(which Tilles had built) when the building was razed. Well before this razing, county employees had pulled down the much smaller Windegger caretaker's home closer to the McKnight gate. A large barn and stable near this home had a second-floor ballroom and chauffeur's quarters and downstairs bays once used for horses and cattle but later for wagons and large cars.

Some 100 feet inside the McKnight gate is a commemorative English oak tree, brought from England's Sherwood Forest as a seedling nearly 70 years ago. The surrounding grounds are packed with magisterial oaks, hickories, cottonwoods, willows, and bald cypress trees. Taylor says there are so many "memorial trees" (all 440 of them bearing plaques) that there is no more room for them at Tilles. "I had to prepare a grid map of these trees because so many of the donors came here wanting to see them," Taylor adds. (The St. Louis county parks department has promoted its very successful memorial heritage program for years in all of its parks.)

Walk by a rocky stretch near the bald cypress trees; the rocks are used for bank stabilization. From here you can look directly across the lake to see the man-made earthen dam and spillway. As you round the lake, notice the chain-link fence at the baseball diamond to the right. Instead of completely circling the lake, walk right onto a wide gravel path at the spillway. Follow it as it cuts past the park maintenance sheds, then turns abruptly right and aims for the bleacher area of the ball-park, which is used regularly in the summer by several softball leagues.

On the old stone walkway at the ballpark comfort station, walk to the nearby roadway, and then proceed briefly right until you see the parking area to your right. From the parking area, get on the grass and head toward the park's west boundary fence. Walk south along the fence that abuts homes on Deer Creek Drive. Around this remote part of Tilles, some people persist in releasing squirrels that they have trapped in their yards. "They do it all the time," laughs Taylor. "It usually happens, however, that in two or three days those same squirrels will find their way back to the same yards. They seem to know instinctively where their old neighborhood is."

Continue walking along the fence in a pleasantly shaded area. When you reach the southwest corner of the park, head back on the grass—encountering another comfort station or two and some cookout sites—to reach the main park roadway. Walk to the right, following the circular road back to your car or accessing the asphalt trail to the right that again takes you to the Litzinger Road fence, the handicapped rest room, the stone gate, and the flagpole circle—and then to your car.

Taylor estimates that around 50 people are regular daily walkers at Tilles, but hundreds hike in the park on busy summer days. He and his staff keep their eyes peeled for the unusual. "Once we had a man who was under doctor's orders to recuperate from an injury. His routine was to walk forward around the park once, then backwards all the way the second time. We never heard if he got well."

19 · Valley View Glades Natural Area

Location: Near Hillsboro, Missouri
Hiking distance: 3 miles
Hiking time: 2 hours
Bicycles: Not permitted

Valley View Glades is a major player in a 2- to 5-mile-wide band of glades (defined as relatively dry open areas with thin, dry soil; exposed rocks or bedrock; prairie grasses; stunted trees; and stunning wildflowers) that stretch for about 100 miles from Morse Mill in northern Jefferson County to near St. Genevieve County, Missouri.

Glades are typically identified by their underlying bedrock, states *Discovering Natural Missouri*, a 1991 Nature Conservancy publication. Dolomite, and some chert, underlies 227-acre Valley View Glades. Elsewhere in Missouri, glades are built on limestone, sandstone, and granite. Each glade supports its own collection of plants and animals.

If you were viewing Valley View Glades and its surroundings from the air, you would see a surfeit of small glades. At least 300 acres of privately owned glades encircle much of Valley View, says Michael Arduser, natural history biologist for the Missouri Department of Conservation's St. Louis region. And about 6 miles to

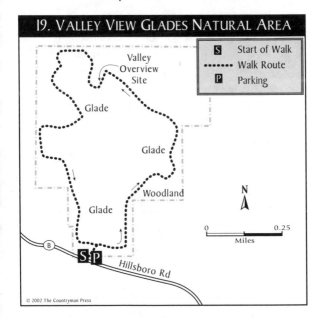

19. Valley View Glades Natural Area

Valley Overview Site

S Start of Walk

••••••• Walk Route

P Parking

Glade

Glade

Woodland

Glade

N

0   0.25
Miles

S **P**

Hillsboro Rd

© 2002 The Countryman Press

the east is Victoria Glades Conservation Area, a 230-acre property with more diverse plant life than, but not as showy as, Valley View. The conservation department manages both properties.

When westbound emigrants settled in Missouri in the 1840s and 1850s, more than 400,000 acres of glades purportedly existed in the state. Nowadays some naturalists believe that Missouri has more glades than any other American state, though they lament that glade acreage is decreasing, due partially to habitat encroachment by the sprawl of homebuilding.

Valley View Glades is one of the few places where one can see the rare wildflower Fremont's leatherflower, which blooms in May and June. Named for General John C. Fremont, once called "America's pathfinder" in recognition of his five major exploratory trips to the West, the plant is said to grow only on eastern Missouri glades and on a glade band near the Kansas-Nebraska border. This white-to-purple flower—the only non-climbing member of the clematis family—can be found in liberal quantities along the trail.

Valley View also has respectable numbers of Missouri evening primroses and pale purple coneflowers, which only grow on glades.

It is home to striped scorpions, the state's sole scorpion species, tarantulas, and red milk snakes. "Some people come into the glades looking for some of these critters," says Arduser, who has seen scorpion hunters armed with crowbars upturning rocks on the trail in their quest for these valuable reptiles. "All of them are breaking the law and damaging the glade."

Butterflies find comfort in the glades, according to reports of butterfly counts sponsored by the Idalia Society of Mid America Lepidopterists and the Webster Groves Nature Study Society, among others. Generally, the counts are conducted from April through late summer to help habitat managers assess the health of the state's butterfly population. It's estimated that 125 of the nearly 700 butterfly species in North America north of Mexico are found in Missouri. Some 70 species have been identified at Valley View Glades.

A final report for 1999 for Valley View provides a good picture of butterfly life on the glades. In April, when violets and Indian paintbrushes were abloom, butterfly species with names like pearl crescent, goatweed, spring azure, and clouded sulphur were noted. In late May 64 gorgon checkerspots were found among the pale purple coneflowers, shooting stars, and

Missouri evening primroses. In mid-June 16 wood nymphs and 7 great spangled fritillaries floated among the St. John's-wort and black-eyed Susans. In August sachems, buckeyes, eastern-tailed blues, and some monarchs flew in, then flew on. Of course, many other species were sighted during the counting. You can see some of them yourself, but we recommend that you bring along a good butterfly field guide.

Bluebirds, some of whom nest in aged pin and chinquapin oaks, are common in the open glades. Olive and bright yellow prairie warblers appear in May, June, and July.

The trail is mostly an extended long loop around the entire property, which encompasses extensive dry woodlands, intermittently dry creeks, and plenty of glades. Naturalists observe that the glades were once grazed by cattle and that much of the peripheral timber was harvested by the early 1900s. As evidence of the land's makeover, fire scars remain on some of the gnarly post and chinquapin oaks.

Access

From MO 141 in southwest St. Louis County, turn right on MO 30. Drive 17.5 miles west on 30 to Jefferson County Highway B. Turn left on B (Hillsboro Road); drive 6.8 miles east, through the village of Morse Mill, to the Valley View Glades turnoff on your left. Park in the lot.

Trail

To reach the loop path from the parking area, walk downhill some 400 feet through dry upland woods spotted with post and chinquapin oaks, shagbark hickories, and sugar maples. Its thin soil is another sign that cattle once found this hillside and adjoining land good for grazing.

The trail begins in earnest at the bottom of the hill. Take a right; proceed along the glade edge where eastern red cedars are plentiful. "See how those cedars hang on tenaciously," says Ramon Gass, a former conservation department forester and entomologist. "They seem to be about one hundred years old." Arduser and other department professionals who manage the glades view the cedars warily. "If we allow too many of them to encroach, our glades will turn into cedar thickets," says Arduser. "We have to selectively cut our cedars—you can see some of them lying along the glades—and then we have to periodically burn the glades." The trail surface is largely composed of eroded rock.

Early on, Fremont's leatherflowers, suspended bell-like from stalks that reach 2 feet tall, appear along trail borders. Ladies' tresses—"the one orchid in Missouri that can be found in stands of hundreds," according to *Missouri Wildflowers*—are on view from August through early November. These small, drooping white flowers emit a fragrance that resembles that of the lily of the valley. Two ladies' tresses species are on the glades; one blooms in August, the other in October and early November. Common prairie grasses such as side oats grama (their seed heads grow on only one side of their stems), Indian grass, and little bluestem are well represented.

The trail fords the dry, intermittent creek many times. Near an early crossing in the woodland section, ancient cedars—larger and knottier than cedars on the glades—grow by the creek bank or in the dolomite rock.

Walkers and old cedar trees on Valley View Glades

"Some of these trees are four hundred to five hundred years old," estimates Gass.

The trail weaves through glade and woodland for most of its length. Serving as trail steps on some upward passages are rocky ledges that support clinging cliff-brake ferns. The rock protects the plants from being washed away by heavy rains. "The ferns don't know that, of course, but that's why they live there," jokes Gass. Hikers will encounter what Gass describes as "hardcore glades," where little but grasses grow on the shallow, rocky soil. "Any trees that appear on this glade are stunted. And look at the streaks of gravel on the glade," says Gass. "The rock simply eroded that way!"

Pale purple coneflowers brighten the glades in mid-summer. "We have coneflowers here by the truckload," says Arduser. Unfortunately, some trail users are interested in the roots of these perennial plants, which are used by pharmaceutical companies to prepare tonics and herbal products such as echinacea. J. Marshall Magner, an entomologist who is a stalwart of the Webster

Groves Nature Study Society, said that as they were to
begin a butterfly count about five years ago, "something
looked different on the glades. Quickly, we perceived
that someone had come in and dug out many of the
coneflowers, taking the roots, and leaving the stems on
the ground and many mounds of dirt. It looked like
someone went through the glades with a plow. It infu-
riated me." Arduser warns that if caught, coneflower
thieves will be prosecuted.

Missouri evening primroses also grow copiously on
the glades. *Missouri Wildflowers* states that the pale-yel-
low flowers "open very suddenly in late afternoon and
close early the next morning." Arduser says he enjoys
sitting in a glade around dusk and watching the primroses open. "They come out like stars in the sky. The
petals just fall open. If you're quiet, you can almost hear
them open up." Bat-sized hawk moths, with tongues 6
to 8 inches long, hover around after dark to pollinate
the fresh flowers. So do small black sweat bees that exist
solely to feed on primrose pollen. Arduser said he's seen
six to eight nocturnal sweat bees on one flower. A western species of solitary bee lives to collect pollen from
pale purple coneflowers and no other flower.

As the hike progresses, you'll walk into and out of a
ravine, then settle in for a long stretch of woodland
trekking. After about 1 mile of walking, take a sharp left
on a linear ridge path that defines the area's northern
boundary. Local historians think that this artery is most
probably an old service road, perhaps a connector
between Hillsboro and Morse Mill from early settlement
times. After you walk for a while, a brown directional
post will point you to the left for a short jaunt to a broad
overview of the valley and cedar-studded glades to the

south. After a breather, follow the side path around until it reconnects with the main trail; resume your hike by walking left.

After 1.5 miles the trail meets a barbed-wire fence that marks the western property line. Turn left and head downhill for a while through more woodland and small glade openings. This final 1.5 miles is the rockiest part of the hike; the woods seem older, the hills steeper. At least two of the hills—both heading up—will greatly test your aerobic strength.

On some of the glades on your left, you'll see fallen cedars, evidence of the conservation department's effort to stop cedar encroachment and keep the glades open to healthy growth. You'll see two more species of drought-tolerant trees: gum bumeilas, with thorns and spatula-shaped leaves, and white ashes. The final section of the trail follows creek beds and takes you past boulderlike chunks of dolomite and chert; gray rock ledges where ebony spleenwort and sensitive fern can be found, and small-scale waterfall activity fed by general groundwater seepage. After the 3-mile point on the hike—quite often, people feel as if they've walked 4 or 5 miles through these glades—you'll reach the last hill, ready to reclaim your automobile and head home.

If you want one lasting look at the hills around Hillsboro and Valley View, drive east on County B to the Outpost General Store.

Walk to the bar area in the rear of the store, and look out the window. On the far horizon are forests, haze, and dim mountaintops. "You're looking as far as Potosi, 30 miles to the south," a bar regular informs us.

20 · Hilda J. Young Conservation Area

Location: Near Eureka, Missouri
Hiking distance: 2.8 miles
Hiking time: 1.5 hours
Bicycles: Not permitted

On a trip down the picturesque Meramec River one summer, attorney Truman Post Young paused on a gravel bar while floating with friends. "Who owns that hill up there?" he asked, pointing. "I do," a fellow floater replied. "Want to sell part of it?" Young asked. A deal was done, and Young was the owner of 13 acres that reached back from the river and up the hill. Young's friends helped him build a small cabin or shell, which the family later called "the Shack" and his friends jokingly labeled "the Workhouse on Chigger Hill." Now razed, the Shack was located across present highway FF and slightly to the west.

"My father owned the property for a while before he married my mother, Hilda," says one of Young's daughters, Pat Jones of Callaway County, Missouri. "My mother had to pass a litmus test before my father would marry her," adds Jones. "She had to prove that she liked country life—and that meant coming out to my father's property on the Meramec." The couple was so captivat-

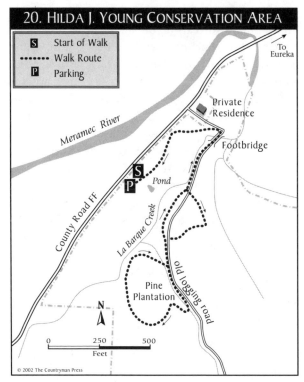

20. HILDA J. YOUNG CONSERVATION AREA

S   Start of Walk
•••••••   Walk Route
P   Parking

Meramec River

County Road FF

La Barque Creek

S
P   Pond

Private Residence

Footbridge

old logging road

Pine Plantation

To Eureka

N

0   250   500
Feet

© 2002 The Countryman Press

ed by the land that they honeymooned there, says another daughter, Ann Lloyd, who continues to live nearby. "My father warned my mother not to bring in any exotic plants to what they called Shack Hill," says Jones. "Well, she didn't bring in *too* many exotics," says Jones, laughing. "But she did plant some autumn olive bushes and multiflora roses and let the honeysuckle take hold."

Truman Young, who in 1929 helped found the downtown St. Louis law firm of Thompson, Mitchell, Thompson, and Young, died in 1942. Ten years later,

Hilda Young built a home north of FF and resided there until 1984, two years before her death at 90. Joseph Logan, a longtime member of Young's old firm, now known as Thompson Coburn, recalls visiting Hilda Young with his wife. "We'd be invited out to walk in the woods and then stop by at Hilda's for conversation. Our aim while taking a walk in what is now the Young Conservation Area was to head back into the woods and picnic at a large log cabin with a massive fireplace and a stable nearby. It had once been a retreat for Rotarians, but by the time we were hiking there, it had been abandoned. We've been hiking there for years and still walk up to the site, although the cabin and other buildings are gone." Hilda Young preferred to drive her Jeep or take her horse over the trail network.

"Mother called herself a farmer," says Lloyd. "We had cattle that grazed the land back then. And we had a horse barn that since has been torn down. It was located east of the present parking area."

Over the years a prominent neighbor was YMCA Camp Taconic, a facility for delinquent boys that operated from 1918 to 1950. The camp had a main lodge/dining room, at least 10 wooden cabins, a log-cabin post office, and much recreational land that abutted the Meramec River and touched both sides of LaBarque Creek. Hilda Young eventually bought all 1,000 acres of the YMCA property and built a home on part of it.

Hilda had a lifelong interest in conservation. She forbade hunting on her land and wanted it preserved in its natural state after her death. Five hundred acres of Hilda's property was donated in 1986 to the Missouri Department of Conservation; the other parcels were sold to the department by family members.

Conservation staffers call the Young walking trail "the Taconic Trail." *Taconic* is the Osage Indian word for "beautiful hills," plus the name recalls the one-time presence of Camp Taconic. The Young Conservation Trail fords LaBarque Creek several times, explores bottomlands and forested hills, circles a pine plantation, and in the spring encounters showy wildflowers by the thousands. Massive spreads of Virginia bluebells are found in mid-April near the creek.

Access

From I-270 in south St. Louis County, take I-44 west 12 miles to exit 264 at Eureka. Turn left on County Road W, drive 2 miles to County Road FF, and turn right onto FF. Drive 2.5 miles to the Young Conservation Area entrance, and park in the lot.

A note of caution: After a rain or during flooding, this loop trail will either be extremely muddy or inaccessible, so make sure you monitor the weather. Also, since the paths are very grassy in many places, it's mandatory that you spray for ticks and chiggers and dress wisely.

Trail

Before starting your hike, note the fishing pond some 75 yards south of the parking lot. This 1-acre pond is the more accessible of the two ponds at Young; it's regularly stocked with fish by the conservation department.

Begin walking east on the Taconic Trail, a wide grassy path set off on the left by rows of eastern red cedars and autumn olive bushes. Closer to the path, prairie grasses—Indian grass, big and little bluestem, and switch grass—have been planted by conservation work-

A bedrocky stretch of the Taconic Trail

ers to combat erosion, says Dave Platt, in charge of site maintenance here and at 17 other conservation properties. This early section of the trail was once a fescue field where Hilda Young's cattle roamed, Platt observes.

As you proceed, note a small hill with honey locust saplings near the only private residence that abuts the loop trail—probably the residence of the Camp Taconic caretaker. Shortly, the grassy trail swings to the right and passes a quartet of ancient cedars that crowd the path as well as a mixed hardwood forest on the right with oaks, hickories, ashes, silver maples, and Ohio buckeyes. Mutiflora roses nearby, possible descendants of those planted by Hilda Young, are springtime bloomers near the path. (Multiflora, or Japanese rose, is an invasive nuisance that "can only be taken out by a bulldozer," according to *Missouri Wildflowers*.)

Small cottonwoods are part of the landscape as you approach the footbridge over LaBarque Creek. (La bar-que means "small boat" in French. Expect to see none of them on your hike.) Gravel bars, fallen logs, and fast-moving bluegill and small bass help define this clear country creek where conservation workers have put in tulip poplars and other species to stabilize the stream banks. "The flood of 1993 damaged this area and the bridge," says Platt, pointing to sand deposits left by plundering floodwater on the trail and the banks.

A sign saying NATURE TRAIL is posted some 500 feet beyond the bridge. Take a left at the sign, head up a hill on the still-grassy trail, and then swing to the right where pine saplings and prairie grasses pop into view. At another NATURE TRAIL sign, turn right. As you head north, you'll see near the crest of the creek bank old trees that were cut down to make way for a nearby fishing pond. Walk to LaBarque Creek, turn left at the trail sign, and begin an uphill trek on a bedrocky old logging road. The forest was last logged in the 1950s when Hilda Young was active in its management. Mules were still being used to drag the logs from the woods. In 1993 much of the bottomland across the creek was "a big lake" due to flooding, Platt recalls. As the trail climbs, glades appear on the hillside.

A cedar plantation crowds the trail before you reach

a power-line clearing. Healthy clusters of rose and purple wildflowers appear on ledges on the left at the edge of the clearing. Occasionally pileated woodpeckers and hawks are seen gliding across the opening, and deer feed in the open space, then retreat into the cover of the forest. "Stand still and you can hear the power lines' static and popping," Platt suggests.

As you continue, bear left at the first trail sign after the clearing (the sign marks the first mile of the trail.) Stay on the grassy path to the creek, which you must step across. The creek setting here is very pastoral: ferns climb the hill from the water; songbirds sing away; white violets, white and purple larkspur, and phlox are scattered everywhere. Steep green hills sweep down to the creek and its gravel bars.

Walk the bottomland to another trail sign; turn right and walk uphill to the 10-acre Missouri shortleaf pine plantation. The path encircles much of the plantation, planted about 50 years ago under the direction of Pat Jones's husband, Edward, who purchased a tree planter specifically for the conservation department's use at the Young Conservation Area. Says Pat Jones, "It was the first time the department ever used a tractor-drawn planter."

At the plantation's southwest corner, make a sharp right. Here, the path strays from the pines to wander among cedars and glades before it resumes its route by the pines. At the next power-line clearing, you can look out to see how the transmission lines separate the two halves of the plantation. (Platt says that the pines— which "are a great place to see migrating warblers in the spring and fall"—are getting too crowded. "We need to do some thinning so they won't get stunted," he says.

"This will also permit healthier growth for our understory trees like small oaks and sugar maples.")

After an hour's walk there's a bench (thanks to Eagle Scouts) where you can rest awhile and listen for woodland critters. An oak-hickory forest lies in front of the bench as you sit; downhill from there is LaBarque Creek. Continuing on, the path skirts the last of the pines, recrosses the power corridor, and moves downhill to the creek. Ford the creek, and then walk straight ahead to another trail marker. Take a left, and walk uphill through the forest (which marks the second mile of your walk).

Keep walking straight ahead on this stretch, where spring beauties, phlox, bluebells, redbuds, and strong white oaks seem to flourish on a spring afternoon. The path should be familiar to you as you keep following the trail signs, recross the footbridge, and retrace your steps on the wide grass path that ends at the parking lot.

Illinois

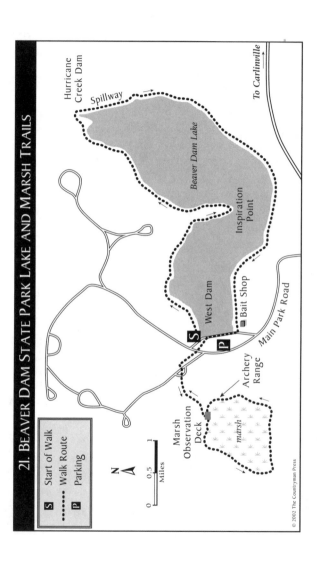

21. BEAVER DAM STATE PARK LAKE AND MARSH TRAILS

Hurricane Creek Dam

Spillway

Beaver Dam Lake

Inspiration Point

West Dam

Bait Shop

Main Park Road

To Cartinville

Archery Range

Marsh Observation Deck

marsh

S Start of Walk
···· Walk Route
P Parking

N

0   0.5   1
Miles

© 2002 The Countryman Press

21 · Beaver Dam State Park Lake and Marsh Trails

Location: Plainview, Illinois
Hiking distance: 2.5 miles
Hiking time: 2 hours
Bicycles: Not permitted
Disabled access: Lake trail only

"We're loved to death," said Matt Tueth, former superintendent of this 750-acre peanut of a state park. "People like us because we're homey; there's only one way in and one way out which means good security, and our quiet hours for campers—10 PM to 7 AM—are easy to enforce. We also have white squirrels—they're not albinos but gray squirrels in their white-color phase."

White-colored gray squirrels are extremely rare, says Jerry Garver, who directs statewide squirrel, woodcock, and wild turkey inventories and programs for the Illinois Department of Natural Resources. "The squirrels at Beaver Dam State Park are probably from a long genetic line of squirrels that reside in a territory that hasn't been hunted for years and years," Garver assumes. "Somehow these squirrels have survived." Garver points out that in other parts of Illinois, such as the city of Olney, true albino squirrels reside. "They're pure white with pink eyes." And not to be confused with the rare gray squirrels at Beaver Dam. According to park historian Jim Frank, who lives next door, recalls that "a lot of white squirrels were seen around here 25 years ago. A ranger back then put up a sign at a feeder that said: FOR WHITE SQUIRRELS ONLY."

The park's 59-acre lake—9 to 12 feet deep and loaded with largemouth bass, bluegill, sunfish, crappie and channel catfish—is circled by a nearly 2-mile-long hiking trail. Nearby, another trail loops around an ancient marsh.

The park is situated in the Macoupin Creek Valley, which was created by the presence of two creeks: Macoupin, a tributary of the Illinois River, and Hurricane. A strong Native American heritage imbues the parkland. Ninety-three prehistoric Indian sites have been identified along Macoupin Creek; many Indian gravesites are nearby as well, says historian Frank.

A magnificent red sandstone ceremonial clay pipe was discovered in the valley in 1875 and was traced to the Mayan culture from Central America. This finding suggests that Indians lived around here from 900 to 1150 A.D.—at about the same time the Cahokia Mound Builders were residing farther south, in the vicinity of present-day St. Louis. A replica of the pipe is displayed at the Smithsonian Institution in Washington, D.C., says Frank, whose written history of the park has been widely distributed.

The park is located on one of Illinois' rare "experimental roads," developed between 1934 and 1938 to test possible bases such as black dirt or clay that would underlie an asphalt surface. The road has no official county or state designation or number other than being called "the hard road" or "the Shipman-Carlinville blacktop." Highway officials call the 15-mile stretch a "state aid" road, meaning that the state and not the county must maintain it.

The pasture and small lake that eventually became the park was leased in 1890 to area investors who built two earthen dams so the water would rise and fishing could thrive. A quasi-resort was formed, called the Beaver Dam Lake Club. Sportsmen who came from St. Louis and elsewhere were met a mile away at the Macoupin Station of the old Chicago & Alton Railroad. For horse-drawn taxi service, they were charged a stiff fee. Amtrak trains between St. Louis and Chicago roll along the tracks today.

In 1901 Sarah Rhodes inherited the property. She and her husband constructed a three-story 16-room hotel and advertised for customers in St. Louis newspapers. When meals were ready at the hotel, Mrs. Rhodes blew a fox horn loudly to summon her guests. Although women stayed at the hotel, Mrs. Rhodes prohibited women from overnight camping on the resort grounds. "That was a moral no-no at the time," Frank says.

Mr. Rhodes was a wary proprietor, Frank says. "Rather than pay the fishing fee, some folks would try to sneak into the lake grounds the back way, but Mr. Rhodes had watchmen looking for trespassers and would nab them as they climbed the fence."

In a small shed near the hotel, blocks of ice cut from the frozen lake were packed in sawdust and stored for the warmer months. Mrs. Rhodes used some of the ice for summertime iced tea. After a meal her habit was to salvage leftover sugar from the bottoms of tea and coffee cups, dry it, and use it again in cakes and pies.

The hotel closed in 1937. Severely downsized, the hotel building became the park ranger's residence but was torn down in 2001 to make way for a park office.

The park maintains two satellites: Denby Prairie Nature Preserve and the Gillespie Railroad Prairie. You can explore the 2.5-acre Denby preserve, halfway between the park and Carlinville along the railroad tracks. "This prairie has survived elk, buffalo, burning, and spraying along the tracks," says biologist Todd Strole of the Department of Natural Resources. "It's a good place to tramp about." The 7-mile long Gillespie prairie lies along IL 16 and former Illinois Terminal Railroad tracks northeast of Gillespie on the way to Litchfield.

Access

From I-270 East in north St. Louis County, drive 10 miles on MO 367 north to Alton, Illinois. Leaving the Mississippi River bridge, follow US 67 north through Alton, Godfrey, then Brighton, to IL 16, about 18 miles. Turn right on IL 16; drive 5 miles to the Carlinville Road in Shipman. Make a left on Carlinville Road; drive 9 more miles to the park entrance. Drive in, and then park at the concession stand.

Trail

The lake walk begins at the boat launch site north of the Beaver Dam Bait Shop, the concession stand popular for biscuits-and-gravy breakfasts and hot sandwiches and, of course, its fishing aids. Bald cypress trees, girded with wire to shield them from potentially hostile beaver action, are seen early on the walk. The namesake beavers are seldom seen near the lake anymore, however. Post oak trees are strong in numbers in the neighboring woods. "Their presence often indicates that the land was once dry and pastured," reminds forest entomologist Ramon Gass. As the trail continues, elms and hickories come into view, as well.

Directly across from the second girded bald cypress is a prickly aster, or toothache tree, laden with thorns. "If you remove the thorns and rub the leaf across your gums, you'll get rid of your toothache," Gass says, repeating an old folk remedy. Ahead, a pair of monstrous black oaks stand guard by the path.

On good days, fisherman troll the lake, often making some remarkable hauls. A 65-pound channel catfish is the record catch, says Dan Strubberg, coproprietor of the Bait Shop. "I caught a 40-pound catfish here myself." Strubberg keeps his eyes peeled for wildlife, having seen in the past common loons and a whistling swan on the lake. "We have our share of deer and foxes, and some people say we have bobcats, but I've never seen one," he adds. "We sometimes hear coyotes at night, especially when a train goes by. Even with the noise of the train, you can hear the howling." Tueth said he's at least seen bobcat footprints in the park. "I heard bobcats on some rainy days," he maintained. "Maybe their dens flooded, and they got mad and screamed. We mainly heard coyotes, though."

Near the first wooden bench, oaks and hickories are still thick—even a chinquapin oak, usually more at home on dry glades, can be seen. At water's edge a lone black willow appears to be stressed. Wildflowers are found in abundance on this section of trail. In April and May, for instance, a handsome colony of white-flowered beard-tongue brings color and texture to the trail.

"Once I saw something memorable over the lake—a bald eagle," biologist Strole says. "They don't normally come around here because they're big river birds, meaning that you expect to find them in flyways above the Illinois or Mississippi Rivers, not here."

Turn right, and walk out to the tip of post-oak filled "Inspiration Point," site of many local weddings and picnics. Twenty-five years ago, before trail rules were set up, campers drove out here, pitched tents, and spent the night. Turn around and return to the main path, continuing right; head toward the Hurricane Creek dam area.

Be alert for turtles basking on partially submerged logs or turtleheads peering out of the water at you near the logs. Look for muskrats, too, because they like to feed near the lake. At the dam area, make a sharp right onto a grass path leading to the spillway. Frank noted the preponderance of white or pinkish multiflora rose bushes along the trail, especially near the spillway. "The state of Illinois planted the roses here, intending them as rabbit habitat among other uses. The roses just kept spreading and were everywhere. I wrote the state a letter of complaint, but they didn't reply." In the summer, wildflowers such as yellow wood sorrel or sour grass, a "low spreading plant [with] clover-like, sour-tasting leaves," according to the *Audubon Society Field Guide to North American Wildflowers*, covers much of the dam area as does the daisylike golden ragwort. Massed behind the spillway are wet-soil tree species that include willows, silver maples, and box elders.

After the spillway the trail becomes curvier, hillier, and often muddier. For much of the way, white and northern red oaks seem to prevail in the woods; poi-

The lake-encircling footpath at Beaver Dam State Park

son ivy shrubs with large pawpawlike leaves are quite visible near the pathway. (*Missouri Wildflowers* reminds us that poison ivy plants produce very small, spiked, and scraggly white or greenish-white flowers that bloom from May to July. Look for them—but not too closely.)

You're apt to see fishermen in boats in some of the coves at this end of the lake, mainly because there are more fish around here. Along the trail are more bench-es, some footbridges, and evidence of measures to fore-stall erosion. As the trail makes one of its final turns before heading back to the concession stand, a narrow path leads up a hill to the new park office passing on the way the concrete block remains of the early-20th-century icehouse. If you take this shortcut, or "social path," you must turn around and return to the main trail. In five minutes or so, you'll be back at the conces-sion stand and ready for the second notch of your hike in the park.

To reach the Marsh Trail, walk across the main park road in front of the concession stand. At the road inter-section, make a left to the dumping station, and look there for the path to the marsh. Walk down to the 40-acre marsh in a woods where tulip poplars and walnut trees reign. Buttonwood bushes ring the marsh, while oaks, hickories, sweetgums, American elms, and more tulip poplars dominate the marshland woods. Climb onto the wooden observation deck.

From the deck it's not unusual at dusk to see a dozen or more colorful wood ducks fly in and land on the marsh or an osprey swooping low to capture a frog, small bird, or a baby wood duck. With the prey in his claws, the osprey speeds to a branch high in a perime-ter tree and begins to dine. "I saw a barred owl fly down and nail a frog while I stood on the deck," recalls Tueth, who comes here at night to listen to the barred owls. Blue-winged teal, kildeer, snipes, kingfishers, double-crested cormorants, and bitterns are commonly seen around the marsh. Strole says he once observed a pie-billed grebe, a swimming and diving bird that's endan-gered in Illinois. "They don't belong on a marsh, so the sighting was an unusual one." In the spring water iris is abloom; green duckweed covers much of the marsh edge.

Walk to the right to begin the walk around the marsh. The wide trail swings past several smaller paths that lead to the park campground. After walking through the woods for about a third of the way, the marsh again comes into view at its south end, where there are chickadees, sparrows, cardinals, and wrens that dash among the brambles and fallen trees.

The trail continues to the left. As it meanders, you'll cross some handicapped-accessible footbridges and pass the park archery range (where bow hunters come to practice) on the right. Keep walking to the left, with the marsh almost always in view, to complete the trail.

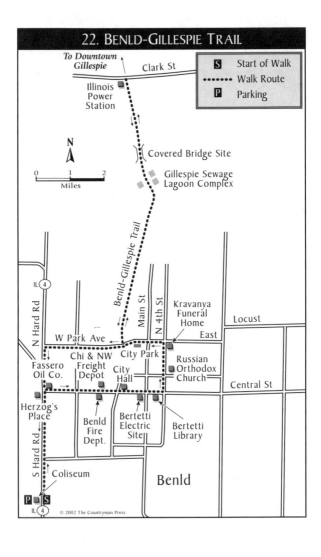

22. BENLD-GILLESPIE TRAIL

S Start of Walk
•••••• Walk Route
P Parking

To Downtown Gillespie — Clark St

Illinois Power Station

N

0   1   2
Miles

Covered Bridge Site

Gillespie Sewage Lagoon Complex

Benld-Gillespie Trail

IL ④

N Hard Rd

Main St
N 4th St

Kravanya Funeral Home

Locust

W Park Ave

East

City Park

Chi & NW Freight Depot

Russian Orthodox Church

Central St

Fassero Oil Co.

City Hall

Herzog's Place

Benld Fire Dept.

Bertetti Electric Site

Bertetti Library

S Hard Rd

Coliseum

Benld

P **S**

IL ④

© 2002 The Countryman Press

22 · Benld-Gillespie Trail

Location: Benld to Gillespie, Illinois
Hiking distance: 4.5 miles
Hiking time: 2 hours

This hike starts in Benld, Illinois, traverses the 1.3-mile Benld-Gillespie Trail, then returns to Benld to complete an absorbing small-town loop. "The Benld-Gillespie Trail is a gem of an open space between these two Macoupin County towns," says Marla Gursch, trails and greenways planner for the Illinois Department of Natural Resources, Springfield. "The trail is actually a linear park that brings two communities together."

In Macoupin County, coalfields were discovered near Bunker Hill in the 1860s and around Gillespie in the 1880s, the latter on property owned by the Dorsey family. In 1900 Benjamin L. Dorsey sold 4,500 acres to the Chicago & North Western Railroad and its captive subsidiary, the Superior Coal Company. The new operation sank four mines near Benld. Three mines—in Eagerville, Sawyerville, and Mt. Clair—were a mile or less from Benld; the fourth was 3 miles southwest in Wilsonville. Plutarch Dorsey, Ben's uncle, was reigning patriarch of the family and a successful horse-breeder. Although Plutarch had eight children of his own, he was magnanimous enough to allow the new town that was emerging by the mines to be named Benld, the acronym for Benjamin L. Dorsey.

Once the coalfields were identified and the mines opened, immigrants from Italy, Russia, and various Slavic countries were drawn to the area. "Some of the immigrants had experience digging tunnels in the Alps, so they qualified for mining jobs here," comments 97-year-old John Bertetti, who clearly recalls mining's heyday in the Benld area. The average depth of the local veins was 6 or 7 feet, enabling the miners to work standing up.

With the mines in place, Benld was established as the southern terminus of the elaborate Midwest network of the Chicago & North Western, which became the area's leading coal hauler. Although the C&NW was restricted to freight, it made one exception by providing free rides to and from work for Benld miners who labored at Wilsonville. In 1904 the Illinois Traction System, later renamed the Illinois Terminal Railroad, opened a passenger depot in Benld with cars going to Springfield and Peoria, Illinois, and into St. Louis. The line shut down in 1958; its tracks lay abandoned for decades. At a local Rotary Club meeting in the early 1980s, member Louie Bertetti suggested that the nearly 2 miles of track between Benld and Gillespie be converted to a hiking-biking path. His motion carried, and several years later the blacktop trail opened—named in memory of Bertetti, who had since died.

Benld, as the site of a 12-engine roundhouse for the Chicago & Northwestern, hosted rail crews that stayed overnight in local hotels or boardinghouses and patronized Benld saloons and restaurants. Miners, too, stopped by the saloons after work, often lingering into the night. With the arrival of Prohibition around 1920, Benld became a kind of frontier town—it had gambling, 32 saloons (by John Bertetti's personal count), prostitution, and visiting gangsters who ran a large still, called "the fifth mine," and other illegal moonshine ventures. It was said that Al Capone, America's best-known Prohibition-era hoodlum, was a frequent visitor to Benld, although most old-timers strongly disagree. Still, despite no passages or footnotes about Benld, Gillespie, or anywhere else in Macoupin County in Capone's three leading biographies, some lifelong residents insist that they saw Capone and his bodyguards strolling Benld's streets or that Capone talked to them or patted them on the head. One woman, for example, maintains that her father was Capone's chauffeur in Benld. Other stories hold that Capone—apparently with no chauffeur in the picture—drove a black Buick, purchased gas at a Benld station, then drove off to Chicago on Sunday nights with a trunk full of moonshine.

In 1924 the Coliseum Ballroom opened in Benld. It had a 10,000-square-foot dance floor, three bars, and a stage that hosted some of America's greatest dance, jazz, and swing bands led by, among others: Tommy and Jimmy Dorsey, Glenn Miller, Harry James, Gene Krupa, Benny Goodman, Duke Ellington, Count Basie, Wayne King, Louis Armstrong, and Sammy Kaye. In the early 1950s Vaughan Monroe broadcast a live radio show, *CBS Camel Caravan*, from the building. As coal mining ebbed in the 1950s, so did the Coliseum, which did its best to offer rock-and-roll bands for a while. Eventually the building became vacant, then reopened as a roller rink. It now is an antiques mall. Some area residents insist that tunnels under the Coliseum helped Capone and his mobsters evade raids by police and Prohibition agents. No such passages have been found.

Many local leaders and Macoupin County Historical Society members tend to treat the Capone and gangster stories as urban legends, choosing to focus instead on Benld as a flourishing coal-mining town that was hospitable to immigrants, home to one of America's few Russian Orthodox churches, and an important junction in early-20th-century railroading. Some of them remember the day in 1933 when a meteor dropped on Benld (it now is displayed at Chicago's Field Museum) as well as the "Benld Independents," a mid-1920s semipro football team that menaced foes in southern Illinois, and the Benld Military Band, a municipal ensemble that competed against and outplayed most other bands in Illinois.

Access

From downtown St. Louis, take I-55 in Illinois north to exit 44, IL 138. Turn left on IL 138; drive 3 miles to Benld. Head through town on Central Street. At IL 4, turn left, and drive about 0.5 mile to the parking lot of the Coliseum antiques mall.

Trail

Start by walking into the redbrick Coliseum building, where Guy Lombardo and his orchestra performed annually for decades, and take a look around. Three original bars remain, as does a balcony that wraps around three sides of the place. The stage door remains—a sign reads OWNERS ONLY. A mall manager likes to relay the story that actor John Wayne once came to the Coliseum to hear a band. "They closed the whole upstairs balcony for him. Apparently, he didn't want to be bothered by fans looking down at him."

Exit the building. During Prohibition, in what is now an open field to the south, stood a house of prostitution called Bessie's Place. "I put in a master circuit breaker at Bessie's," recalls retired electrician George Lacy. "We built a panel in each of the six bedrooms, so in an emergency a prostitute could shut off the electricity, open a panel in the wall, step down some stairs, and escape through the cellar door. All the girls had their own flashlights. On Saturday nights a man would sit in his darkened car in front of the place, and if he saw the sheriff coming could push a button, and the lights in the house would go out. Across the highway was Benny's; he served meals and also had prostitutes."

Walk north on the narrow sidewalk along IL 4. Several blocks off to the right are remaining tracks of the Illinois Terminal railroad and vestiges of the once-popular Benld brickyard, a veritable playground for Benld kids early in the 20th century. Near the brickyard was the building where the 4-pound chunk of meteor landed in December 1933. "The distinction of that meteor is that it never hit the ground," explains John Fassero. "It came down through a garage roof, then through the roof of an automobile, then lodged in the car's floorboard." John Bertetti's older brother, Frank, the high school principal back then, drove the rock to the Field Museum in Chicago, which brought the town much publicity.

Just before turning right onto Central, Benld's main thoroughfare, note the two-story dark-brick building on the west side of IL 4. "This was called Herzog's Place," said 91-year-old Antone Fassero. "There was a tavern below, and the railroad crews slept overnight in the rooms above."

Across Central—on the northeast corner of IL 4—is the small brick office of the former Fassero Oil Company. Behind it is a large white garage used for storing bulk oil when Fassero was an active oil wholesaler—the nation's oldest Shell oil jobber, going back to 1919. In the next block are St. Joseph Catholic Church and its rectory at 310 Central. At 216 Central is the handsome six-pillared home of the Tarro family, whose forebear, Dominic Tarro, built the Coliseum in 1924. Down the street on the right is the Benld Fire Department building, occupying the site of the Illinois Terminal Railroad depot. The train ride to Gillespie cost a nickel, while the round-trip fare to Carlinville was 37 cents. Directly across the street, the Sundae Best Catering Company was once the doctor's office for the Chicago & North Western. "When a miner was injured, he was transported to the doctor's office, then taken across the street to wait for the Illinois terminal car to take him to Staunton," said John Fassero. "At Staunton they'd be carried into the depot to wait for the train to Litchfield, where there was a hospital. The injured miners were always put in baggage cars. If miners died, they'd be taken directly home, where the funeral was held, since there were no local morticians in the early days of the coal mines."

The Chicago & North Western freight depot was located behind the doctor's office on what is now a large cinder lot. A green Vietnam-era army tank is parked behind the doctor's structure, a gift of the Marines in memory of an area man killed in that war. "In the early days, a side track was located near the C&NW depot," says John Bertetti. "You'd see two or three train cars filled with zinfandel and other grapes from California." Bertetti explained that many of the miners who hailed from Italy or the Slavic countries continued the practice of making wine at home to drink with their meals. "People would walk by the tracks to buy parcels of grapes directly from the cars."

Cross the railroad tracks. An old storefront on the right with broken pale-green blocks once housed the Log Cabin. "There was a bookie joint in the basement, and instead of booths, there were 10 miniature log cabins where people ate sandwiches and drank," according to George Lacy. Benld's Municipal Building and Civic Center (city hall) is on the north side of Central. Once a bowling alley and a furniture store, the structure began life as Wesley's Theater, one of two movie theaters in town during the 1920s and 1930s. A coin and collectibles shop at 211 is the former Benld Dairy. Many of Benld's saloons were on Central, some of them merely the front parts of residences.

Though banks once occupied the northeast, northwest, and southwest corners of Main and Central Streets many of the miners shunned them as places to put their money. Frank Bertetti wrote in *The Story of Macoupin County: 1829 to 1979*, that many of the immigrants didn't trust banks. "Benld once held the record for having the most money deposited in any one post office branch in the entire United States."

The parking lot north of the First of Benld Bank on the right side of Central is the site of Bertetti Electric, where for decades Louie Bertetti sold radios, television sets, and appliances. On Main just to the right off Central, is a large wooden shed covered in tin. "My grandfather, Ben, had a livery stable in that building and rented horses from the lean-to on its north side," says John Fassero.

Continue down the hill on Central. On the right is one of the town's newest buildings, the Frank Bertetti Public Library, which was financed in part by Frank's brother, John. (Two blocks east on Sixth Street during the Depression years and beyond was the Prosperity Club, where beer was a nickel a glass. On their walk to the mines, some brave miners would stop by the Prosperity for an early beer—sometimes adding a raw egg to the brew.) Turn left onto Fourth Street. The unattractive building with the fading shingles on the northeast corner is the shabby remains of Pete Jones's house of prostitution, a lively spot in the heavy days of gambling and Prohibition. "There was a runway on stilts that lead to a long row of small rooms where the girls were," said Anton Fassero.

One block north is the Holy Assumption Russian Orthodox Greek Catholic church, on the corner of Fourth and Willow since 1915. It's the parish's second building. A simple frame church, put up in 1907, burned to the ground in July 1915 taking a prized Bible, rare Byzantine banners, and gold-and-silver-trimmed vestments given by the Czar of Russia to the congregation at Benld. In its nearly one hundred years, the parish has been a pivotal part of the community. In 1928 a group of Don Cossacks, performing in St. Louis, visited the church for a special concert. The parish had picnics in the Prosperity Club park near Benld and dances at Sosenko's Hall, Dmytryk's Hall, or Zboyovski's Hall. A Russian parochial school was next door. At Easter, Russian Orthodox families still march three times around the church at midnight, then enter the brightly lit building to celebrate Christ's ascension.

Two blocks north on Fourth Street is the Kravanya

Funeral Home, site of the Ben L. Dorsey home—which is still extant, hidden under the brick façade. Turn left on East Locust by the city park. The municipal band played its weekly concerts here, approximately where the water tower stands. (North on Fourth is the site of the old C&NW roundhouse, coal chute, and water tower—behind what is now the Benld municipal storage depot and garage.)

Under the viaduct and trestle for the old C&NW tracks, used now as a spur for Monterey Mine #1 north of Benld—the only mine left in the area—was a pond for cooling steam engines. Kids from Benld regularly swam and played in this as well as ponds at the three mines closest to town. "Those ponds were built for washing coal and cooling the engine boilers, but they were great for swimming," Anton Fassero explains. Those at Mt. Clair and Eagerville even had diving boards. Walk under the viaduct. A gravel road to the right leads to the site of the former C&NW roundhouse complex. The Benld-Gillespie Trail is next on the right.

Turn right at the trailhead to begin your walk to Gillespie (hometown of actor Howard Keel). Early on, the western edge of the blacktopped onetime Illinois Terminal Railway bed consists of silver maples, osage oranges, and other trees that typify Illinois fencerows, says Ramon D. Gass, the forester and entomologist, as we walk along. Behind the fencerow are oaks, hickories, hackberries, and saplings as well as intermittent coursings of a stream network. Honeysuckle bushes dominate the right side of the trail (and much of the left), and then farm fields enter the picture.

An oily farm road also comes into view on the right; it parallels the trail for a spell. "During Prohibition that road may have led to an illegal distillery on the other side of the railroad tracks about 300 yards off to the east," a neighbor tells us. Those tracks constitute the freight spur for the Monterey #1 coal mine, which still operates in the area.

As the trail proceeds, mostly cornfields flank the path until you reach the city of Gillespie sewage treatment lagoon, which consists of three distinct treatment ponds located on either side of the trail. Foating aerators apply oxygen to assist bacteria decomposition. "The plant treats the sewage water so thoroughly that you can almost drink it," says Dan Fischer, Gillespie mayor. The filtered water becomes part of the creek bed that is visible mainly on the left side of the trail.

Beyond the sewage lagoon, the trail takes a noticeable dip. "The railbed here once had a wooden covered bridge, but vandals burned it down a couple of years after the trail opened—about 1987," says Fischer. "You can still look down from the trail here and see the stream below and the nearby bottomland forest."

From the sewage plant northward, Gillespie has installed streetlights. "Gillespie is responsible for one-third of the trail; our city limits are somewhere between the sewage lagoon and the end of the trail," Fischer said.

The trail ends by an Illinois Power Company electrical booster station at Clark Street in south Gillespie, and you must now turn around and walk back to the trailhead in Benld. If you wish, however, you can continue straight ahead on a dirt path leading to Macoupin Street, which takes you in about a half mile into downtown Gillespie. The Benld-Gillespie Trail may be extended in the near future, says Marla Gursch of Illinois DNR. "It could extend north on the railbed to Carlinville, east on an abandoned right-of-way to Litchfield, or south to Staunton," she said. "We're working with the Macoupin County Trails Association and the county to decide what to develop and where to find the money."

Surrounded by mines, Gillespie—along with Benld— was critical to the organizing efforts of the Progressive Mine Workers Union, especially in the early 1900s, says Fischer. "We were part of the hotbed of American labor around here. Even Mother Jones was around this area helping to organize the union. As she grew older, she requested to be buried at the Union Miners Cemetery over in Mt. Olive. After she died and before she was buried, the cemetery had to hire armed guards, they say, because some Progressive Miners from Gillespie wanted to steal her body and bury it here because of so much strong local sentiment. That didn't happen, of course, and that story is probably just another legend."

Once you return to Benld from Gillespie, turn right on Fourth, which becomes West Park Avenue. Across from the Benld trailhead at Trolley Street a ball field has been laid out on the site of what old-timers remember as "Hoboes Village." Until the Illinois Terminal Railroad ceased operations in Benld in 1958, hoboes camped in the brush, then hopped trains to continue their travels.

Walk west on Park in what locals refer to as "the new addition" of Benld: a collection of homes erected in the 1920s and 1930s. Walk left on the North Hard Road, which is "old Route 66," a rare remaining patch of the country's once most famous highway.

Once you arrive at Central—and its junction with IL 4—walk left on the sidewalk along IL 4 back to your parked car at the Coliseum.

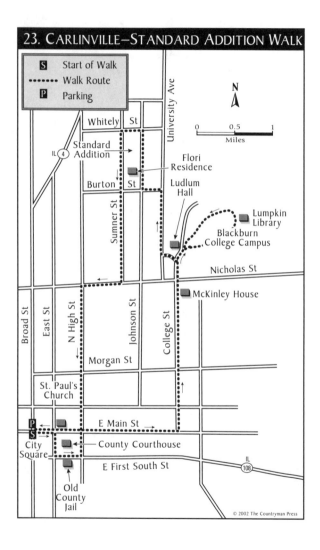

23. CARLINVILLE–STANDARD ADDITION WALK

S Start of Walk
••••• Walk Route
P Parking

N

0   0.5   1
Miles

Whitely St

University Ave

IL 4 Standard Addition

Flori Residence

Burton St

Ludlum Hall

Sumner St

Lumpkin Library

Blackburn College Campus

Nicholas St

McKinley House

Broad St

East St

N High St

Johnson St

College St

Morgan St

St. Paul's Church

E Main St

P

S

City Square

County Courthouse

E First South St

IL 108

Old County Jail

© 2002 The Countryman Press

23 · Carlinville–Standard Addition Walk

Location: Carlinville, Illinois
Hiking distance: 3 miles
Hiking time: 2 hours

First settled in the late 1820s, Carlinville, the Macoupin county seat, has evolved into a peaceful college town of nearly six thousand situated some 50 miles south of Springfield, Illinois. Blackburn College, founded in 1837 as a seminary by the Reverend Dr. Gideon Blackburn, a Presbyterian minister, is the major cultural fixture in town. It is one of seven American four-year liberal arts colleges requiring students to assume tasks ordinarily undertaken by full-time employees at other institutions. Student labor is responsible for at least 10 of the campus's 17 major buildings.

Nine square blocks located northwest of the college are known as the Standard Addition. This unassuming neighborhood, raised on a wheat field, sustains what devotees believe is the largest collection of Sears Roebuck mail-order-catalog homes in the world.

Requiring more coal to fire its refineries in World War 1, Standard Oil of Indiana opened three mines north of Carlinville in 1917. A sudden influx into the area of at least a thousand miners forced Standard Oil to deal seriously with worker housing. From the Sears catalog (which was labeled "the Farmer's Bible" or "Wish Book" in its day), Standard Oil ordered 196 five- and six-room homes, ranging from $750 to about $1,900. The order broke down to 26 homes for Wood River, Illinois, where Standard had a refinery; 14 homes for Superville, Illinois, which changed its name to Standard City, and 156 homes for Carlinville. It took six railroad boxcars to deliver one home, says Laurie Flori, president of SANTA, the Standard Addition Neighborhood Tourist Association in Carlinville, headquartered in Flori's showplace Sears home on Johnson Street. Mail-order kits contained just about everything for the home, except its foundation: precut marked lumber, doors and windows, plumbing and lighting fixtures, roof shingles, paint and varnish—even the furnace. Elaborate floor plans and a pair of trees came, too. Some of those trees are still in the ground.

Usually, the typical Sears home could be erected in five days, says Flori, whose residence has been the subject of a BBC-TV documentary as well as national media features. She says she knows the history of most of the 152 surviving Sears homes in Carlinville. And she relishes describing the female construction superintendent, Marie Pictorius, who rode her horse from homesite to homesite "hiring people in the morning and firing them in the afternoon if their work was not up to snuff." Some residents like to pass on the lore that the horse is buried somewhere under the Addition. Nobody knows where.

Just north of Carlinville off IL 4, a horse of some prominence lies buried on a piece of land once known as the Meadows, home of Richard Rowett, a Carlinville resident who served as a Union general in the Civil War.

Carlinville's "Million Dollar" courthouse

Rowett's thoroughbred horse Charley, who dropped dead in the pasture in 1886, was buried with full military honors and lowered into the ground facing north. Rowett later disinterred Charley and had him turned around so he would "face the enemy" to the south. Charley probably saved the general's life twice in battle, once when Charley walked the remaining plank of a blown-up bridge and again, with the general aboard, when he leaped a "broad chasm" to evade a possible Confederate ambush. Rowett became an importer and breeder of thoroughbred and Clydesdale horses on his Carlinville farm—and bred the 1889 Kentucky Derby winner, Spokane. He had already gained prominence in the 1870s by introducing the first true-bred beagles to America, says his biographer, Tom Emery, in *Richard Rowett: Thoroughbreds, Beagles and the Civil War.* "The Rowett strain or pedigree is still found in some beagles today."

Carlinville was also the home of John M. Palmer, an early chairman of the board of Blackburn Seminary. Raised as a Democrat, he was the Republican governor of Illinois (1869–1873) who left his party protesting the Republican Grant administration. Later, he went to the U.S. Senate (1891–1897) as a Democrat and at age 79 was the presidential candidate for the National, or "Gold Democrat," party. Like Rowett, Palmer (and three other Carlinville residents) was a Civil War general.

Beyond any doubt, the centerpiece of the downtown Carlinville historic district is the massive Macoupin County courthouse, which opened in 1870. The building cost $1,340,000, a mere $1,165,000 more than the original $175,000 estimate. Touted back then as America's largest county courthouse, it was larger than the Illinois state capitol in Springfield. The lavish structure contained a 7-foot judge's chair so heavy that the bailiff had to push it up to the Italian marble bench on a special set of tracks. The magnesium limestone building was adorned with wrought-iron window frames, and walls and ceilings of sheet iron instead of plaster.

Carlinville citizens were irate over the excessive costs and unneccessary massiveness of the domed building, quickly tagged the "Million Dollar Courthouse." No one was ever indicted for the overage, but circuit clerk George H. Holliday took the brunt of the accusations. One day in late 1870 he was seen with a "mysterious briefcase" boarding a train for St. Louis. Some time later, a man resembling Holliday was arrested and brought to Carlinville. Holliday's wife, Cinderella, was asked to identify the man. "He is not my husband," she said. Despite a long nationwide manhunt, Holliday was never found. Meanwhile, it took 40 years to retire the bonds needed to finance the project.

Thaddeus L. Loomis, the presiding county judge during the courthouse debacle, fared well in its wake. With leftover magnesium limestone from the courthouse, he built a 50-room hotel—the St. George—on the east side of the city square. No longer a hotel, the building—Loomis House—contains several businesses including the St. George Room. Loomis was never charged.

Access

From St. Louis, follow I-55 north to IL 108. Drive 12 miles west on IL 108 to the Carlinville city square, and park on its east side by Loomis House.

Trail

From the square, which contained the county's second courthouse and which one resident describes as "a picturesque island surrounded by a circular drive," walk south to East Main Street then one block east where the "Million Dollar" courthouse comes into view. Walk right on East Street for a better perspective on the large building, then take a left on East First South Street for a full-frontal view. Walk in and look around if the building is open. Across from the courthouse is the 1869 county jail, last used in 1988. The building was built in the "jailer residence" style popular in the 19th century. The "medieval-inspired fortress," as the local chamber of commerce calls it, was built to accommodate 17 prisoners. Each stone in the jail was hollowed at the end. "A cannon ball...was placed in each joint to prevent any single stone from being moved by a prisoner" in an escape attempt, wrote Lucille Carney in the *Illinois State Journal*.

Turn left on High Street, and then make a quick right on East Main Street, the start of one of the pre-eminent residential neighborhoods in the city. In the 1820s, on what is now the southeast corner of Main and High, stood the first county courthouse, a log cabin, says Emery, the local historical writer. At least one home on East Main—long since razed—was the site of Underground Railway activity in the 1850s and 1860s. The sizeable white frame Victorian home at 616 was where two West Point grads who were to be generals in the World War II era, Truman H. (four stars) and Kurt M. (one star) Landon, were youngsters in the 1920s and 1930s. On December 7, 1941, Truman, the future four-star general, commanded a squadron of B-17 bombers en route from California to Hickham Field, Hawaii, landing unscathed during the Japanese attack on Pearl Harbor. During the war, he headed a bomber command in the central Pacific area as well as a joint task force under Admiral Chester Nimitz. He later commanded U.S. Air Forces in Europe. After the war he directed the Caribbean Air Command as well as the National War College. Brother Kurt headed the Air Force Pacific command in the 1960s. At 630 East Main is a yellow-brick Civil War home, purchased in 1904 by the generals' grandfather, A. Lincoln Hoblit, founder of Carlinville National Bank.

Turn left onto College Street, and walk north to the Blackburn College campus. At Ravine and College is

McKinley House, since 1926 the official residence of Blackburn presidents. A gift from U.S. Senator William B. McKinley financed the five-bedroom Georgia Colonial residence. McKinley was founder and president of the McKinley Lines, which some said was the largest interurban train system in the United States. A ranch-style brick home just south of the president's home on College was the official residence of Blackburn deans for a while but was later sold to a private party. Cross Nicholas Street and enter the Blackburn campus through the stone gates.

Walk straight ahead, and then bear right in front of Hudson Hall and the next door Clegg Chapel. Constructed by student help and dedicated in 1932, Hudson is the main academic building, housing the humanities and social sciences. "The building was dependent almost entirely on faith," wrote Glenn L. McConagha in *Blackburn College 1837–1987*. Construction was halted from time to time until more funds could be secured, he said. Hudson replaced "Old Main," the school's original administration building, destroyed in a 1928 fire. Stroll east to Stoddard Hall, a three-story women's residence put up in 1928, the first structure built by Blackburn students. Occasionally students hear voices coming from the vacant Stoddard third floor. Some people think the voices may originate with the ghost of Mrs. Sara Stoddard, perhaps upset that her original women's building has gone co-ed. At least one other campus ghost has been seen or heard: Isabel Bothwell "appears" occasionally in the music building that bears her name, possibly distressed that her conservatory has been used for other purposes, such as a theater.

From Stoddard, continue walking in an eastward

direction past Lumpkin Library, another student building dedicated in 1970. "Books and other library materials were moved from their old home to the new one by a human chain that extended across the campus," according to a 1996 orientation booklet. Walk left to the F. W. Olin Science Building, another student construction project, named in memory of Alton, Illinois, industrialist John M. Olin's father, Franklin W. Continue west to the gymnasium complex, then south on the main campus roadway to Ludlum Hall, which houses the president's office and admissions. Turn right to University Avenue, then right again for a walk along the athletic field to Burton Street.

On Burton walk one block west to Johnson, which is the main artery of the Standard Addition. Turn right on Johnson; Flori's five-room, two-bedroom, one-bath Sears catalog home at 910 retains its original kitchen sink and cabinet, toilet, dining-room chandelier, bathroom tile, oak hardwood flooring, and five-panel doors. Sears sold eight different home models to Carlinville buyers. The Flori family lives in the Roseberry model, the only model with an L-shaped kitchen. A while ago Chicago-based Sears began to take some archival interest in its Carlinville legacy (it ended catalog sales of homes in 1942). "Sears asked me in 1986 if we could open seven of our homes for a tour," says Flori. "We had two thousand visitors in four hours. The line for my house was all the way down the street."

Flori adds that the neighborhood was thought of as a slum when she and her husband, David (who had grown up in the Addition) moved in and commenced their arduous home restoration. In the ensuing years she has been a passionate champion of the area, coaxing local residents who grew up in a Sears home to move back into the neighborhood. One group that meets regularly is the Standard Addition Gang, original Sears dwellers who have returned. "I didn't like living here back when I was a girl," maintains returnee Mary Alice Shaw, whose Sears home was at Whiteley and University. "The sidewalks were curbed and went all around the block. You couldn't really get off your block as a kid." She now extolls the historic nature of her neighborhood.

Walk to Whiteley for a short trek to Sumner, then south all the way to Nicholas. From the sidewalks of Johnson and Sumner, you'll see between 90 and 100 Sears homes, most of which have kept their original frame shapes and squarish front porches. At Nicholas, walk right to North High Street, then left all the way to East Main Street, where you must take a right. On your way back to the town square, you'll pass St. Paul's United Church of Christ, in the same building since 1878. German immigrants from the province of Brunswick had founded St. Paul's Evangelical Church, its original name, in 1858. In 1883 a women's organization called Frauen-Verein was organized; their initial act of charity was donation of the church bell. It wasn't until 1918 that the congregation decided to conduct services in English—alternating with German every other Sunday!—and in 1919 the church constitution was translated into English.

Finish your 3-mile hike with a walk around the rather bare Carlinville square, where just recently city officials removed four large sweetgum trees. One reason for the cutting was citizen complaints about slipping on sweetgum balls. Ironically, just weeks earlier Carlinville had received a Tree City USA designation.

24·Fults Hill Prairie Nature Preserve

Location: 8 miles southeast of Maeystown, Illinois
Hiking distance: 1.5 miles
Hiking time: 2 hours
Bicycles: Not permitted

What do Tennessee's Reelfoot Lake, Georgia's Okefenokee Swamp, California's Torrey Pines Preserve, and Illinois' Fults Hill Prairie Nature Preserve share in common? Designation by the U.S. secretary of the interior as National Natural Landmarks. The nation's nearly six hundred such landmarks are among "the best examples of a type of biotic community," states the National Park Service, which administers the 40-year-old program.

On 532-acre Fults Hill, a limestone bluff that reaches some 300 feet from street level, there are eight separate hill prairies, limestone glades, forests, ravines, old croplands, rare and endangered plants and small animals, and eye-opening vistas. Some of the state's most extensive caves are located in the vicinity; an Indian mound may lie near the base of Fults Hill. Its landmark status, however, is based on the astounding array of prairies that collectively cover some 33 acres. Specialists from the Illinois Department of Natural Resources,

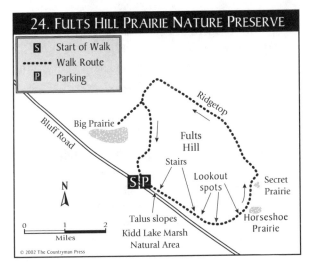

24. FULTS HILL PRAIRIE NATURE PRESERVE

S Start of Walk
...... Walk Route
P Parking

Bluff Road

Big Prairie

Ridgetop

Fults Hill

Stairs

Lookout spots

Secret Prairie

S P

N

Talus slopes

Horseshoe Prairie

0   1   2
Miles

© 2002 The Countryman Press

Kidd Lake Marsh Natural Area

which owns Fults Hill, marvel at the mostly undisturbed nature of the prairies—that is, they haven't been grazed or plowed, due chiefly to their steepness or bluff-edge locations. "It is the most exemplary hill prairie and limestone glade area along the Mississippi River in Illinois," reported the biologists who recommended landmark designation. Years ago an Illinois DNR biologist told a reporter that Fults Hill was the largest hill prairie group in the state and "possibly in the entire country."

It is estimated that around 450 hill prairies are located along 240 miles of Mississippi River bluffs through Illinois but that only 13 percent of them (including those on Fults Hill) are relatively undisturbed. "Many of the important grasses of these [hill] prairies are the same species that were seen, but not described, by the early travelers on the western prairies and plains," wrote David F. Costello in *The Prairie World*.

Across Bluff Road is Kidd Lake Marsh Natural Area,

a "representation of a river bottom prairie marsh" on the sprawling American Bottom section east of the Mississippi. The marsh area is an extension of the Fults Hill Prairie Nature Preserve. Researchers have said that the lake, situated on a French land grant, was originally a very shallow 800 acres. "The old French land plots of long narrow strips in the rich bottomland are still the legal divisions of property," one historian noted recently. Birders and others have reported seeing nesting king rails, least terns, and common gallinules near the marsh—plus an impressive colony of muskrats.

Fults Hill has significant neighbors. Seven miles southeast is Fort Chartres State Park. The French built the two-story fort, less than a mile from the Mississippi, around 1718; three years later it served as headquarters for the French governor of Illinois. With three hundred troops on hand, "it became the strongest fortress in the New World," stated Georgia M. Engelke in *The Great American Bottom*. Others maintain that the fort's original powder magazine may be the Midwest's oldest building. Thirteen miles to the southeast is Prairie du Rocher, perhaps the oldest surviving town in the state.

For half a century wildlife experts, teachers, students, and history buffs have tramped up Fults Hill to see the wildflowers and grasses, hike the rolling ridgetops, explore the cliff ledges, and even watch the sunset. "You get a different view every time you climb Fults Hill," says Bill Gonterman, a native Illinoisan who resides in St. Louis. He's scaled Fults Hill for at least 35 years. "After you've climbed Fults Hill, you feel like you're sitting on top of the world. You almost always have a sunset up there, and they are some of the most beautiful you'll ever see... they're spellbinding."

Access

From Jefferson Barracks Bridge in south St. Louis County, drive east on I-255, and then join IL 3 south. Follow IL 3 through Columbia, then to Waterloo. At Waterloo turn right on IL 156, then immediately left on Lakeview Drive (a county road). Continue south through Wartburg, then into historic Maeystown. Take Mill Street south through Maeystown. Two miles or so below Maeystown, turn left onto Bluff Road. Fults Hill is 6 miles ahead on the left, after passing Steffen, Stringtown, Ivy, Fults, and Kidd Lake Roads. Park in the small lot.

Trail

In 1980 a proposal was made to loop a branch of the Great River Road, which parallels the Mississippi, along Bluff Road by the foot of Fults Hill. Neighbors and wildlife managers complained that the "improved" road would bring unwanted automobile noise and exhaust and more road kills of animals. Compromisers suggested elevating the road by the parking area so that rare and endangered snakes from Fults Hill could slither underneath while migrating between the bluff and the marsh. Both plans fell by the roadside.

This walk begins to the right of the parking area with a steep climb up two flights of stairs—some 130 steps—that flank eroded path sections along the limestone bluff. Near the base of the bluff are imposing limestone outcrops under which are chunky, rocky, thin-soiled talus slopes that may shield nocturnal plains scorpions that reside on Fults Hill and nowhere else in Illinois. Threatened and endangered—and very secretive—flat-headed snakes, which are less than a foot long, are the scorpions' neighbors. Whip snakes

On Big Prairie at Fults Hill

and narrow-mouthed toads are other residents that live exclusively among the river bluffs. Nearby you may find sugar maple, chinquapin oak, and Kentucky coffee trees. Fox dens may exist near the talus slopes. Fragile fern can be found along the upward path.

Just above the second flight of stairs, off a side path to the right, is the first of several minioverlooks that offer panoramic views of the river valley below—the still-busy railroad tracks first laid by Missouri Pacific around 1900; the distant Mississippi River; Kidd Lake Marsh, and the Ameren UE Rush Island power plant. Located on the west bank of the Mississippi in Jefferson County, Missouri, the plant burns 633 tons of coal per hour at full capacity, supplying electricity to 125,000 homes. One concrete exhaust stack—easily seen from Fults Hill—is 700 feet, taller than the Gateway Arch in downtown St. Louis.

The first distinct Fults Hill prairie is on the third overlook. Wild onions and side oats grama are prairie plants in evidence here, as is a chinquapin oak, a Carolina buckthorn, and small blue ash tree, with its unusual squarish twigs. As the trail continues, you'll see plenty of multiflora roses blooming in the spring as well as rows of fragrant sumac, then some old cedar trees. The presence of cedars in this nonprairie woodlands stretch of the walk suggests that cattle grazed here in open land years ago, says Illinois DNR natural heritage biologist Diane L. Tecic, who has a commanding knowledge of Fults Hill.

A second prairie upcoming on the right is more challenging. Because of its shape, it's known as Horseshoe Prairie. You must wander down into it to explore its richness in seasonal flora: Indian grass, big bluestem, round-headed bush clover, goat's rue, white flowering splurge, woodland sunflowers, and yellow resin weed. "We burn our prairies here every two or three years to re-invigorate them and get rid of invasive, nonprairie plants that may have appeared," says Tecic, pointing to the flourishing and colorful hillside.

Return to the main path, and walk to the right, continuing upward. Sassafras trees, which are spreading too fast and reducing growth opportunities for native plants, occur in abundance on this part of the trail, along with raspberry bushes and white oaks. "This woodland area was really open in the past; we want to restore it so that it more resembles a glade," says Tecic. Soon another prairie appears, this one a kind of secret prairie since it's off the main path. As you take the downward path into the prairie you'll see Indian grass and side oats grama, the principal grasses, and perhaps—as we did—an eastern hoghead snake. "It looks like a cobra, hisses but never strikes or bites, and loves toads," explains Tecic as she picks up and strokes the reptile. At the tip of the bluff, you may see—in August mainly—the Missouri orange coneflower, which is on the Illinois endangered species list. "This plant almost always grows on bare rock and usually only at the edge of the prairie," Tecic says. Small, pinkish false foxgloves bloom nearby in late summer.

Return again to the main path, and continue walking to the right. At the trail's 0.5-mile point, the trail divides. Walk to the left where the path widens and gets grassier as it follows the ridgetop. Bordering the path are upland oak-hickory forest sections, logged in the early 1930s, then the early 1950s, and old farm fields. Heavy amounts of rough-leaved dogwoods line the trail edge for a while; behind them are persimmons and more oaks and hickories. Blackjack oaks with leaves resembling the fleur-de-lis are ridgetop residents, as are aggressive kudzulike racoon-grape vines with heart-shaped leaves. "This noxious vine seeks sunny openings in the woods and tends to choke off everything else," says Tecic. Fast-spreading sweet clover, which flowers most of the summer and crowds out its neighbors, is abundant in the vicinity.

Just beyond the 1-mile point, take a sharp left, staying on the ridgetop. (If you continue straight ahead, you'll enter what Tecic calls a "degraded prairie," one of several on Fults Hill. "We've let that prairie go. It's been taken over completely by white sweet clover.") After a short stretch of woodland walking where there are more rough-leaved dogwoods—they flower white in May or June—the trail comes into a formidable hillside prairie where big bluestem, also known as turkeyfoot because its slender seed heads are reminiscent of turkey feet, is the reigning grass. Walk slowly downhill until you see a dirt path with graduated concrete steps early on that leads to the left. Mark the spot carefully (although a trail direction sign may be in place), and then continue straight down to Big Prairie, the largest hill prairie on Fults, where there are New Jersey tea shrubs and wildflowers such as silky asters, tall boneset, and blazing star. Missouri orange coneflowers and prickly pear cactus occupy space near the tip of the prairie's edge. "If you were to visit the prairie edge in the spring, you might see dwarf bedstraw, Whitlow grass, and slender heliotrope. For the most part, these plants are only found here in Monroe County," Tecic says. Long-blooming rose verbena and bluish wild sweet William are wildflowers that blanket the glade by Big Prairie in the spring and early summer. You can't miss them!

"This is the place where we can see lots of bald eagles in the winter," says Tecic. "I once saw 20 eagles flying by at eye level on thermals along the bluff lines," she says. Enthusiasts from the Kaskaskia Valley Audubon Club come here to chart autumnal hawk migrations. (The extra walk to the tip of this large prairie and back to the path that you have marked adds about a quarter mile to your hike. Be careful on your walk back up the bluff. If it's wet, the path can be very hazardous.)

Return to the downhill path that you have marked. Begin the last leg of the walk. On your way down, you'll see cliffbrake and woodsia fern. Chinquapin oaks and cedars, in which long-eared owls occasionally roost, are plentiful in the descending woods where nodding ladies' tresses show off in the spring. Elms, walnuts, and hackberry trees are other residents of the forested areas. In the spring wildflowers such as waterleaf, trillium, phlox, violets, and larkspur add a final burst of color near the end of the trail.

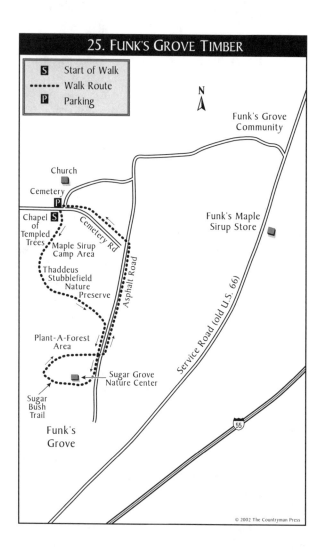

25. FUNK'S GROVE TIMBER

S Start of Walk
•••••• Walk Route
P Parking

N

Funk's Grove
Community

Church

Cemetery

P

Chapel **S**
of
Templed
Trees

Cemetery Rd

Asphalt Road

Funk's Maple
Sirup Store

Maple Sirup
Camp Area

Thaddeus
Stubblefield
Nature
Preserve

Plant-A-Forest
Area

Service Road (old U.S. 66)

Sugar Grove
Nature Center

Sugar
Bush
Trail

55

Funk's
Grove

© 2002 The Countryman Press

25 · Funk's Grove Timber

Location: Shirley, Illinois
Hiking distance: 3 miles
Hiking time: 1.5 hours
Bicycles: Not permitted

For motorists headed for Chicago or St. Louis on I-55 south of Bloomington, Illinois, familiar signs point to the turnoffs to the Funk's Pure Maple Sirup store as well as the Funk's Grove interstate rest stop. The local vendors of pure maple syrup prefer to spell it "sirup," as opposed to "syrup."

To reach the heart of Funk's Grove, you must leave I-55 at either the Shirley or McLean exits. What lie ahead are the maple sirup store, the tiny community of Funk's Grove, and, farther west, the grove itself. On the grove's periphery is a tranquil family cemetery started by the first settlers; in a cemetery corner is a white frame church building described as "midwestern carpentry classic revival" that has been used continuously since it opened in 1865.

In the woodland south of the cemetery is the man-made Cathedral in the Trees with log pews and altars carved from a giant white oak.

Behind the cathedral are the "maple sirup camp," majestic woodlands, showy spring wildflowers such as Virginia bluebells and white and prairie trillium, and pathways to explore one of Illinois' largest spreads of old-growth, or virgin, forest. "This forest is historic. It has been a continuing forest for several thousand years, a forest that has never been completely cleared," says Don Schmitt, horticulturist at Illinois State Normal University and revered regionally as the "Dean of Green." "In presettlement times, the area nearby was 90 percent prairie and 10 percent forest, so Funk's Grove was a historic prairie grove, one of the finest known examples of its kind. Back then, this forest lay in the center of a sea of grass."

Funk's Grove was settled in 1824 by Isaac and Absalom Funk, who were joined later that year by brother-in-law Robert Stubblefield and his wife, Dorothy. Clearly, Isaac Funk was the leader of the group. He acquired nearly 30,000 acres of fertile land—"more land than is owned by many large Southern plantations," said one writer at the time. As a land and livestock owner—and breeder—Isaac was referred to as "the cattle—or beef— king of Illinois." He was "one of the first to see the advantage of wintering cattle and fattening them on the corn of the prairie lands," wrote his biographer in *Funk of Funk's Grove*. Isaac was proud of his livestock production and especially of the two cows he sold Sylvester Marsh in 1850. One of the animals weighed 3,500 pounds and together the two of them totaled around 6,000 pounds. The *Prairie Farmer* said in 1851 that "the so-called Marsh cattle are the largest pair of cattle ever raised in North America."

Funk was not just a wealthy gentleman farmer. He was a founder of Illinois Wesleyan University in Bloomington and on the committee that laid the groundwork for Illinois State Normal University. Furthering his passion for public service, he was elected to the Illinois legislature, completing terms in the 1840s and attending meetings and hearings with fellow legislator Abraham Lincoln. It was said that Lincoln visited the Funk home and that they were friends. Before his death, Funk was elected to the Illinois senate.

In the early days of the Civil War, Isaac served on a county committee to raise money for the Union side and to pay bounties of $150 each to male citizens who volunteered to join an Illinois regiment and fight the Confederates. Three of his sons—he had 10 children— joined the regiment. "When the 94th regiment of Illinois Volunteers left Bloomington in box cars without ventilation, he (Funk) provided hatchets and handsaws for the troops accompanied by instructions to cut the necessary holes in the sides of the cars," wrote Helen Cavanaugh in his biography.

Funk and his wife, Cassandra, who died within four hours of each other in January, 1865, are buried in Funk's Grove cemetery, a piece of land so pristinely historic that it is listed on the U.S. Department of Interior's National Register of Landscapes. Isaac and Cassandra and their immediate family lie in a plot surrounded by a black wrought-iron fence in the center of the burial ground. Ever since 1884 Funk-Stubblefield family reunions have been held on or near the cemetery grounds, says Stephen Funk, a reigning patriarch of the Funk family and once the owner of the sirup store. "We have twelve thousand family names on our index, but I know there are more than that."

"Part of the novelty of Funk's Grove is that more than one hundred years ago, in the late 19th century, the Funks and Stubblefields were talking of land conservation and preservation," said Schmitt. "Many of them stipulated such practices in their wills. The interaction between natural and human history with these families has been amazing."

Access

From St. Louis, take I-55 north to IL 136 in McLean. Turn left, drive past the entrance to the historic Dixie Trucker's Home, then look for the sign to Funk's Grove. You'll be driving on a service road that is a remnant of old US 66. Drive to the maple sirup shop. After your visit, turn right on the service road and continue 1 mile to the turnoff to Funk's Grove. Drive through the tiny Funk's Grove community, then on to the cemetery, about 1 mile farther. Park outside the cemetery; enter the grounds.

An important note: Funk's Grove is in an exciting period of development. That means changes—in trail layout and direction, new buildings, new plantings. Trail markers have recently been installed from the Chapel of the Templed Trees down to the Sugar Grove Nature Center. Plans are to have Funk's Grove maps available inside the old church in the cemetery and at the nature center.

Trail

Begin the walk by wandering the cemetery grounds, which contain around 750 burials dating to 1830 when Isaac Funk's father, Adam, was laid to rest. The large picnic shelter near the cemetery entrance is constructed in part from timber from a massive white oak felled on the farm of Eugene D. Funk Sr., father of Funk's Seeds and a grandson of Isaac. The tree was said to be 215 years old with a girth of 15 feet.

Walk toward the church, which retains its original walnut pulpit, altar rail, and glass windows, and many original pine pews. The building is usually open—you can enter through either of its two front doors. The church is used almost every weekend in summer months by church congregations in the region who come to worship and picnic, says Steve Funk. If the weather is nasty, the congregations will use the church building; if it's fair, they'll adjourn to the Chapel of the Templed Trees. In the early 19th century, a log-cabin schoolhouse existed on the grounds; a stone marker west of the church marks the spot.

Beautiful trees, including a strong showing by oaks, stand in the cemetery. A dawn redwood and a neighboring northern arbor vitae are deployed near a bench close to the church. Large ashes and mammoth spruces spread their protective branches over the graveyard. (The state's largest known blue ash, sycamore, locust, and walnut trees lie on nearby Funk's Grove property, but none are seen on our walk.)

A replica of a Celtic cross near the church is a recent commemorative marker. Dedicated in 2000, it memorializes 50 or so Irish immigrants buried here. Most were laborers who toiled on the Chicago and Alton Railroad in the 1840s. The Irish Monument was erected by the McClean County Historical Society.

Wander in a westerly direction to find the gravesites of the Funk's Grove founding families. A black wrought-iron fence surrounds the Isaac and Cassandra Funk plot. Across the road to the south are Robert and Dorothy Stubblefield, who died in the 1870s. Nowadays, the Funk's Grove Cemetery Association decides who gets buried where. The cemetery board is divided among descendants of Funks and Stubblefields, says its president, John Rehtmeyer, a Funk descendent. The cemetery has two parts, the 12-acre "old section" where Isaac and Robert rest, and the 10-acre "new addition" just around the corner. "Generally the Funks were buried on the north side of the old section and the Stubblefields on the south. These days, however, we're pretty intermingled," says Rehtmeyer. "It's now the policy of the board to bury people on a first-come, first-served basis. Some of the descendants are fighting to be buried in the last remaining spots of the old section."

Leave the cemetery and walk south to the Chapel of Templed Trees, about 400 feet in from the road. "I came here to find myself; It is so easy to get lost in the world," declares a sign along the path. The signage is the work of the chapel's founder, Lafayette Funk III, a son of Eugene Funk, the seed king. Some 20 rows of elm logs serve as pews and seat nearly 200 in this nondenominational gathering place. "The elm logs last about six years, then they rot and must be replaced," comments Rehtmeyer, who manages the propery for the Funk/Stubblefield interests. Rehtmeyer, who was married in the outdoor chapel in 1981, says that on average about three weddings a week occur in the chapel from March through October. Most knot tiers are family members although some outsiders receive wedding privileges. "Notice what I call the wedding guest 'registration stump' as you approach the chapel, and then the two 'usher stumps' near them," Rehtmeyer points out. The two altars are made from one white oak log. "I carved one altar from the top end of the log and the other altar from the bottom end," says Rehtmeyer. Behind the altars a magnificent white oak backdrops the clearing in the woods.

The old church by the Funk's Grove cemetery is still used.

From behind the pulpit, walk south on a path that's bordered by stinging nettle and waterleaf. This area is in what Steve Funk calls the "maple sirup camp," the area in the grove where maple trees are tapped for a period of three to six weeks anywhere from February 1 to the end of March each year. About three thousand maples are tapped in this 80-acre parcel known as "the sacred 80," says Funk. "We generally hang two buckets on each tree and let the sap run," he says of the process that's continued since the frontier days of 1825. "The wind always seems to blow in the tapping area," adds Gary Woith, director of the nearby Sugar Grove Nature Center. "There is a sense of sound and smell that's activated in here. Listen to the wind shift—it blows hard, then blows soft. You look up to see how the canopy is moving. You hear wind, but you don't feel it. But it's up there."

Follow the trail markers to continue your walk through the tapping area, then into the Thaddeus Stubblefield Nature Preserve. The Stubblefield preserve is a 30-acre woodlot characterized by high-quality, old-growth maples, a healthy understory that includes pawpaws and dogwoods, and dazzling seasonal wildflower exhibits. "Some of the black walnut trees around here produce fruit the size of baseballs," observes Rehtmeyer.

Leave the nature preserve and follow the path left toward the asphalt road that bisects the grove. Walk right on the road, which was probably an old trail from Bloomington to Springfield, says Rehtmeyer. "I assume that Abraham Lincoln traveled here on his way to Springfield," he says. On the far left are railroad tracks laid originally in 1854 by many of the Irish immigrants who are buried at the cemetery. Today Amtrak uses the tracks.

Walk to the end of the road, then hike the gravel lane up to the Sugar Grove Nature Center, where there is a visitors center crafted from a one-time machine shed and cattle barn and a picnic shelter that doubles as a "sugar shack" in winter where school groups learn how to make maple syrup from sap.

Look around the center then walk west to cross a small bridge which acts as trailhead to the short Sugar Bush trail. (Be sure to pick up an interpretive booklet at the trailhead.) Walk left after the bridge; follow the path clockwise. On the way are plenty of maple saplings and some one-hundred- to three-hundred-year old maples and oaks. Cross another bridge where you may see a Native American wigwam erected by local school children. The path then enters a walnut grove. The trail booklet explains that old photos "show no evidence of walnut trees [here], so the [tree] population began by external forces—squirrels—bringing the nuts into the area."

Continue walking east on a border path in a section that Woith calls the "Plant-a-Forest Area" where school-children plant trees and prairie plants, then return periodically to study and evaluate and learn from their planting actions. "We want to establish among the kids a physical attachment to the land," he says.

"We plan to restore about 60 acres of prairie in this section," says Schmitt.

As you leave the nature center area, stop by the Buena Vista Veranda Corn Crib for a last look at the prairie. "Inside the corn crib we have cut four windows so visitors can sit down and view our 5-acre prairie plot, watch the sky, see turkey buzzards and hawks soaring overhead, and relax before walking back to the cemetery to finish their walk," said Woith. Continue walking until you reach the blacktop service road; walk left, and return to the cemetery area to complete the loop.

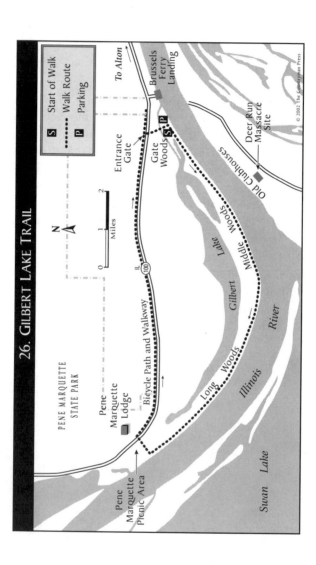

26. GILBERT LAKE TRAIL

PENE MARQUETTE STATE PARK

Pene Marquette Picnic Area

Pene Marquette Lodge

Bicycle Path and Walkway

IL 100

N

0 1 2
Miles

To Alton

Brussels Ferry Landing

Entrance Gate

Gate Woods

P

S

Old Clubhouses

Deer Run Massacre Site

Long Woods

Gilbert Lake

Middle Woods

Illinois River

Swan Lake

S Start of Walk
······ Walk Route
P Parking

© 2002 The Countryman Press

26 · Gilbert Lake Trail

Location: Near Grafton, Illinois
Hiking distance: 6 miles
Hiking time: 3 hours
Bicycles: Not permitted
Note: *Trail closed October 15 to December 15
during waterfowl migration peaks*

Nearly 430,000 vehicles annually use the two boats
that comprise the Brussels free ferry fleet, located 3
miles north of Grafton, Illinois, off IL 100. A good guess
is that fewer than 5 percent of the vehicle occupants—
people who come to hike or dine at Pere Marquette
State Park, view autumn leaves, or explore the shops or
sights of Grafton—are aware of the existence of Gilbert
Lake, about 300 hundred yards west of the ferry landing, and its richly diverse riverside and bottomland forest trail.

A hike on the Gilbert Lake trail would be incomplete
and much less adventuresome without first making a
five-minute crossing on the Brussels Ferry. A ferry operation across the Illinois River has been in existence at
this site or nearby since 1817 when Thomas Reynolds
was licensed to do business "2 miles from the confluence" of the Illinois and Mississippi rivers at Grafton.
Old Madison County court records reveal the mandat-
ed rates for that first ferry: foot man, 12½ cents; man

and horse, 25 cents; horse, $12\frac{1}{2}$ cents; "waggon," $1; meat cattle, $12\frac{1}{2}$ cents, and hogs and sheep, $6\frac{1}{4}$ cents each.

Following the Reynolds ferry, in the 1880s Henry Wheeler established "the Deer Plain Ferry" at the present site of the Brussels landing. Wheeler is said to have pulled his barge manually across the river via a long cable attached to it. Later he bought a push boat with a one-cylinder engine. In 1960 the state of Illinois acquired the ferry, cutting the crossing fee from 80 cents to zero, and stretching the operation to 24 hours a day.

In a five-minute crossing, much can occur, says veteran operator Darrell W. Coughlin. "One night a lady left her car and proceeded to do cartwheels down the length of the ferry. Another time, an older lady who had been watching eagles while waiting to board the ferry continued to be so intrigued by them that once aboard, she continued to watch the eagles and forgot to take her car out of drive as she stepped out to get a better view. Her car accelerated straight into the siderails; no one was hurt." Other deckhands and operators recall weddings aboard the Brussels and the Golden Eagle ferries (the latter operation, 5 miles southeast of the Brussels ferry, is situated on the Mississippi River) as well as family members who strew ashes of the recently cremated into the bosom of the Illinois.

During the calamitous flood of 1993, the Brussels Ferry continued to function, although the round-trip took 105 minutes instead of 10. The temporary landing was about 1 mile south of the current landing. Gilbert Lake, a kind of natural backwater slough, is geographically positioned under the globally significant Mississippi river flyway, the world's busiest migrating bird highway. Some estimate that the flyway carries 44 million birds during their annual migrations. The lake and nearby open waters were created in the 1930s after the U.S. Army Corps of Engineers built Lock and Dam 26 on the Mississippi River at Alton, some 20 miles south.

Thousands of ducks, geese, and shorebirds, such as great blue herons and egrets, rest or fish in the Gilbert Lake area and are often quite viewable to hikers. A parallel attraction is the closeness of the Illinois River. The trail meets the river at about the 2-mile marker on the river, according to Corps of Engineer measurements. (Mile 0 is at Grafton; mile 327 is at the spot where the Chicago River, northernmost span of the Illinois River, meets Lake Michigan near the downtown Loop area of Chicago.) The Illinois River, according to Chuck Theiling, then with the Illinois Natural History Survey, is "the most studied river in the world." Scientists continue to examine its fish population; barge-carrying capacity; sewage and sediment volumes, and commercial and recreational benefits and potential.

In 1818, said Theiling, "the Illinois River lay alongside the most important fur-bearing region in the Northwest; in the early 1900s, the river was the most productive inland fishing spot and the most productive mussel stream in America. A century ago, nearly 24 million pounds of fish were harvested annually; about one thousand commercial fishermen plied the river. Now, with all the dams [six exist to maintain the river's nine-foot channel] we have dropped below six million pounds of fish per year."

Aside from the river, the area attracts birders and bird researchers. Helen Wuestenfeld of Jerseyville, Illinois, is engaged, along with experts elsewhere in the state, by the Illinois Department of Natural Resources to conduct sandpiper censuses, a task she has cheerfully handled for more than 30 years. "In a good year we'll spot about a thousand sandpipers, especially if Gilbert Lake is low or drained by the Corps so it can plant food for the birds," explains Wuestenfield. (Sandpipers are small birds "with long thick bills and little legs and feet that seem to twinkle as they run rapidly along our ocean beaches, mudflats, and lake shores in search of food at the fringes of the water," writes John Kieran in *An Introduction to Nature*.)

Wuestenfield leads the Audubon Society's annual Christmas bird count in the area. Her surveyors have traced some ten thousand snow geese and thousands of Canada geese. "We see snow geese in fields next to Gilbert Lake but not in the lake itself," she says. As to Canada geese, she relates the story about a decline in Canadas around the United States at least 20 years ago. "So the Department of Natural Resources decided to raise their own Canadas," she continues. "DNR sent one thousand of them down here in boxes, hoping they'd migrate with wild Canadas. They were turned loose at Gilbert Lake, and some of them have remained here year-round ever since. There is a group of one hundred to two hundred at Gilbert Lake and another bunch of one hundred or so along the shoreline at Grafton."

White pelicans are another species seen in large numbers. "I have no theory why whites settle here," Wuestenfield confesses. "We used to say that a white pelican was sick if it stayed over during the winter, but not anymore. We see them by the hundreds all in a mass resting at Gilbert Lake. But when they want food, they fly across the Illinois River to Swan Lake in search of fish. They can probably probe deeper with their bills than about any other bird." No brown pelicans, indigenous to the southeastern and Gulf Coast waters, have ever been recorded in the area.

Ducks are seen in profusion at Gilbert Lake. "February and March are good months to see them," Wuestenfeld suggests. "Males are in their prime colors in March. Some of them actually shimmer; they're magnificent to watch. The ducks are mainly puddle ducks that fish in shallow water as opposed to diving ducks that prefer deeper water. You will see wood ducks, blue- and green-winged teals, redheads, widgets, gadwalls, pintails, and shovelers."

Access

From I-270 east in north St. Louis County, take MO 367 north into Alton, Illinois. From the Alton bridge, turn left and follow signs to the Great River Road. Take the Great River Road west, with the Mississippi River on your left and majestic limestone bluffs on the right, to Grafton, Illinois. In Grafton, continue on IL 100 about 4 miles to the Brussels Ferry landing. Continue briefly on IL 100, then turn left into the parking area.

Trail

Veteran hikers divide the trail into three sections: the gate woods, the middle woods, and the long woods, the latter of which emerge into the Pere Marquette State Park picnic grounds. Between the woods lie Gilbert Lake itself, the Illinois River, and other open waters.

After parking, walk south on the gravel path in the "gate woods" bottomland. Across from a water pump

Observing Gilbert Lake from the "gate woods"

on the left, Gilbert Lake looms large. Frequently hikers might catch sight of hundreds of huddled white pelicans clustered on one of several small islands in the lake. If you don't see them on the lake, they may be soaring overhead. "When you observe hundreds of pelicans flying in a stream, it looks just like a ballet," Wuestenfeld marvels. "The first bird flaps its wings, then the second bird, and so on, but never at exactly the same time. Pelicans put flying eagles to shame."

During summer months, bright-blue morning glories, rose or white hibiscus, and rose-red smartweed may be in full bloom by the lakeshore. Nearby are willows or buttonwood bushes. "Unfortunately, people have come along and cut down some of the willows to construct duck blinds," Wuestenfeld laments.

When the trail reaches the Illinois River, it veers right onto a riprap walkway that appears to be a form of natural levee. Heavy flooding has deposited enough silt on the banks to slightly elevate the levee; the riprap maintains it. Look to the left for a perspective of the

Brussels ferry operation, which connects with Calhoun County in Illinois. Through the years politicians and others have proposed bridges to replace the ferry. In 1932 the Father Marquette Memorial (toll) Bridge was suggested by the U.S. assistant secretary of war, but the idea faded for lack of support. A major four-lane thoroughfare was proposed in 1967—the Calhoun Jersey County Bridge—but the state couldn't afford $5 million for the feasability study, so that idea evaporated, too.

Most of the eagles are seen along this close-to-the-river stretch. "Eagles love it here by the river," observes Wuestenfeld. "They perch in tall trees so they can watch both the lake and the river for floating fish. The annual volume of eagles fluctuates from fewer than one hundred to up to six hundred or seven hundred. The optimum time to see them, from my experience, is around the tenth of January." Alton biologist Mark Hall, who visits Gilbert Lake often, has seen hungry eagles kill rabbits and squirrels along the trail as well as ducks initially crippled by duck hunters. "When the temperature hits around zero, eagles become stressed about finding food," he says. "For some reason, at this low temperature, the eagles allow the most proximity to people."

Some of the old clubhouses still stand on the opposite side of the river, but many have been removed after irreparable flood damage. The Army Corps of Engineers, the landowner, no longer allows clubhouse construction or leasing. About a half mile up the river, well past the end of the clubhouses, is the probable site of the Deer Run Massacre. Francis Parkman in *The Discovery of the Great West* recalled the travels of Sieur de La Salle, the French explorer of North America. Parkman reported that La Salle passed Indian settlements as he floated the Illinois Valley in 1680. The La Salle party landed by the spot thought to be the massacre site. They saw, said Parkman, "half-consumed bodies of women, still bound to the stakes where they had been tortured." About seven hundred persons, mostly women and children, were killed by raiding Iroquois and Miami warriors, historians estimate.

To the right, on or near the lake, snowy egrets and great blue and little blue herons are frequent visitors in the warm months. The first cut on the right side of the trail—about 0.8 mile from the trailhead—is a dredge cut made by the Corps of Engineers, possibly to station a new pump. "Look out to the lake from here and you may have a direct sighting of pelicans at rest on land and in the water," says Wuestenfeld. "March and October are the best viewing months for pelicans. We saw four thousand of them at Swan Lake in September 2000. We discovered for the first time that pelicans are actually nesting at the lake, not just roosting there.

"Every now and then," continues Wuestenfeld, "one can see pretty rare birds around here. One year a sandhill crane dropped by. It was obviously lost, for its natural habitat is in the north and the west. We call this happening 'an out-of-range occurrence.'" Late in 2001 she identified a very rare rose-throated becard, normally a resident of the southern tropics.

The trail passes several leased farm fields where corn and soybean are grown. Farmers must leave half their crop on the ground each year to feed the ducks and geese in the winter.

Well into the second mile of the walk, you reach the "middle woods," which is tree-rich and dense and a great place to see or hear songbirds. Prothonotory warblers, with brilliant golden heads and blue-gray wings, are habitual visitors, as are yellow-throated warblers that nest in sycamore trees and sing like canaries. About 20 pairs of American redstarts nest in trees by the trail. They're beautiful black specimens with bright orange and white tail patches. "They quit singing about July 1, as do many other songbirds, so you better get here early in the summer to appreciate them," says Wuestenfeld, who explains that most songbirds that nest in the summer refrain from songs but, of course, still call. "Only a few songbirds sing all summer long," she says.

Before arriving upon the "long woods" and finishing the hike, you'll pass some abandoned farming plots and home sites from the early 20th century. By the time you reach the "long woods," Gilbert Lake has been left behind, and the river lies out to the left. The path through the woods is on a farm road established enough to appear on maps from the late 1800s.

After completing the walk through the last stretch of woods—about 1 mile in length—you finish the hike on the fringes of Pere Marquette Park. You now have two choices: 1) retrace your steps back to the trailhead, or 2) walk through the picnic grounds, cross IL 100, and walk to the right on the bike/hike blacktop path that parallels the busy highway.

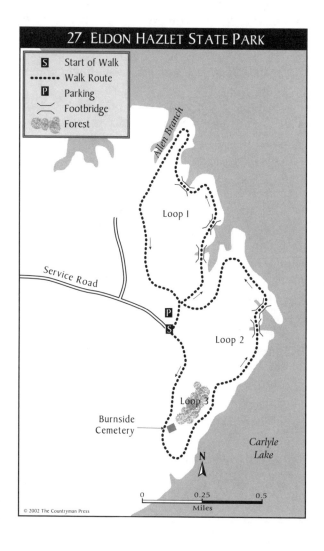

27. ELDON HAZLET STATE PARK

S Start of Walk
······· Walk Route
P Parking
≍ Footbridge
🌳 Forest

Allen Branch

Loop 1

Service Road

P
S

Loop 2

Loop 3

Burnside
Cemetery

Carlyle
Lake

N

0   0.25   0.5
Miles

© 2002 The Countryman Press

27 · Eldon Hazlet State Park

Location: Near Carlyle, Illinois
Hiking distance: 3 miles
Hiking time: 1.5 hours
Bicycles: Not permitted
Note: *Closed during November and December for hunting season*

In sole possession of the southwest shore of Carlyle Lake, Illinois's largest man-made lake, Hazlet is no ordinary park. It's a destination, says superintendent Gary Tatham. He points to the lake itself—sailor's paradise, fisherman's dream, camper's delight. "We're the largest class-A campground in Illinois, with 327 campsites [all with showers and electricity]," Tatham says.

Ironically, Hazlet owes its existence to hundreds of years of punishing floods in and around the Kaskaskia River Valley, especially near Carlyle and Shelbyville, where farm and business interests were repeatedly damaged. (The Kaskaskia is a 325-mile stream that starts near Champaign, Illinois, and meets the Mississippi River near Kaskaskia, Illinois. The river's watershed is said to be the largest in Illinois.) In 1952 Carlyle attorney Eldon Hazlet formed the Kaskaskia Valley Association with one major goal: Stop the flooding by converting the valley into a productive river basin that provides fish-and-wildlife conservation, recreation, and flood controls. Through perseverance and a major partnership with the

U.S. Army Corps of Engineers, a dam was built and finally opened in 1967. And thus the lake was born and then the park.

In the first years of the 19th century, the Goshen Road—which ran from Shawneetown on the Ohio River, through wilderness, to communities that would become Edwardsville and Alton, Illinois—passed through Hill's Ferry (now Carlyle), the settlement on the Kaskaskia River founded in 1812 by John Hill, who also erected a fort against Indian raiders. Settlers and salt traders traveled the road "on horseback, in two-wheeled carts, covered wagons, donkeys . . . and bare feet," wrote Jane E. Rosinos in the *Edwardsville Journal* in 1968. Traders and settlers also arrived in the area via the Vincennes Trail, which roughly paralleled the present US 50 from Vincennes, Indiana, on its way to Cahokia and St. Louis. By 1837 the river settlement, where English immigrants were predominant, was incorporated as Carlyle, honoring the English writer Sir Thomas Carlyle.

A 264-foot suspension bridge with wooden planks, supported by 32-foot stone towers and suspended from handmade wrought-iron cables, was opened in 1860 in the Lower Town part of Carlyle, near where Hill ran his ferry." [The bridge] is free to all citizens of the county but foreign travelers [people from the next county and beyond] are required to pay toll," stated the 1881 *History of Marion and Clinton Counties, Illinois*. "People came from all over just to see a swinging bridge," one newspaper said. By the 1920s its wooden floor was rotting, its cables were weakening. By 1936 state officials closed it to all but pedestrian traffic. Meanwhile, a more modern highway bridge across the Kaskaskia had opened next door.

For years local youngsters used the bridge area as a favorite place to fish, swim, and play. One lad, William Dean, was a regular swimmer, even though he almost drowned in the river in 1916. He went on to a distinguished military career—which included seeing action in World War II and then the Korean War, during which time he was captured and imprisoned by the North Koreans for three years and awarded the Congressional Medal of Honor in absentia. He was honored by his hometown in 1953 when the restored suspension bridge he had known so well as a boy was rededicated as the William F. Dean Memorial Bridge. No trip to Carlyle Lake would be complete without a walk over the Dean bridge.

Carlyle Lake covers 26,000 acres of water; the contiguous public land totals 11,000 acres, including 3,500 acres at Hazlet and 900 acres at the smaller South Shore State Park. Four sailing harbors are located on the lake. Probably the best-known harbor is operated by the four-hundred-member Carlyle Sailing Association, which enrolls owners of 15- to 19-foot racing sailboats. "We have the best harbor and facilities of any sailing venue in the United States, sailors tell us," says St. Louisan Jim Harris, a past commodore of the association. "This is a big bathtub of a lake. You can set a course in any direction and just take off. The lake is a very level playing field. As such it attracts Olympic sailors and some of the elite in sailing." (One harbormaster, Ric Golding, observes that "the lake is unique because of the basic flatness of the land surrounding it. There is nothing to block the wind on Carlyle except maybe the [Gateway] Arch—and that's 50 miles away in downtown St. Louis and has a hole in it.")

Races involving Carlyle Sailing Association boats are scheduled for most Sundays during the sailing season from May through October; regional, national, and international regattas occur during the summer. On Saturdays the lake is dominated by larger recreational sailboats from the other three Carlyle Lake harbors. "Out on the lake, sailboats tend toward the middle to get the best winds," comments Gerald Donaldson, longtime harbormaster (along with his wife) of the Carlyle Sailing Association and its four 300-foot floating docks and clubhouse. "Powerboats tend to run closer to the shore. The best sailing winds are from mid-May to mid-June; they pick up again in September and October. On a given weekend there are more sailboats than powerboats on the lake."

Bank fishing is extremely popular with fishermen who reel in white bass, walleye, bluegill, bullhead, crappie, and catfish. One prize catch, a 78-pound flathead catfish, is displayed in the U.S. Army Corps of Engineer visitors center. Ten percent of all Illinois fishing is done at Carlyle Lake, Illinois DNR's fisheries division estimates.

Birders also know the park and the lake well. During migrations, hawks, white pelicans, and songbirds such as warblers stop by. Herons and terns are year-round residents, and eagles have nested on the north end of the lake. Among the raptors, red-tailed hawks stay year-round. "We have a high predation population here," says park superintendant Tatham. The shoreline of Carlyle Lake and nearby farm fields provide a continuing food supply for red-tails and other hawks: rabbits, mice, voles, snakes, squirrels, doves, insects, and chipmunks. In recent years a smallish northern saw-whet owl roosted in a cedar tree near the park adminis-

The William F. Dean Memorial Bridge in Carlyle

tration building. "It stayed for weeks and was easy to see," recalls Jim Birdsell, assistant park superintendent. Traffic among bird enthusiasts increased tenfold on weekends during the owl's visit, Birdsell said.

The 1.5- to 3.25-foot-long eastern massasauga rattlesnakes (which belong to the pit-viper family of venomous creatures along with copperheads and diamondbacks) are among Illinois-listed endangered and threatened wildlife species at Hazlet. Massasauga habitats, ranges, and populations are being researched in the park—the most viable site in the state—by specialists from the Illinois Natural History Survey. The snakes are identified by a row of black-brown splotches along their backs and rows of dark spots on their sides. Massasauga bites are rarely fatal, but if you're bitten, contact the park headquarters to find the nearest medical help.

In winter, anywhere between fifty thousand and three hundred thousand Canada geese, plus an appreciable number of snow geese, can be seen on or near the lake if there is no ice. However, in exceptionally cold weather, up to a foot of ice may form. "When that happens, we call it 'Minnesota-quality' ice," says Birdsell.

In November and December the Cherokee and Hazlet's four other trails close to allow pheasant hunting. Up to eight thousand hunters come to the park seeking to harvest some of the thirteen thousand pen-raised pheasants released by park workers. "There is something in the soil south of I-70 that doesn't allow pheasants to breed naturally," says site interpreter John Bunnell of the park's imported pheasant population.

Access

From downtown St. Louis, take I-55 to I-64 in Illinois; take I-64 east to the IL 50 exit. Take IL 50 through Lebanon to IL 127 in Carlyle. Drive 4 miles north to the Hazlet entrance. Follow signs to the park administration building. Continue east on the road in front of the building until it dead-ends. Take a left, and then watch for the road on the right that leads to the Cherokee Trail parking area. The Cherokee Trail consists of three well-marked loops.

Trail

From the parking area, walk on a wide meadowy stretch bounded by oaks and hickories on the left and an old farm field that now contains autumn olive trees and silky dogwoods. At one time small farms and riverside clubhouses were scattered around here. Head to the pre-Civil War Burnside Cemetery, which operated from the 1840s through the 1860s and contains 17 burials, nine of them Burnsides. James Burnside Jr. arrived in 1817 as "the first white man to make settlement," states the 1881 *History of Marion and Clinton County, Illinois*. He and wife, Eliza, had six children, four buried here.

After roaming the cemetery, follow the path to the edge of Carlyle Lake, marked by steep, riprapped banks to forestall erosion. The main channel of the Kaskaskia River flows close to the shoreline, explains Bunnell. "The deepest part of the lake—from 10 to 15 feet—is right here," he says. "We're comparatively shallow here, definitely not a Lake Tahoe," adds Tatham.

Deer thrive in the oak-hickory forest through which we walk. "People come here all year long just to look at the deer," says Bunnell. "Deer love acorns, and this place is filled with oaks, so it makes sense." Birdsell says that several Indian mounds are suspected to exist nearby. "There was much presettlement activity involving Indians, who used the Kaskaskia River as a kind of superhighway," Birdsell said. Standing on the shore one can see South Shore State Park and campground straight across the lake and slightly to the right (the lake is 3.5 miles wide). To the far right, the Corps of Engineers dam is viewable. Across the lake to the left are the town of Boulder and the Coles Creek and Boulder campgrounds. Although recreational fishing is extremely popular on the lake, commercial fisherman may only fish—mostly for carp and buffalo—in January.

Continue following the meandering path northward by the lakeshore and through the woods of oaks, hickories, elms, and sycamores. "You'll find morel mushroom hunters around here in abundance [up to two hundred a day] in late April and early May," says Bunnell. "You should pick morels and put them in onion bags so their spores will fall out as you look for more morels," Bunnell adds. "This helps redistribute the mushroom spores and keeps our crop at the same level year after year. It takes a spore five years to make a mushroom."

At the end of the trail's first loop, white pine trees whose lower trunks have been scraped by the racks of buck deer make an appearance. The second loop, which begins the second mile of the walk, starts by the lakeside where there is a bench, nearby cottonwoods, and more deer-scraped white pines. "Too much scraping will eventually kill the pines," says Birdsell.

In the spring healthy clusters of white trillium, spring beauties, trout lilies, bloodroot, Dutchman's breeches, and other wildflowers can be found along the trail.

Walk by more white oaks and shagbark hickories, where sassafras and ash trees provide much of the understory. A footbridge erected in 1977 by the Youth Conservation Corps crosses a ravine; from there the trail veers to the left. Another footbridge isn't far away. From it you can see trees gnawed by beavers or strangled by overpowering grapevines. After the second footbridge you again face the lake. The waterway on the left is the Allen Branch, main entranceway into the lake for everyone except sailboaters.

Look out into the lake. If the day is clear you'll most probably see structures rising from the water about 2.5 miles out. Looking like silos, the structures are water intake towers used by the city of Salem, Illinois, 20 miles to the east. One tower is abandoned; the other supplements summer drinking water for Salem when there's a shortage of rain. The water flows from the lake via a transmission line to the Salem reservoir. "Those towers have probably saved the lives of several fishermen who got caught up in storms when the waves were 4 or 5 feet high," John Bunnell says. "The fisherman waited out the storms by tying up to the towers."

Continue hiking the shoreline. Make a detour to visit

an overlook, and then return to the main path. Out on the horizon—again, only if the day is clear—you may be able to see "Party Island," one of the lake's several islands; the others are found on the north part of the lake, which lures mostly fishermen. The islands are slowly eroding away due to constant wind and wave action, says harbormaster Donaldson. "Lots of power-boat owners use Party Island, but not many sailors. People have brought power generators there so live bands can come in and perform at their parties," Donaldson adds. To the left of the island is a railroad trestle that separates the north and south halves of the 18-mile-long lake. The Burlington-Northern railroad runs 27 trains a day—most carrying coal—over the 4.6-mile-long lake trestle from Carlyle to Keyesport, Illinois, says Ric Golding, the harbormaster and history buff who also operates the *Spirit of Carlyle,* a jet-drive tour boat that leaves at 2 PM Wednesdays, Saturdays, and Sundays from his harbor at West Access Marina. "Those tracks were put down in 1868 along the Kaskaskia River by the old Jacksonville & Southeastern Railway," Golding adds. Paddle-wheel steamers offered rides on the Kaskaskia River between Carlyle and Keyesport in earlier days.

Follow the connector path to the final loop of the Cherokee Trail. This last lap, where wildflowers are copious in April, is a marked nature trail; descriptive leaflets may be available at a nearby signpost. Beyond trees number one (a honey locust) and two (a shag-bark hickory) are four wildlife nesting boxes installed by Bunnell using a ladder and scoop bucket. "We hope to attract small owls, hawks, or woodpeckers—maybe even flying squirrels," he says. For a stretch, the path becomes a woodchip berm that rises above a small section of wetland.

Follow the path to an intersection; bear right. Just ahead along the path, Bunnell says he has seen at least a dozen green dragon plants—considered comparatively rare by wildflower experts. Green dragons, which bloom in late April and May, are cousins to the more common jack-in-the-pulpit wildflowers that grow abundantly in this part of the park. Three- to 4-inch greenish "dragon's tongues" rise from the plant's hood, distinguishing it from its better-known relative. "You have to go looking for the green dragon with your mind intent on it and nothing else, or you will scarcely find one in 20 miles, even when it blooms," wrote botanist Donald Culross Peattie in the 1935 *An Almanac for Moderns*. Its flower is green, wrote Peattie—"[a] queer, elvish, secretive green, thrusting out a little reptilian tongue."

Continue walking to another footbridge. Off the bridge in the ravine to the right are dense stands of yellow-orange jewelweeds that bloom in late summer and whose nectar attracts bees as well as migrating ruby-throated hummingbirds. The slender-beaked birds "stay for three or four minutes, then shoot away like rockets," wrote Edwin Way Teale in *Circle of the Seasons*. Jewelweed, a member of the Impatiens family, is also called touch-me-not because, if touched, the seedpods explode, and seeds scatter everywhere. The path next takes you to another overlook, thought by park officials to offer the best perspective on the lake, where you are very near the mouth of the Allen Branch, the narrow waterway that conveys fishermen, duck hunters, water-skiers, and powerboaters onto the lake. From this final overlook, it's a short jaunt to trail's end at the parking area.

28 · Lincoln Memorial Garden

Location: Lake Springfield, Springfield, Illinois
Hiking distance: 2 miles
Hiking time: 1.5 hours
Bicycles: Not permitted

In the 18th century, the "Old Indian Trail" up into central Illinois began at the settlement called New Design, located on the American Bottom southeast of the confluence of the Missouri and Mississippi Rivers. The trail angled northward, cutting through unrelieved prairie, then through bountiful sugar groves until it reached the Sugar Creek valley near the creek's merger with the Sangamon River near what is now Springfield, Illinois.

As John Mack Faragher points out in *Sugar Creek: Life on the Illinois Prairie*, the Indian Trail was but a "narrow rut" across the prairie, a ribbon road, albeit a vital one. During the War of 1812, Kickapoo Indians moved south on the trail to harass and even kill American settlers. Ninian Edwards, who governed Illinois territory, countered by ordering American militiamen and their wagons up the trail to burn the main Kickapoo village beyond the Sangamon River. That maneuver is said to have broken the will of the Indians and turned the tide for Illinois in the war. The trail was soon renamed the

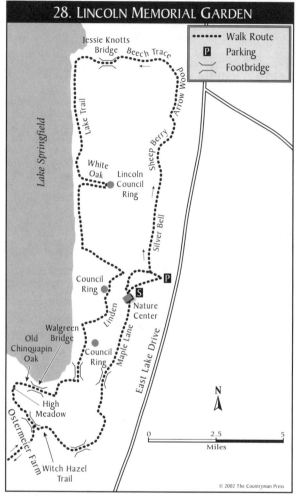

28. LINCOLN MEMORIAL GARDEN

• • • • • • Walk Route

P Parking

⌣ Footbridge

Lake Springfield

Jessie Knotts Bridge
Beech Trace
Lake Trail
Arrow Wood
White Oak
Lincoln Council Ring
Sheep Berry
Silver Bell
P
S
Council Ring
Nature Center
Linden
Walgreen Bridge
Old Chinquapin Oak
Council Ring
Maple Lane
East Lake Drive
High Meadow
Ostermeier Farm
Witch Hazel Trail

N

0   2.5   5
Miles

© 2002 The Countryman Press

Edwards' Trace in honor of the fighting governor.

In 1822 Congress designated Edwards' Trace as a post road, certifying it to support regular mail runs between St. Louis and Springfield. The new post road was called the St. Louis Road. In the 20th century, the road would be partially incorporated into a new highway between Chicago and St. Louis: US 66.

Sugar Creek Valley, and its major trail, was a factor in the settling of Springfield and its satellites such as Auburn, Chatham, and Glenarm. Near the valley were hardwood forests, prairies, and settleable marginal land—just right for farming and the formation of communities of migrants from the south and the east. And there was plenty of water, what with Sugar and Lick Creeks nearby and the Sangamon River not far away.

More than one hundred years later, as Springfield's population expanded, its municipal water supply consisted mostly of suspect wells. Facing the challenge to do something drastic, visionary civic leaders decided to create a mammoth new supply of water by damming Sugar and Lick Creeks. Years after the concept was announced, the new Lake Springfield was producing the area's drinking water and offering countless recreational possibilities.

On July 12, 1935, the lake—actually, a reservoir—was dedicated incrementally. First the spillway was dedicated, then the Vachel Lindsay Memorial Bridge, then the Beach Stadium. A motorcade of dignitaries was at each dedication. The most famous personage was poet Carl Sandburg, a colleague of his fellow poet Vachel Lindsay, who had died in his native Springfield at age 35 in 1931.

While the lake was filling in, leaders of the Garden Clubs of Illinois mulled the idea of commemorating Abraham Lincoln's domineering presence in Springfield in the last century. Mrs. T. J. Knudson, a board member of the group, persuaded other members to take on the memorial project and place it on the shore of the new Lake Springfield. Mrs. Knudson knew of the reputation of Jens Jensen, considered the dean of American landscape architects at the time. She wrote to ask of his interest and availability and, with trepidation, his fee. Jensen replied that he had been honored the world over, but the greatest honor of all would be to design the Lincoln Memorial Garden—for no fee at all.

Jensen's ultimate design consisted of eight council rings with numerous fingerlike walking lanes radiating from them. Most of the lanes were designed to exhibit clusters of trees or wildflowers and to effect partial openings in the land to let in the sun or to view the lake. "[Jensen] saw the rings, essentially circular stone benches, as a means for fostering friendly gatherings within the garden... the kind of gatherings associated with the Indian campfire," wrote Leonard Eaton in *Landscape Artists in America*. For nearly 13 years, until his death in 1951, Jensen visited Springfield, attending to the further design and growth of the garden. Near St. Louis he found six huge boulders and ordered them set in pairs by each garden entrance. He also designed several architecturally relevant bridges. "The only additions to the garden made without his approval are the sturdy benches [at least 30 of them], contributed by state garden clubs, each one bearing a quotation from Lincoln," reported Eaton. "Today, Lincoln Memorial Garden is one of the few remaining Jensen landscapes ... that has not been consciously changed and that is still used as Jensen originally intended," writes Robert E. Grese in *Jens Jensen: Maker of Natural Parks and Gardens*.

One longtime supporter, Thelma Sibley, still leads tours of the garden, starting from its Nature Center headquarters. In 1934 she and her husband moved into the third home to be built on the lakeshore, and she saw the lake fill with water. "I saw Jens Jensen here once digging with a shovel . . . turning ground for something," she recalls. "He wore a light tan suit and a flowing tie. He looked so out of place."

By the way, Grese notes that despite Jensen's initial surge of altruism, he sent the garden board a $500 invoice for his layout. He said he was too poor to "give the plan outright."

Access

From St. Louis, take I-55 north to exit 88. Turn right onto East Lake Drive; proceed 7 miles to the Lincoln Memorial Garden entrance. Park, and then walk to the Nature Center to begin your hike.

Trail

Leave the Nature Center building, and turn right. Follow the sidewalk, where in late April or early May what garden administrator Jim Matheis calls blue and gray "Confederate" violets are in full bloom as are some amazing masses of white trillium, one of the least seen of the trillium family. A large stone wheel ahead on the trail came from a local rock quarry. Says Matheis, "This stone was supposed to be part of a pillar for the old state capitol [in Springfield] but the wagon carrying it broke down and ended up here. We call it 'the Big Rock.'"

Turn left onto Silver Bell Lane. A handsome silver bell tree, which produces showy, white bell-shaped flowers that, observes Matheis, "dangle up and down and come out around the first of May," stands near the intersection. One of the garden's rarer trees, and on the Illinois endangered-species list it's distinguished by its smooth reddish-brown bark with whitish stripes.

Rows of purplish-blue periwinkles border part of Silver Bell Lane. These plants were favorites of Mrs. Knudson, said Matheis, so they occur in some profusion along the way. Scattered among the periwinkle, which flower in late April and early May, are clumps of wild ginger and white Solomon's Seal. The garden's map shelter/information kiosk appears next on Silver Bell Lane.

A grove of sugar maples is a highlight of Silver Bell Lane. Jensen designed this cluster, referring to it as a "maple room." The garden staff and local volunteers and schoolchildren tap about 150 maple trees in February and March, with most of the syrup used up at the annual pancake breakfast in March.

Continue ahead on Sheep Berry Lane, where viburnum and other thick understory species add contrasts in color along the pathway. At least two more Jensen "maple rooms" are seen along this stretch of trail. If you look to your left when you come to Prairie Path, you'll see the garden's oldest prairie.

After this intersection Sheep Berry Lane becomes Arrow Wood Trail and proceeds straight ahead. Cross the first bridge over a no-name tributary of the former Sugar Creek. Under the bridge, along the banks, Virginia bluebells thrive in the spring, along with more of the stunning white trillium.

Turn left on Beech Trace, where white bluebells, also rare regionally, come alive in April. At the end of Beech Trace, with Lake Springfield now in sight, is a Jensen half council ring. Look toward the lake and you'll spot a

Heading toward the Nature Center at Lincoln Memorial Garden

grove of about 20 bald cypress trees scattered along the shore. "Those trees don't know that they're located too far north of their typical range," says Matheis, proud of the way the garden staff has nurtured them. Jensen had brought the cypress trees from the tip of southern Illinois as a representation of swamp habitat found in that part of the state.

Cross Jessie Knotts Bridge (she was one of the garden's founders), and then turn left on the Lake Trail. Straight across the lake is the Island Bay Yacht Club, home of most of the sailboats that ply the lake in warm months. Smokestacks on the horizon belong to the city powerplant. At the far right on the lake is the Vachel Lindsay Memorial Bridge. Turn left on White Oak Trail, and walk up to the Lincoln Council Ring, largest in the garden, where Matheis and his wife were married years ago. "Our families sat outside the ring that day," he recalls. "The white oaks overhead give this place a cathedral-like feeling. You get another view of our prairie from here, too." These white oaks sprang from acorns collected in the early 1930s by Illinois schoolchildren—plants were difficult to come by then—that were then planted by Boy Scouts and adult volunteers. White oaks were deemed an appropriate Lincoln memorial because they live for centuries and will probably outlast any artificial or man-made memorials. Turn around and return to the Lake Trail; continue to the left.

Turn left, and walk up Dogwood Lane. "You are entering one of Jensen's designed landscapes here," says Matheis. "You see a sugar maple on top of the hill ahead; dogwoods here at the bottom, and the prairie in between. Each fall the maples are gold, the dogwoods are red, and the prairie is both red and brown. Jensen plotted this spot according to the place where the sun would set in the fall. Late in the autumn day, the sun reflects off the golds and reds."

Turn right on Linden Lane, where midway along the path, the garden's most used council ring is seen. Continue on to the Buckeye Trail; turn right, then left onto lakeside Shadbush Lane. After crossing another footbridge and council ring, walk right onto Hickory Lane, following it as it bends left toward Shady Lane. Turn right on Shady Lane, which, says Matheis, resembles an old railroad right-of-way. "Railroads ran all over this place in the late 19th century," he says.

Shady Lane will take you up to and over the garden's largest and best-known span, the Walgreen Bridge. This structure was named in honor of Mrs. Myrtle Walgreen, another key garden founder. "Mrs. Walgreen had a birthday coming up one year, and her husband, Charles [founder of Walgreen Drugs], asked her what she wanted for her birthday," recalled Mrs. Sibley. "'I want a bridge for Lincoln Memorial Garden,' she said." As it happened, the couple had an agreement that any gift would have to fit into a certain corner cupboard in their home. So Mr. Walgreen gave her a blueprint for the bridge and a check for $1,500 to build it (in 1939 or 1940). For years, Mrs. Walgreen helped raise funds for plantings for the garden by presiding over spring tours of her home up in Dixon, Illinois. "She was always on her knees planting bulbs," says Sibley.

After crossing the Walgreen Bridge, you'll come upon the garden's oldest tree, a 250-year-old chinquapin oak that is so important, a Decatur, Illinois arborist has volunteered to tend it and give it an occasional trim. "Only seven trees were on this land, which was an old pasture, when the garden began," says Sibley. "Everything else we have here was planted deliberately."

After paying tribute to the old chinquapin, find High Meadow Trail, which follows the rim of this small isthmus on the lake. Proceed to the left until you arrive at a new path that makes a right and goes to Ostermeier Farm, a later residence of Sibley and her husband and where 30,000 to 40,000 prairie plants have been put in by the garden since 1995. After viewing the Victorian home and its outbuildings, turn around and walk back to Witch Hazel Trail, taking a right turn. Follow Witch Hazel past its intersection with Hawthorne Trail, then Shady Lane. After a footbridge, Witch Hazel becomes Maple Lane, which takes you back to the trailhead at the nature center. Mementoes of the garden as well as crafts and books are sold in the gift shop within the nature center.

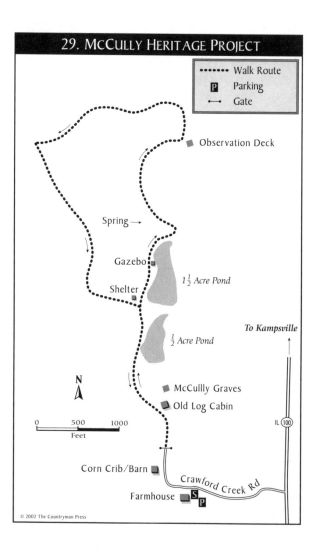

29. MᶜCULLY HERITAGE PROJECT

- •••••• Walk Route
- Ⓟ Parking
- •—• Gate

Observation Deck

Spring →

Gazebo

Shelter

$1\frac{1}{2}$ Acre Pond

$\frac{1}{2}$ Acre Pond

To Kampsville

McCully Graves

Old Log Cabin

IL ⑩⓪

N

0   500   1000
Feet

Corn Crib/Barn

Crawford Creek Rd

Farmhouse Ⓢ Ⓟ

© 2002 The Countryman Press

29 · McCully Heritage Project Nature Trail

Location: Kampsville, Illinois
Hiking distance: 2 miles
Hiking time: 1 hour
Bicycles: Not permitted
Note: *Closed in November for hunting season*

Howard McCully made the most of his 85 years. His biography includes four years as a coordinator for a Chautauqua-like road show company that traversed America as well as 18 lively years clerking in a St. Louis bookie joint where, he said, his customers ranged from doctors to pimps. During that time, he met Eva and proposed marriage, taking "half a day off [in 1935] to tie the knot—borrowed $50 from my boss, which I had to pay back. These were the Depression years," he later recalled. Sometime later his boss was indicted for income tax evasion, and "the job disappeared ... and that was when I decided I wanted to start a nursery."

Eva wasn't keen on a nursery. So when Howard opted out of a trip to Florida—telling his pals to "take Evie, I have too much work to do"—he speedily plowed his ground, and by the time of her return, he had planted hundreds of evergreen saplings to formally debut the new family business—in 1945—in Hazelwood. Eva forgave Howard his stealth and became an active partner in the nursery, which existed until 1971. With thoughts of postretirement, the McCullys searched for land in the Crawford Creek Valley suited to tree farming. Shown some Calhoun County timberland, Howard decided it was the most beautiful woodland he had seen and had to have the farm—"and I don't care what it takes." A price was agreed on, and in 1982 the McCullys moved to Illinois to settle on what was then 565 acres and is now 940 acres.

"I helped Mr. McCully plant 25,000 to 30,000 trees," says site superintendent Tony Brady, still on the job after nearly 20 years, seven of them while McCully was still alive. "We used up all the available ground [hillsides and old farm fields] to put the trees, so we stopped around 1990. Mr. McCully drove the tractor, and I sat behind, dropping in saplings. Mr. McCully liked walnut trees the best. We also put in a lot of white oaks, white pines, and bald cypress." All the prodigious planting by the McCullys won them the Illinois Tree Farmers of the Year Award in 1984.

Aided by his friend and adviser, William McCartney, executive director of the Two Rivers Resource Conservation and Development Area in Pittsfield, Illinois, McCully produced a master plan, plotted a trail network, restored an old log cabin, constructed and stocked two ponds, and invited in professionals from the Center for American Archeology, up the road in Kampsville, to do some digging. When McCully died in 1995, the project earmarked as his "heritage" was off and running and open for public use. The McCullys, seeking to leave their land in better condition than when they arrived, set up a trust, deeding their property to the foundation. "There is nothing like this in Illinois," McCartney said at the time.

The main trail, on the north end of the property, is where deer and wild turkeys rival the trees in volume. "There are tons and tons of deer here," says Brady. "In cold weather we can see 50 to 60 deer at a time. We have seen as many as 100 wild turkeys right by the trail. Bald eagles often fly over since we're close to the Illinois River." Goldfinches are also seen in abundance. On the property's south side, on higher ground overlooking the Illinois River, equestrians and hikers share a less-developed trail network. "Equestrians accustomed to the trails at Pere Marquette State Park have now found our place," says Brady.

From the south overlooks one can see parts of at least two islands in the Illinois River: Shell Island, literally covered with mussel shells, and Hurricane Island, near Michael, Illinois, a favorite with duck hunters each fall. (A larger island, Diamond, lies south of Hurricane.) It wasn't unusual, either, to see the mighty *Delta Queen*, one of the nation's best-known steamboats, float up the Illinois in the years before bankruptcy closed down its operations. In the endowment's future is a nature center, farm museum, expanded wetlands, and primitive camping sites, says the board. Although hiking is free, contributions are welcomed. For information, phone 618-653-4687.

Access

From I-270 in north St. Louis County, take MO 367 north over the bridge into Alton, 10 miles. From the bridge, turn left on IL 100, which becomes the Great River Road along the Mississippi River, to Grafton, 17.5

miles. Continue on IL 100 through Grafton, past Pere Marquette State Park, to Hardin. Cross the Illinois River drawbridge, and then continue north on IL 100 through Michael to Crawford Creek Road, 9 more miles. Turn left; take Crawford Creek Road 0.75 mile to the McCully parking lot.

Trail

From the parking lot, walk west past the farmhouse, and head for the gate on the right, where the walk begins.

With an English walnut, old maples, and a century-old white pine in its front yard and two abandoned cisterns nearby, the farmhouse is the provisional visitors center. It has served as a science/nature classroom, and in November, when the property is closed to the general public, provides sleepover rooms for bow hunters. "Deer hunting has become big business in Calhoun County," explains Brady. "We have another house on our land where we can put up more hunters; we even have a professional guide who stays here throughout November to assist the hunters."

Near the farmhouse on the left are an old-time corn-crib and a red barn. Inside the barn is another corn-crib, framed with ancient white-pine logs. Rusted farm equipment and antique hand tools that McCully collected are on display in the barn. "It's worth walking inside and having a look," says Brady. Once through the gate, you'll get a feel for McCully's planting ventures: tall black oaks backdrop both sides of the path; so do white pines, white oaks, and some ashes.

A prized McCully possesion was the 19th-century log cabin that sits on the right side of the trail and is equipped with desks for schoolchildren and artifacts to examine. McCully had discovered the cabin in a ravine and had it moved trailside. WELCOME CHILDREN OF ALL AGES says a sign out front. Old Calhoun county court records suggest that John Surbeck, who had purchased 40 acres for $20 in 1854, built the cabin around 1855. By 1860 six Surbecks resided in the smallish cabin. In 1863, say census papers, Surbeck owned 12 cows, 17 hogs, 9 acres of corn, and 1 carriage. By 1870 a subsistence farmer owned the cabin and adjoining land, which yielded winter wheat, corn, and Irish potatoes. In 1887 Michael Kinscherff bought much of the present McCully land.

When his son, Albert, married Katherin Daak in 1901, the pair moved into the empty cabin, living there for 11 years. In 1914 Kinscherff cousins took over the cabin, furnishing it with a "rag rug over straw ticking, a grand piano, and red-plush overstuffed furniture." A hired farmhand who moved from the cabin in 1923 is said to have been the last person to inhabit the building.

As the McCullys aged, they debated their burial site. First choice was to be near the observation deck, which lies farther up the trail, McCartney, the McCullys' executor, once recalled. "They wanted to be buried high up on their land so they could watch over us as we developed it." But when Eva died in 1994, adverse weather conditions dictated burial in the bottomland. So she was interred behind the log cabin, as was Howard, who died a year later.

By the stream just beyond the cabin on the trail, McCully planted a stand of bamboo that he had saved from his nursery in Missouri. A half-acre pond, accented by a bankside solitary white pine, lies just ahead.

Across from it are a McCully-planted hemlock and a handsome pecan tree. Nearby is the first of four shelters on the property. "Howard put the shelters up because he didn't want his guests to get caught in the rain," says Brady. The fire pits by the shelter were designed for fishermen and others who camped nearby.

Another pond—about 1.5 acres in size—is next on the trail. "Howard personally bought the original fish for his ponds and continued to stock them," McCartney once explained. "He and Eva liked to feed the catfish in the ponds." Brady says it isn't unusual to catch a four- or five-pound bass or healthy numbers of bluegill, catfish, and crappie and for some of the fishermen to camp overnight by the water. Boy Scouts donated the flagpole. Brady and McCully erected the nearby gazebo, following instructions from the box it came in. "Howard was always pitching in on projects," says Brady.

At a fork in the path, veer to the right, and walk uphill. A quick side trip to the left, however, takes you to the natural spring that feeds the fishing ponds. The uphill trek is through timber dominated by white oaks and joined by dogwoods, elms, sassafras, and hickories. Along the way, a path to the right—the Woodland Loop—will return you to the pond area. Unless you must end your hike early, keep walking straight ahead on the rocky, rutted, and sometimes muddy old logging road. Pass two more shelters, stands of black walnuts with autumn olives, and a mammoth ravine to the left. "This whole farm is pretty much ravine," observes Brady, who credits squirrels, in addition to his late boss, for seed dispersal. "Those squirrels really helped us with black oaks on this hillside. Most of the oaks around here are from acorns dropped by squirrels."

Atop the hill is the observation deck that faces the Illinois River about 1 mile to the east and the Crawford Creek Valley to the right. Brady and McCully helped local contractors erect the stand. A trail—the Grassland Loop—takes off from the right of the deck and returns hikers to the second shelter. Our walk continues to the left, however, on a southbound ridgeline path between two impressive ravines, one of which yielded the cabin in McCully's early days as landowner. A barbed-wire fence on the right defines the property line for a while.

This section of the walk is through an oak-hickory woodland where understory dogwoods and redbuds bring the forest to life each spring. Notice how white-tail bucks have left rack marks via rubs or scrapes on the lower bark of cedars scattered through the woods. Occasional tree stumps indicate that timber operations once occurred here. Several forks in the path appear on the ridgeline stretch; keep walking left at the forks, disregarding secondary and dead-end loops that lead to the right.

Once the road starts downhill, the property's deepest ravine prevails on the left. A large concentration of cedars is found on a hillside to the left near the bottom of the hill. "This makes a great bedding place for deer," observes Brady. "In a clearing inside the woods, the deer can lay down and hide and no one knows they're there." Persimmons are so profuse nearby that "you can almost smell their fruit in the fall," Brady says. As the ground levels out, you'll see once again the first shelter that appeared on the trail. A right-hand turn will take you to the parking lot and the end of your hike.

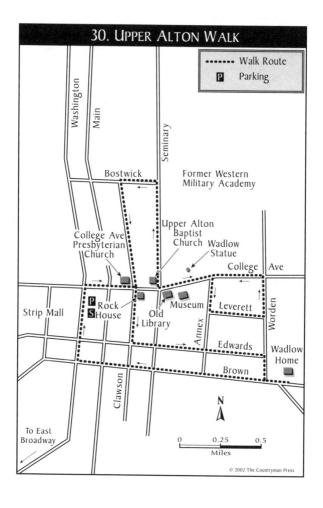

30. Upper Alton Walk

•••••• Walk Route

P Parking

Washington

Main

Seminary

Bostwick

Former Western Military Academy

College Ave Presbyterian Church

Upper Alton Baptist Church

Wadlow Statue

College Ave

Strip Mall

P
S Rock House

Old Library

Museum

Annex

Leverett

Worden

Edwards

Wadlow Home

Clawson

Brown

To East Broadway

N

0   0.25   0.5
Miles

© 2002 The Countryman Press

30 · Upper Alton Walk

Location: Alton, Illinois
Hiking distance: 4 miles
Hiking time: 1.5 hours

First settled by Joseph Meacham, a Vermonter, in 1816, the log cabin village of Upper Alton—on an "elevated prairie" where panthers, bears, and buffalos also resided—was said to resemble a New England town. Many of the early settlers in the village were from the old states east of the Mississippi River. In fact, wrote Illinois governor Thomas Ford in 1854, "They were just a slice off the great loaf of Old States."

"There is the same wealth of foliage, generous lawns and gardens and the quiet air of culture in the atmosphere which pervades the college towns of the east," stated the Alton Glass Company in a 1912 booklet. "A fine-toned morality is said to characterize its inhabitants," said the *History of Madison County, Illinois and Its People* in 1914. Among the log cabins there were mansions, too. One building, the Bostwick home (its site is at the present corner of Seminary Street and Bostwick Avenue) was said by some to be the "most elegant and costly residence west of the Alleghanies." It was erected in 1836 and has long since disappeared.

From its earliest years, Upper Alton was a cultural center. The culture was manifested in Shurtleff College

(1827–1957), Western Military Academy (which began as the Wyman Institute in 1879 and closed in 1971), and two key churches, the College Avenue Presbyterian Church, whose first pastor was the Reverend Elijah Parish Lovejoy, one of America's first Civil War–period abolitionists, and the Upper Alton Baptist Church.

Upper Alton was also the home of Robert Wadlow, 1918–1940—at 8'11.9" the world's tallest man known to medical science. Wadlow was a familiar presence on College Avenue in the late 1930s. He walked from his home on Brown Street to the soda fountain at Kerr's Drug Store as well as to Alton Senior High School farther west on College Avenue. At maturity Wadlow wore size 37 shoes and worked as a spokesman for the International Shoe Company, St. Louis. Wadlow spent one year studying prelaw courses at Shurtleff College, then traveled nationally as a pitchman for the shoe company. In the last four years of his life, Wadlow, his father, and his road partner traveled at least 300,000 miles, visiting 800 towns in 41 states. Just before he died, Wadlow had been fitted for a larger shoe size, 39 AAA. He is buried in Upper Alton Cemetery.

Upper Alton is still called Pie Town by some old-timers. The story goes that in 1846 when the United States declared war on Mexico, Alton was designated a mustering point for all of the Illinois regiments. In an area now known as Rock Springs Park, about 1 mile west of Upper Alton's business center on College Avenue, volunteers camped and waited for the call. The ladies of Upper Alton were persuaded to bake pies for the soldiers. Later on they also baked pies for Civil War soldiers while they were camped nearby, awaiting mustering.

In its lifetime Shurtleff (now Southern Illinois University–Edwardsville School of Dental Medicine) was celebrated as being the oldest college in Illinois (founded in 1827), followed by McKendree College in Lebanon, (1828) and Illinois College in Jacksonville (1829). The Baptist-oriented college, one of whose graduates was General John Pope, the Civil War Union officer, was said to be run as if it were an Ivy-League school. In 1864 the entire student body enlisted for the Union cause, forming a regiment in the Civil War. The college was closed for six months while the regiment was on short-term duty.

Access

From I-270 in north St. Louis County, turn north on MO 367, and enter Alton via the new Lewis Bridge. Turn right on IL 143; then quickly spot the IL 140 sign. Follow 1L 140 to the right, onto East Broadway, where it passes Fast Eddie's Bar and Grill on the way to Washington Avenue. Turn left onto Washington, following it north to Upper Alton. After crossing Edwards Street, find the Family Dollar/Schwegel's Store strip mall, and park there. The trip from the bridge to the parking area is slightly less than 2 miles.

Trail

From the parking lot, walk right on Washington Avenue, then turn right onto College Avenue. At 2572 is the former Speed B. Kerr pharmacy, which boasted an active soda fountain operation until 1996 when it closed after decades of service. "We had to turn off the ceiling fan over the front door whenever we heard that Robert Wadlow, the Alton giant, was coming in for ice cream,"

Gail Kerr once recalled. "We were afraid he might cut his neck if we didn't."

Down the street at 2520 College was the shoe store once owned by Robert's father, Harold. "Following Robert's passing, Mr. Wadlow opened a retail shoe store . . . where Robert, in a large framed picture, looks with quiet eyes upon the scene below," wrote Frederic Fadner, a Shurtleff teacher, in *The Gentleman Giant*, a florid biography of Robert, in 1942. Cross Main Street, and continue east toward Clawson.

College Avenue Presbyterian Church is on the northwest corner at Clawson. Organized in 1837 as the Upper Alton Presbyterian Church, its first pastor was the abolitionist Elijah Parish Lovejoy, whose tenure was short because he was assassinated late in 1837 by thugs who protested Lovejoy's antislavery stand and his editorials in the *Alton Observer*, the Presbyterian newspaper that circulated in Illinois and Missouri. The original church burned in 1858. The present stone gothic church building was dedicated in 1927.

In October 1837, before Lovejoy's death, his church hosted a meeting that formed the Illinois Anti-Slavery Society. But, says the church's 150th anniversary booklet, "A near riot [near the church] made it necessary for the delegates to leave the church." They moved to the Rock House, a course rubble white-stone double building across the street at 2705 College Avenue. One day later the society was officially started; Lovejoy was named corresponding secretary. Considerably altered over time, the Rock House was said to have been a stopover on the Underground Railroad.

(The Underground Railroad Movement stretched from the 1830s through the 1860s, says Charles L.

Blockson in *The Underground Railroad*. He indicates that Illinois had five lines of the railroad, including one from Alton. "Fugitives were hidden in livery stables, attics, and storerooms, under feather beds, in secret passages, and in all sorts of out-of-the-way places," Blockson writes. "They moved on to the next station at night by wagon, by boat, and by train. Routes of travel were changed at a moment's notice.")

Continue walking east on College Avenue. The Upper Alton Baptist Church, organized in 1830 by Baptist missionary John Mason Peck, is on the northwest corner at Seminary Street. In 1818 Peck and a fellow missionary had founded the First Baptist Church of St. Louis, which soon started a Sunday-school class for black slaves. He moved to Illinois in 1821 to start organizational work in the Alton-Edwardsville area. In 1827 he opened Rock Springs Academy, which eventually moved to Alton in 1832 and became Shurtleff College. As they grew, Shurtleff and the Baptist church became somewhat interdependent. College buildings were used for Sunday-school classes; the college graduation service was held at the church. Faculty members filled the pulpit when the church was without a pastor.

Diagonally across from the church is the Southern Illinois University–Edwardsville School of Dental Medicine, the former Shurtleff College. Walk through the wrought-iron gate by the one-time Shurtleff library, now the biomedical library. A $15,000 Andrew Carnegie gift originally funded the building. (An oil portrait by Shurtleff graduate Alban J.Conant of Abraham Lincoln smiling, the only such representation of the 16th president, hung in the Carnegie library. It now is displayed at the Southern Illinois University–Edwardsville main library.) Next door is the Alton Museum of History and Art, once Loomis Hall, the first Shurtleff building. The Reverend Hubbell Loomis, first Shurtleff president, is the structure's namesake. Now on the National Register of Historic Places, Loomis is reputed to be the oldest college building in Illinois still used for teaching purposes. That explains why the museum has set up a teaching classroom in the building. (The college name evolved from Rock Springs Academy to Alton Seminary to Alton College of Illinois, until in 1835 its leaders received $10,000 from Dr. Benjamin Shurtleff, a Boston physician, to establish a professorship in oratory and erect a small building. A grateful board of directors quickly named the college for its benefactor.)

Shurtleff's four-story limestone-faced administration building was the central presence on campus. Its top floors were designed to accommodate 40 male students, and each of their 40 rooms had a fireplace—until a fire of unknown cause consumed it in 1939. A new building took its place in 1940 and continues as the main classroom edifice on campus.

Behind the large classroom building is the old Shurtleff gymnasium, a 1924 relic that's still used daily, says Norman Showers, an Alton museum docent and 1950 Shurtleff graduate who is Alton's respected expert on the college. At one time the gym hosted AAU industrial-league basketball games as well as a guest appearance by the fledgling Harlem Globetrotters. "Our Olympic basketball teams were once recruited from the industrial teams of their day, such as the Owens-Illinois and Olin teams located in Alton," Showers says. He reminds us that SIU–Edwardsville actually started in Upper Alton in the fall of 1957 after Shurtleff had officially

The old Carnegie Library (now the biomedical library) on the SIU-E dental school campus

closed. "In 1965 SIU moved lock, stock, and barrel to Edwardsville."

Continue wandering through the campus, then return to College Avenue, passing the new dental clinic as well as the former chapel building on the southwest corner near Annex Street. Assemblies and convocations were held upstairs in the chapel building; classrooms were located downstairs. Walk south on Annex Street, where stuccoed Hunter Hall, the Shurtleff biology building, is on the southeast corner at College Avenue. On your way to Leverett Street, notice Shutleff's army barracks storage and auxiliary buildings that are now bricked over by SIU. Turn left on Leverett, where some of the 19th-century brick homes have been converted to dental school use, particularly the Washington Leverett home at 3006 (he was an early Shurtleff president) and the Bulkley home at 3003, both erected around 1865. At 3030 was the 1870 home of Mrs. John Leverett. At

Worden take a left, and walk to College Avenue. Walk across College; turn left. Upcoming is the 1985 bronze statue of Robert Wadlow on the north side of the dental school campus.

Labeled "the tallest man in authentically recorded history" by his biographer, Wadlow was an icon in Upper Alton. Wadlow's one-story frame "birth home" is scheduled for removal to a spot just west of the statue and near the elegant stone Cole-Clark carriage house (a satellite of a one-time huge turreted redbrick mansion, or "cottage," as it was called) that is being restored to become an interactive children's museum behind the Wadlow complex. Wadlow's mammoth easy chair, now on view at the nearby Masonic lodge, will be replicated in bronze and installed by the statue, thanks to efforts by Alton Rotarians.

Wadlow attended primary and secondary schools in his hometown. As a young teen he joined the Boy Scouts, which turned him into a walker. He often walked up to 6 miles a day until his size, weight, and balance made walking more treacherous. Even in high school, however, he walked the mile to and from school most days, often stopping at the Speed Kerr soda fountain. He entered Shurtleff College in January 1936, intent on becoming a lawyer. Because of his increasing weight, more than 400 pounds, he was forced to take a taxi to his classes, which were no more than a mile from his home on Brown Street. He left Shurtleff after a year, primarily because his weight made walking and sitting in lecture seats very uncomfortable. He went to work as a spokesperson for the children's shoe division of International Shoe Company and died in 1940 in Manistee, Michigan, while on a shoe promotion tour.

From College Avenue turn right at Seminary Street. At 1859 Seminary (corner of Walnut) is the Federal-style frame home on land once owned by Ninian Edwards, first territorial governor of Illinois. At 1821 is the 1900 home of Paul S. Cousley, once the editor of the *Alton Telegraph*. And at 1831 is Castle House, designed in the shape of a cross by Orlando L. Castle, a Latin professor at Shurtleff in the old days. At Bostwick Street is the main entrance to the Mississippi Valley Christian Academy, formerly Western Military Academy. In 1879 the site was occupied by the Wyman Institute, founded by Dr. Edward Wyman, a 75-year-old St. Louis educator who had established two previously successful academies in St. Louis. Wyman was well-known in St. Louis as founder in 1843 of the "English and Classical High School,"—which welcomed Tom Thumb and the great singer Jenny Lind (dubbed "the Swedish Nightingale" by P. T. Barnum) to his Wyman's Hall—and, in the early days of the Civil War, of City University, where all the students were uniformed and instructed in military marching and in the manual of arms.

In the late 1890s Western issued a notice to students: "Immoralities of all kinds are strictly forbidden." Wardrobe instructions for students in 1895 stipulated three nightshirts, three sets of white underwear, three sets of summer underwear, six napkins, and a ring and blacking brick. As late as 1954 the school issued its policy on smoking. "Smoking by boys is frowned on, but cadets of 16 may smoke with their parents' permission at designated campus spots." Uniforms resembled those of the U.S. Military Academy at West Point, New York.

Western had its own hiking club, and cadets would

wear their "workaday" uniforms on their walks—
though Sunday afternoon parades had cadets wearing
their dress uniforms. Cadets marched through Upper
Alton whenever Shurtleff had its homecoming parade.
At times the parading became lengthy. Every now and
then the cadets marched to downtown Alton, nearly 4
miles, to board excursion steamers on the Mississippi
River. A Thanksgiving day tradition in Alton for years
was the annual football game between Alton High
School and Western Military Academy. "It was always
Alton High's last home game and we almost always
won," recalls Harold sparks, a 1950 graduate of Alton
High and football running back. "Even though the
game was a tradition, I think the only people who came
were the families of the football squads, cheerleaders,
the Alton band, and recent graduates."

Among Western graduates were Lieutenant Commander Edward (Butch) O'Hare (class of 1932), the
heroic World War II navy pilot for whom O'Hare airport
in Chicago is named; Bob Barker, the television master
of ceremonies (class unknown); the painter Thomas
Hart Benton (1906); William S. Paley (1918), once
chairman of the board of CBS Radio, and Brigadier
General Paul W. Tibbetts (1933), commander of the
Enola Gay, the plane that dropped the atomic bomb on
Hiroshima. In 1931 and 1932, O'Hare and Tibbetts
were roommates.

After Wyman died in 1888, Colonel Albert Jackson
purchased the complex and changed the name to Western Military Academy. In its earliest days, the Wyman
Institute had been located on the grounds of the old
Bostwick mansion. (Earlier the mansion had been used
as a seminary by Shurtleff College.) When the home

burned in 1903, Western erected a new administration building along with a handful of other Bedford-stone English-style buildings, some with battlement parapets. A drill hall and gymnasium large enough for indoor baseball, a dining hall, bowling alley and shooting gallery, plus militarylike barracks buildings comprised the bulk of the campus. If you choose to explore the grounds, you'll note that Western's old gymnasium plus the building that housed the cafeteria on the ground floor and the library, study hall, and classrooms in its upper floors remain. Although four of the five barracks have been torn down, one survives. It apparently is the administration building for the academy, but 50 years ago it served as the WMA executive office.

Return to Seminary Street; walk west on Bostwick to Clawson, making a left. Take Clawson across College Avenue to Edwards Street, with Horace Mann School on the corner. Turn left and walk to Worden, then right to Brown Street. Robert Wadlow lived at 3204 Brown. In the summer of 1934, according to his biographer, Robert opened a soft-drink stand in his front yard and did a thriving business—which created traffic jams on his street. Curious visitors trampled the grass and shrubs in their eagerness to buy soda from the giant. An Alton policeman was often on hand. Seated in a chair borrowed from the front porch, Robert was cashier while his brother and sister poured. "Sometimes [would-be customers] would ask [Robert] to stand and then leave without buying anything," his biographer wrote.

Turn around and walk west on Brown to Washington. Turn right, pass Masonic Lodge 25, where Robert Wadlow became a Mason, and then walk to the shopping area to retrieve your car.

Index